This series is a forum for up-to-date empirical and theoretical contributions on the subject of media reception. One area these studies investigate is how people deal with the media messages they receive, which ranges from which forms of the media on offer they select and why, the quality of what they receive and how they process it, to media reception in everyday life and its consequences for individuals and society. In short, the series addresses the question of what people do with the media.

Reihe Rezeptionsforschung

Edited by
Ass.-Prof. Dr. Tobias Dienlin | Jun.-Prof. Dr. Anna Sophie Kümpel
Dr. Frank Mangold | Dr. Anna Schnauber-Stockmann

Editorial board:
PD Dr. Marco Dohle | Assoc.-Prof. Tilo Hartmann
Dr. Matthias Hofer | Prof. Dr. Thomas Koch
Prof. Dr. Holger Schramm | Prof. Dr. Carsten Wünsch

Founded by Uwe Hasebrink and Patrick Rössler

Volume 42

Elena Pelzer

Living with Cultivating Messages

What Are the Constructs that Compose
Media Messages in Cultivation Theory?

 **Nomos**

The Deutsche Nationalbibliothek lists this publication in the
Deutsche Nationalbibliografie; detailed bibliographic data
are available on the Internet at http://dnb.d-nb.de

a.t.: Münster, Univ., Diss., 2021

ISBN   978-3-8487-8304-5 (Print)
         978-3-7489-2694-8 (ePDF)

British Library Cataloguing-in-Publication Data
A catalogue record for this book is available from the British Library.

ISBN   978-3-8487-8304-5 (Print)
         978-3-7489-2694-8 (ePDF)

Library of Congress Cataloging-in-Publication Data
Pelzer, Elena
Living with Cultivating Messages
What Are the Constructs that Compose
Media Messages in Cultivation Theory?
Elena Pelzer
244 pp.
Includes bibliographic references.

ISBN   978-3-8487-8304-5 (Print)
         978-3-7489-2694-8 (ePDF)

Onlineversion
Nomos eLibrary

1st Edition 2021
© Nomos Verlagsgesellschaft, Baden-Baden, Germany 2021. Overall responsibility
for manufacturing (printing and production) lies with Nomos Verlagsgesellschaft mbH
& Co. KG.

For Ben

ACKNOWLEDGMENT

This book would not exist without the intellectual support and guidance of my advisors, Prof. Dr. Julia Metag and Dr. habil Jens Woelke. I would like to thank both of them for giving me the opportunity to work on a topic that I feel passionate about, for their invaluable wisdom, and for putting trust in my work style. I would also like to thank Prof. Dr. Benjamin O. Turner and Prof. Dr. Andreas Fahr for their helpful remarks on an earlier version of this manuscript. My thanks also goes to the scholars who crossed my path as collaborators such as Dr. Patric Raemy, Dr. Deborah Castro, Prof. Dr. Tom Fritz and Prof. Dr. Benjamin O. Turner; I truly appreciate all the stimulating discussions we have had.

I also want to thank my family and friends, who are the most dedicated, caring, and supportive individuals in the world. And finally, I want to thank my husband, Ben Pelzer, whose faith in me and endless patience throughout the research process was unwavering. I am so happy your steadfast belief that I would publish this book was actually realized. Thank you.

ACKNOWLEDGMENTS

Abstract

Cultivation theory assumes that the exposure to messages on television affects people's conception of social reality. Initially, it was assumed that these cultivating messages are uniformly distributed and that the viewers are unselective in their viewing habits. Over the last five decades or so, a large volume of empirical studies has investigated this cultivation effect further and produced significant development and refinement of the theoretical premises.

One of the most substantial developments is the introduction of genre-specific messages and metanarratives as alternative concepts of how messages are conveyed on television and how viewers receive them. Genre-specific messages assume that viewers have preferences for certain genres and that each genre consists of a unique message; metanarratives, on the other hand, assume that there are messages that are conveyed across different genres which are sought out actively by the viewers. Much of the criticism around these alternative concepts of cultivating messages centers around the question of how they differ from the original concept of uniform messages. Moreover, some critiques doubt that there is a need for alternative concepts despite the changes in the media landscape towards online television.

In light of the shift in viewing habits towards online television including subscribed video on demand (SVOD) services such as Disney+ or Netflix, this book explores the constructs and the set of propositions that compose media messages in cultivation theory. To this end, the current conceptualizations of cultivating messages, namely uniform message, genre-specific messages, and metanarratives, are disentangled by evaluating their degree of precision and underlying main theory. From the implications of these three message concepts and against the backdrop of the trend towards a greater fragmentation of genres towards subgenres in the era of online television, an original concept for cultivating messages is introduced: subgenre messages. Including this original concept, the final set of four main concepts for cultivating messages is then synthesized in order to assess how similar or different they are to one another. The result is the definition of two postulates and a number of lemmas that relate the cultivating concepts to one another in a generalizable framework that applies to any field and research area that studies cultivating messages. By using the degree of fragmentation of messages and the level of selective viewing as the framework, a two-dimensional space is developed to situate the four cultivating concepts.

In a unique simulation model, the validity and implications of the postulates, lemmas, and two-dimensional space are tested. The simulation investigates how a bias between true and estimated message concepts affects the results from cultivation analysis. The study consists of a data generating framework in which the true state of the simulated world is defined, such as the way viewers behave and how messages are distributed. The four generating frameworks, each guided by an according message concept, are then analyzed in a second step by a data analyzing framework. This ensures that data derived from each message concept is analyzed through the lens of each message concept. The results show that the cultivation effects differ substantially, although still to varying degrees, depending on the message concept that is applied. The analysis of uniform messages is only convincing in the single case when uniform messages shape the reality. In most cases in which the analysis performed differs from reality, subgenre messages outperforms the alternative message concepts. The simulation also demonstrates the mechanisms of the original concept of subgenre messages which enables future scholars to implement it in their future research.

Table of Contents

List of Figures   15

List of Tables   17

List of Abbreviations   19

Chapter One   Introduction   21

1.1 From Living with Television towards Living with Cultivating
     Messages   26

1.2 Premises, Rationale, and Structure   29

Chapter Two   Cultivation Theory: Then and Now   32

2.1 Origins of Cultivation   33
     2.1.1 Prelude to Cultural Indicators Project   33
     2.1.2 Cultural Indicators Project   38
            2.1.2.1 Theoretical Implications of the Cultural Indicators
                     Project   39
            2.1.2.2 Some Empirical Assessment of the Cultural
                     Indicators Project   42
     2.1.3 Message System Analysis   46
            2.1.3.1 Four Measures for Message System Analysis   47
            2.1.3.2 Analyses in Message System Analysis   50
            2.1.3.3 Example of Empirical Assessment   53
     2.1.4 Some Critique, Advancement, and Refinement   57
            2.1.4.1 Some Critique on Theoretical Implications   58
            2.1.4.2 Some Critique and Advances in Methodology   61

2.2 Digitalization and Cultivation   67
     2.2.1 Gerbner's Idea of Television   69
     2.2.2 Television Today: What Is Online Television?   72
     2.2.3 Consequences of Online Television for Cultural Indicators
            Project   74

Chapter Three Defining Genre, Narrative, & Message   79

3.1 Why to Consider Genre, Narrative, & Message   79

3.2 Four Perspectives to Define Genres   82

    3.2.1 History and Genre from the Linguistic Perspective   84
    3.2.2 Financial Forces and Genre from the Economic
         Perspective   86
    3.2.3 Reality Observation and Genre from the Sociological
         Perspective   88
    3.2.4 Knowledge Structures and Genre from the Psychological
         Perspective   90
    3.2.5 Implications of the Four Moderating Factors   91

3.3 What's in a Narrative?   93

    3.3.1 Narrative Turn Across Fields   93
    3.3.2 Narratives in Communication   95
    3.3.3 Narratives in Semiotics   97
        3.3.3.1 Classical Narratology   98
        3.3.3.2 Post-Classical Narratology   102
    3.3.4 Implications from Semiotics for Communication   105

3.4 What Is a Message?   109

    3.4.1 Defining Messages in Cultivation   109
    3.4.2 Messages in Semiotics   111

3.5 Interim Conclusion   113

Chapter Four Ways to Categorize Cultivating Messages   116

4.1 Uniform Messages   117

    4.1.1 Critical Theory and Uniform Messages   119
    4.1.2 Precision of Uniform Messages   122

4.2 Genre-Specific Messages   124

    4.2.1 Tenets and Critiques of Genre-Specific Messages   124
    4.2.2 Precision and Relevance of Genre-Specific Messages   126

4.3 Metanarratives   129

    4.3.1 Postmodernism and Narratology on Metanarratives   130
    4.3.2 Precision of Metanarratives   132
        4.3.2.1 Multi-Generic Status   133
        4.3.2.2 Nested Structure   135

4.4 Novel Concept: Subgenre Messages   136
   4.4.1 Consequences from Former Message Concepts   136
   4.4.2 Subgenres and Online Television   139
   4.4.3 Assumptions of Subgenre Messages in Cultivation   142

Chapter Five   Synthesis: Postulates, Lemmas, & Research Question   144

5.1 Postulates and Lemmas of Message Conceptualizations   144

5.2 Summary and Research Question   148

Chapter Six   Simulation of the Impact of Message Categorizations   151

6.1 Simulation Model   151
   6.1.1 Data Generating Framework: True Message Concepts   153
   6.1.2 Data Analytical Framework: Estimated Message Concepts
      & Strength of Belief   155

6.2 Results   158
   6.2.1 Differences in Determining Heavy and Light Viewers   158
      6.2.1.1 DAF Results for Viewing Groups when Uniform
          Messages as DGF   160
      6.2.1.2 DAF Results for Viewing Groups when Genre-
          Specific Messages as DGF   162
      6.2.1.3 DAF Results for Viewing Groups when
          Metanarratives as DGF   163
      6.2.1.4 DAF Results for Viewing Groups when Subgenre
          Messages as DGF   163
   6.2.2 Differences in Belief Effects between Heavy and Light
      Viewers   164
      6.2.2.1 DAF Results for Belief Effects when Uniform
          Messages as DGF   166
      6.2.2.2 DAF Results for Belief Effects when Genre-
          Specific Messages as DGF   167
      6.2.2.3 DAF Results for Belief Effects when
          Metanarratives as DGF   168
      6.2.2.4 DAF Results for Belief Effects when Subgenre
          Messages as DGF   169
   6.2.3 Impact of Third Factors on Differences between Heavy
      and Light Viewers & Belief Effects   171

Chapter Seven Implications & Discussion 174

7.1 Implications of the Simulation Results for Assessing the Impact of Message Concepts 174

7.2 Limitations of Simulation Choices 176

   7.2.1 Common Limitations of Simulation 176

   7.2.2 Modelling Viewing Choice Behavior 178

   7.2.3 Distinction between Heavy and Light Viewers 179

7.3 General Implications for the Future of Cultivation Theory 182

Chapter Eight Conclusion 185

REFERENCES 191

APPENDIX 207

Appendix A Tables & Figures 207

Appendix B Narrative Glossary 216

Appendix C R Code for Simulation 221

List of Figures

Figure 2.1 Trends of Violence Index 1967—1975 for various hours of program. Figure re-creation from data by Gerbner and Gross, 1976a.   56

Figure 3.1 Number of times 'message,' 'narrative,' 'story,' and 'genre' was mentioned in an article by Gerbner et al. between 1966 and 2001 per year on average   81

Figure 3.2 Overall number of times 'message,' 'narrative,' 'story,' and 'genre' was mentioned in five articles by Morgan, Shanahan and/or Signorielli between 1997 and 2019   82

Figure 3.3 Defining narratives by the degree of narrativity   108

Figure 4.1 Example for nested structure of metanarratives   136

Figure 5.1 Dimensions of Cultivating Messages   147

Figure 6.1 Graphical illustration for matrix for uniform messages, genre- specific messages, metanarratives, and subgenre messages   154

Figure 6.2 Degree of belief in cultivating message for heavy and light viewers with respect to DGF and DAF   165

Figure 6.3 Degree of belief in cultivating message for heavy and light viewers with respect to DGF and DAF without noise   171

Figure 6.4 Degree of belief in cultivating message for heavy and light viewers with respect to DGF and DAF with noise   172

Figure 7.1 Example of ROC curve to estimate the dependency of cultivation effects on cut-off point choices; each point would derive from a single choice of cut-off   181

Figure A.1 Sum of times the article by Gerbner and Gross (1976a) was cited per year   211

Figure A.2 Overall number of times 'message,' 'narrative,' 'story,' and 'genre' was mentioned in an article by Gerbner between 1966 and 2001 per year   212

Figure A.3 Gerbner's general model of communication (after Gerbner, 1958, p. 93, McQuail and Windahl, 1981, p. 19)   213

Figure A.4 Nünning's axis of degree of theoretical elaboration of legacies in post-classical narratology (after Nünning, 2003, p. 256)   214

Figure A.5 Density functions for degree of belief in cultivating message for heavy and light viewers with respect to DGF and DAF without noise   214

Figure A.5 Density functions for degree of belief in cultivating message for heavy and light viewers with respect to DGF and DAF with noise   215

List of Tables

Table 2.1   Prongs of the Cultural Indicators Project including
            question, analytic approach, and aim   40

Table 2.2   Reliability coefficients for study by Gerbner and
            Gross (1976a) and subsequent studies.   55

Table 6.1   Mean differences in hours of exposure to message 1
            between heavy and light viewers with respect to DGF
            and DAF   159

Table 6.2   Means of exposure to message 1 for heavy and light
            viewers with respect to DGF and DAF   160

Table A.1   Summary of questions and terms of public message
            system analysis.   207

Table A.2   The components of television as a medium for
            delivering audiovisual content in the broadcast,
            cable/satellite, digital and internet eras.   208

Table A.3   Number of times message, narrative, story, and genre
            are mentioned in respective articles on cultivation by
            Gerbner et al.   209

Table A.4   Mean differences in degree of belief in message 1
            between heavy and light viewers with respect to DGF
            and DAF   211

List of Abbreviations

CS	character violence score
DAF	data analytical framework
DGF	data generating framework
DVD	digital versatile disc
DVR	digital video recorder
E-ELM	extended elaboration likelihood model
EPG	electronic program guide
GNP	Gross National Product
HBO	Home Box Office
HV	heavy viewer
IMDb	The Internet Movie Database
LV	light viewer
P2P	peer-to-peer
PPV	pay-per-view
PS	program score
PSA	public service announcement
PVR	personal video recorder
ROC	receiver operating characteristic
SLR	systematic literature review
SVOD	subscribed video on demand
UGC	user-generated content
VCR	videocassette recorder
VHS	video home system
VI	violence index
VOD	video on demand

Chapter One Introduction

How are viewers affected by the depiction of scientists in the TV show *The Big Bang Theory* (2007–2019)? Which element of the ad message led to the purchase of the new smartphone? Will a health campaign with a narrative structure increase people's acceptance of the novel vaccine? Although these questions span across many subfields in communication studies—from mass media effects' research to strategic communication to health communication—one aspect recurs: The importance of *messages*. For communication scholars, messages, along with various ancillary concepts such as narratives, genres, or topics, are generally not of interest in and of themselves, but rather because of the way they are used by communicators, or their putative effects. And the body of research on messages, genres, and narratives in communication is growing rapidly: For example, the number of articles with the term 'narrative' in their title has increased by nearly 8,900 percent within two decades, more precisely from 15 titles in 1993 to 1,346 titles in 2013 (Braddock & Dillard, 2016). Given the centrality of 'messages' and similar concepts to much of communication studies, it is surprising that scholars oftentimes either ignore the question of how to define and compare the concepts, or stick religiously to definitions that were established decades or even centuries ago. Of course, these concepts may still apply today. But a missed evaluation of whether the concepts and their presuppositions remain true in today's new media environment might at least indicate a missed opportunity for refinement and advancement. Especially when scholars undertake the important efforts of drawing theoretical links and conducting empirical research, it is important to re-evaluate whether the concepts move in similar structural boundaries as when they were initially developed. For example, the idea that television sends out the message that the world is a mean and dangerous place was developed in the 1950s when U.S. television consisted of three broadcast channels. Today in the era of online television, however, we can choose from an abundance of television channels, and have developed a new understanding of mobility, accessibility, connectivity, and participation. Hence, online television, and the new media environment in general, forces scholars to re-evaluate the constructs and set of propositions that compose media messages. The focus of this book is therefore on disentangling message conceptualizations in order to allow scientific progress by defining, in a precise, contemporary and well-grounded way, the object of study, and the various ancillary concepts that play a role.

The need for understanding messages and its relatives against the back-drop of the new media landscape is particularly evident in theories whose core relies heavily on messages. For example, both agenda setting and cultivation theory were found to be within the top three of the most-cited theories in the field of mass communication (between 1956 and 2000; Bryant & Miron, 2004) as well as in mass communication research (between 1993 and 2005; Potter & Riddle, 2007). And both theories deal to a considerable degree with messages: More precisely, agenda-setting theory (along with its offspring second-level agenda setting and its other relatives such as framing or priming) is intertwined with issues of news production and consumption (Singer, 2018), with the theory's roots lying in the observation that the media "may not be successful much of the time in telling people what to think, but it is stunningly successful in telling its readers what to think about" (B. C. Cohen, 1963, p. 13). Thus, agenda setting puts forward claims about the salience impact of messages, issues, and topics on the public. Similarly, on an attitudinal level, cultivation theory deals to a great extent with the effects stemming from messages: The theory posits that messages on television shape society's conception of social reality. In this line of research, heavy viewers of the mean world messages on television are more likely to perceive the world as a dangerous and mean place compared to light viewers. The idea of messages is so central to cultivation theory that its founder, George Gerbner, even named one of the three major components of the project after it. The 'Cultural Indicators Project' (Gerbner, 1969a; Gerbner & Gross, 1976a) highlighted the interplay of three components in a macrosystem approach: the media institutions, the *media messages*, and the cultivating effect (Gerbner, 1973; Morgan, Shanahan, & Signorielli, 2015; Shanahan & Morgan, 1999). In accordance, the project aimed to address three major questions, namely 'what are the processes, pressures, and constraints that influence and underlie the production of mass media content?' (institutional analysis); 'what are the dominant aggregate patterns of images, messages, facts, values, and lessons expressed in media messages?' (message system analysis); and 'what is the independent contribution of these messages to audiences' conceptions of social reality?' (cultivation analysis; Gerbner, 1973; Morgan et al., 2015; Potter, 2014; Shanahan & Morgan, 1999).

Messages are therefore central to cultivation theory, and scholars have undertaken great efforts in constructing possible ways in which the messages on television appear and cultivate us: Initially, Gerbner and his associates believed that viewers are presented with a total, unified world of messages (Gerbner & Gross, 1976a; Gerbner, Gross, Signorielli, Morgan, & Jackson-Beeck, 1979; Morgan et al., 2015). The most commonly referred to example of such a uniform message is that television depicts the world as a scary and mean place. This and the other most general messages on television are assessed by a content analysis. The number of hours that a viewer is exposed to these messages then predicts how cultivated they are. This means that a viewer who views television heavily is more likely to have a world view that mirrors the portrayals on television than a person who watches very little television. It does not matter what exactly the viewers are watching on television, nor when, because the assumption is that the messages are equally distributed over all channels and time slots.

The initial cultivation study by Gerbner and Gross (1976a) and the underlying construct and set of propositions of uniform messages was as widely recognized as it was critiqued: One of the main critiques brought forward by Hawkins and Pingree (1981a), Potter (1993) and other scholars was the premise about the uniformity of messages on television and that viewers are unselective when they watch television. They argued that this premise might have been valid decades ago when there were only three channels available. But given the fragmentation of the media landscape and the increasing number of channels and variety of genres available to viewers, scholars started to challenge the assumption that the distinctions between genres are unimportant and that viewers have no preferences for shows or genres. Rather, these scholars believe that messages do in fact vary across genres: Thus, a conceptualization commonly referred to as 'genre-specific messages' evolved (J. Cohen & Weimann, 2000; Hawkins & Pingree, 1981a). In this view, for example the two genres 'crime' and 'romance' are expected to differ in their messages: Heavy viewers of the former are more likely to perceive the world as a scary and violent place, while heavy viewers of the latter genre come to the conclusion that love overcomes all hurdles in life. Proponents of the original conceptualization of uniform messages, however, are undecided whether this concept of genre-specific messages in fact deserves to be labeled as 'cultivation' since the concept comes with new assumptions (Morgan & Shanahan, 2010).

Given the vast interest in cultivation theory in general and the discussion about a valid conceptualization of cultivating messages, it is therefore surprising that hitherto there is no work that aims to define the set of propositions of these message concepts in order to assess their precision for cultivation theory. Moreover, providing a framework in which the similarity of these concepts can be assessed is still a call that is made from time to time, but that has not yet been answered. For example, Morgan and Shanahan (2010, p. 341) call for "a clear rationale for how they [genre-specific messages] are similar to or different from the more global concept of cultivation" which is the concept of uniform messages. Especially given the emergence of another alternative message concept, namely 'metanarrative,' the call seems even more pressing than before. Briefly, the alternative message concept of metanarrative assumes that there are messages that cross the borders of genres liberally and which cause the cultivation effect (Bilandzic & Rössler, 2004; Potter, 1993, 2014). Hence, while the development of genre-specific messages and metanarratives mark one of the most substantial developments in cultivation, they also highlight the need to disentangle the message concepts in cultivation theory to determine how the concepts differ from the original concept of uniform messages. In particular, scholars may begin to ask: How clearly do uniform messages, genre-specific messages, and metanarratives articulate their specific assumptions and propositions so that scholars can understand the concepts and use them in their research? How well do they fit with the underlying assumptions of cultivation theory? And what are their commonalities and differences? These are the questions that this book sets out to begin to answer.

The need for understanding the various concepts of cultivating messages also hews closely to the changes in the media landscape and the emergence of online television within the last decade or two: For example, in today's new media environment, Netflix, Hulu, Amazon Video, Disney+, and other subscription-based video on demand (SVOD) services are growing rapidly. Indeed, half of all households in the U.S. already have access to SVOD services (Nielsen, 2016, 2017), and they are also in a growth phase in Europe (Castro & Cascajosa, 2020). VOD as well as SVOD platforms offer a streaming service of broadcasted shows and movies, but also invest in in-house productions to retain subscribers (Castro & Cascajosa, 2020). Online television includes these VOD and SVOD services in addition to linear television as known from the broadcast and cable era in the 1970s (Johnson, 2019). However, online television is not only defined by the mere increase of TV shows or movies that viewers can watch, but also with regard to implications on mobility, availability, individuality, engagement levels, and algorithmic recommendation systems as the new TV guide. Today, we can watch anything whenever and wherever; we can watch alone, co-view with others, or co-space but not co-view; we can watch TV shows, but also play, like, comment on, and rate them; and if we are undecided what to watch then online television provides individual solutions algorithmically derived based on our demographics, locations and previous preferences—an individualized TV guide magazine (Jenner, 2016; Johnson, 2019; Lobato, 2018).

Hence, there has been a considerable shift in the components of television as a medium ever since its first introduction in the broadcast era. Although Morgan et al. (2015) claim that online television, and SVOD services in particular, have not fundamentally changed how stories are being told, they nonetheless set novel systematic boundaries in which they operate. For example, to a greater degree than ever before, content is being created and presented in a hyper-targeted way (Jenner, 2016): The initial approach of clustering content into genres has been to a large degree replaced by a more granular approach of subgenres and even microgenres. For example, in 2014, Netflix counted 400 subgenres and 75,000 microgenres in its database. These may be subgenre creations such as 'romantic horror' or microgenres such as 'Violent Suspenseful Action & Adventure from the 1980s.' Meanwhile, viewers are not limited to a set of movies and TV shows from a genre such as 'horror' anymore, but can select their content from specific subgenres with a certain focus such as 'zombie' or 'slasher and serial killers.' Given the mechanics of online television, the more the viewer watches a certain subgenre, the likelier it is that the recommendations for further TV shows and movies are from a similar subgenre, an effect known as lock-in effect. Hence, the novel systematic boundaries in which the production system and the audience operate have caused a shift towards subgenres. Given that cultivation theory posits effects from television messages, naturally the question occurs as to how the shift towards online television and the push towards subgenres affects the tenets of cultivation theory.

Against the backdrop of online television, here we explore how to disentangle cultivating message concepts, both as initially conceived as well as advancements thereof, namely uniform message, genre-specific messages, and metanarratives. The scope of the book can be traced back to Potter's idea that cultivation basically exists in three forms: Either as a construct referring to one type of media effect; as a hypothesis predicting a positive association between television exposure and cultivated conceptions; or as a formal theory that consists of constructs and assumptions (Potter, 1993). The focus of this book is on the third form, i.e., approaching cultivation as a theory that consists of constructs and assumptions, since the contribution is to systematically organize the dimensions of the various concepts of cultivating messages. By synthesizing (rather than merely aggregating) the concepts we create a common scientific framework that scholars may use to make substantial progress in understanding their research object in cultivation better. Thus, the question that guides us here is,

> What are the constructs and the set of propositions that compose media messages in cultivation theory?

While reading this book, the reader will notice that there are aspects that are mentioned only as a side note or are missing altogether. For example, the other two prongs of the Cultural Indicators Project, namely institutional analysis and cultivation analysis, and the developments in each domain, will only be discussed briefly. Of course, it is crucial for future cultivation scholars to emphasize more the interdependence between the three prongs. However, this is only attainable if the part of message system analysis is understood in greater depth. Therefore, this work focuses on messages to guide future theoretical and empirical efforts which aim to offer a more complete picture of cultivation theory, and bring together message system analysis, institutional analysis, and cultivation analysis. Moreover, the critiques, developments, and side tracks of cultivation theory that have been evolving over the last nearly 50 years seem virtually endless, and "the more work that is done, the more complex the questions (and the answers) become" as Shanahan and Morgan (1999, p. 3) put it. Aside from the short compilation in the next Chapter, to discuss and appreciate appropriately all of the work that has been done in the realm of cultivation theory would simply go beyond the scope of this work. Thus, we will go by 'less is more' as it allows us to gain deeper knowledge in the constructs of messages in cultivation and its ancillaries, an area that has mainly been neglected previously.

1.1 *From Living with Television towards Living with Cultivating Messages*

In 1976, George Gerbner and Larry Gross published the article *Living with television: The violence profile* which is widely considered a milestone in cultivation theory. Indeed, the cultivation research inspired by Gerbner and his associates proliferated remarkably over the last several decades— leading to nearly 650 relevant studies published by 2015 (Morgan et al., 2015), and making it *the* most-cited communication theory in 16 journals between 1993 and 2005 according to Potter and Riddle (2007). As of March 2020, the aforementioned article has a current count of 3,551 citations according to Google Scholar, and 690 citations according to the Web of Science, reflecting 15.33 average citations per year. Remarkably the citation count of 61 in 2019 represented the peak single-year citation count across all years since publication (see Figure A.1). The title choice of the original work furthermore inspired several spinoffs such as *Living with television: The dynamics of the cultivation process* by Gerbner, Gross, Morgan, and Signorielli (1986), followed by *Growing up with television: Cultivation processes* by Gerbner, Gross, Morgan, Signorielli, and Shanahan (2002), and *Living with television now* by Morgan, Shanahan, and Signorielli (2012). The title chosen for the present book, namely *Living with cultivating messages*, also openly alludes to the original. Still, the slight difference in the exact wording pays tribute to one particular change in the media landscape as well as the main focus of the book, which will briefly be explained below.

First, is the change to the original title by letting go of the term 'television.' From the beginning, television was central to Gerbner's claims, being described as "the central arm of American society" since it "is a medium of the socialization of most people into standardized roles and behaviors" (Gerbner & Gross, 1976a, p. 175), thus, functioning as enculturation. Even in more recent works by associates of Gerbner's, namely Morgan et al. (2015), television is still perceived as the most central device to cultivation research: "We are watching about 150 hours of live TV a month, compared to about 15 hours of time-shifted TV, 5 hours of watching a DVD or Blu-Ray device, 10 hours of online video, and less than 2 hours of video on a smartphone (Nielsen, 2015). To be sure, alternatives to traditional TV viewing are on the rise—and causing seismic shifts in the industry—but the time we spend watching programs live on a traditional TV still dwarfs these other options" (Morgan et al., 2015, p. 694). Five years later, the Nielsen quarterly Total Audience Reports suggest an increasing trend of SVOD services: Over the course of not even two years, from Q1 of 2018 to Q4 of 2019, the percentage of time Americans spent watching SVOD services increased from 10 percent to 19 percent of overall time spent watching TV. Peter Katsingris, Nielsen's senior vice president of audience insights, even predicts that "the proliferation of on-demand streaming services is the most profound media disruption of the last half-century." Moreover, SVOD services and linear television are not seen as antagonists in institutional media study, but rather as creating jointly the era of online television (Johnson, 2019; Lotz, 2017a, 2017b). Thus, while the book still focuses on television, and online television in particular, we want to emphasize more strongly *what* has been affected by the changes in the media landscape in cultivation theory rather than the changes to the institutions themselves. This is due to the focus of the book on cultivating media messages, rather than media institutions or cultivation *per se*, which are the other two prongs of Gerbner's Cultural Indicators Project.

The second change to the title concerns the focus of this book on message conceptualizations in cultivation theory. This is an original approach to cultivation theory since former books, book chapters, and journal articles have mainly focused on validating the idea of enculturation, resulting in empirical studies investigating cultivation effects. Some scholars have also contributed to the advances in cultivation theory by their rigorous critiques (e.g., Hirsch, 1980, 1981; Newcomb, 1978; Potter, 1993)—which continues even now (e.g., Potter, 2014)—which led to several theoretical and empirical improvements such as mainstreaming and resonance (for an overview see e.g., Gerbner et al., 2002; Shanahan & Morgan, 1999). Other scholars have started to focus on integrating a psychological perspective in cultivation theory, taking a closer look at cognitive mechanisms within the viewer (e.g., Shrum, 2002), or the influence of the perceived realism of the stories (e.g., Busselle, Ryabovolova, & Wilson, 2004; Bilandzic & Busselle, 2012a), or the role of transportation and transportability (e.g., Bilandzic & Busselle, 2008) in the cultivation process. A small number of scholars have also linked cultivation theory to other approaches such as the Third-Person Effect (e.g., Diefenbach & West, 2012; Jeffres, Neuendorf, Bracken, & Atkin, 2008), Agenda Setting (e.g., Hetsroni & Lowenstein, 2012), the Uses-and-Gratifications Approach (e.g., Bilandzic & Rössler, 2004), or the Spiral of Silence (e.g., Shanahan & Scheufele, 2012). In other recent works, scholars focused on the applicability of cultivation theory in our new media environment, either in theoretical statements (e.g., Morgan et al., 2015, 2012; Shanahan & Morgan, 1999) or in empirical investigations on social media such as Facebook (e.g., Tsay-Vogel, Shanahan, & Signorielli, 2018) or Instagram (e.g., Stein, Krause, & Ohler, 2019), in relation to gaming (e.g., Chong, Teng, Siew, & Skoric, 2012; Williams, 2006), or with respect to SVOD services (e.g., L. Prince, 2018). In summary, scholars have contributed to advances in cultivation theory enormously. It is therefore even more surprising that there has been no work so far synthesizing the various conceptualizations of messages. Even in his article on *Mass Media Discourse: Message System Analysis as a Component of Cultural Indicators*, Gerbner (1985) focused more on the methodological issues of conducting the content analysis rather than further extrapolating the theoretical foundation of the message system analysis, namely the underlying assumptions and properties of the concept of uniform messages. Given the rise of genre-specific messages and metanarratives, a precise framework to distinguish the various message concepts seems essential to make common progress in cultivation theory and research. The need seems even more pressing given our new media environment and online television, which has elevated the importance of genres, especially in comparison to the era of broadcasting television.

1.2 Premises, Rationale, and Structure

The book operates under the constructivist premise that there is more than one perspective to construct a concept. Therefore, most chapters of the book refer to two or more perspectives in order to define a particular concept. For example, 'messages' and 'narratives' are viewed through the lens of communication and semiotics, and 'genres' is approached by drawing from four perspectives, namely semiotics, economy, sociology, and psychology. For other concepts, the book explains precisely from which theoretical strand the established concept comes. For example, the book addresses how critical theory may underlie the concept of 'uniform messages' from Gerbner, or whether the concept of 'metanarratives' from cultivation theory shares commonalities with the concept of metanarratives from postmodernism or narratology. In summary, here we will consolidate multiple ways to define concepts that have gained attention across disciplines, as well as reveal the field of origin for and philosophy underlying several established concepts in cultivation theory. Combined, both approaches show that there is more than one way to view a concept, and invite scholars to take a closer look (again) at the assumptions that each strand comes with when they use a particular concept in their research.

One goal of the book is to collect theoretical implications from various perspectives, oftentimes supported by empirical findings, for the state of cultivation theory and the state of messages and its ancillaries in general, as well as cultivating messages in particular. The substantive contribution of this book, however, is to integrate these areas and synthesize them. In this effort, there are several advances that arise for each of the areas: In particular, we discuss the impact of the new era of online television for cultivation theory; we integrate perspectives from semiotics, economy, sociology, and psychology to increase the precision of defining genres, narratives, and messages, and distill a definition for each concept; we assess the degree of precision for the concepts of cultivating messages and give advice how to increase the precision in future work; and we propose an original new concept of cultivating messages named 'subgenre messages' by advancing the defining elements of the current concepts and linking them to the trends of online television. Thus, this book will show that by integrating and synthesizing (rather than merely aggregating) all aspects together enables development in each area separately. The foundation of this theoretically sound understanding of cultivating messages and the other areas then allows the articulation of a comprehensive framework in which to put the concepts in relation to one another, and to test it empirically.

In the following, we first give a short overview of the origins of cultivation theory including the Cultural Indicators Project; what makes messages central to cultivation theory; and some critique targeting the message system analysis in the past but also other aspects of the initial cultivation project. From this short overview of the past, we then articulate why online television requires scholars to take a fresh look at the conceptualization of cultivating messages. Next in Chapter 3, given that online television, and SVOD services in particular, emphasize the importance of genres, we consider how genres can be defined through the lens of several perspectives. In this Chapter, we also discuss how Gerbner may have defined messages and how this connects to the ideas of signs in semiotics. As a short textual analysis reveals, Gerbner paid little attention to narratives, while his associates give the term increasing space in their articles. The Chapter therefore also entails a consideration of how the concept of narratives is treated in communication and semiotics. The consideration of narratives is also relevant for understanding metanarratives in the next Chapter.

The synthesis on defining genres, narratives, and messages then enables us in Chapter 4 to explore the ways that the system of messages has been categorized in cultivation theory up until now. The recapitulation of the theoretical concepts starts with the original conceptualization of uniform messages, then moves on to genre-specific messages and metanarratives. In each of the Sections, the respective message construct and its set of propositions is explored by assessing the philosophical strand or super-theory that underlies it. This original approach allows us to evaluate the precision for each cultivating message concept. Finally, we present a novel conceptualization, namely subgenre messages, that arises naturally from the implications of online television on message concepts such as the trend towards subgenres and microgenres in SVOD services.

The implications of the four message conceptualizations are then abstracted even further in Chapter 5 and distilled into two Postulates and a number of Lemmas. The goal of this Chapter is to relate the various concepts to one another in order to show how similar or different they are. By using the degree of fragmentation of messages within a genre and the necessity of genre-selective viewing as the framework, we develop a two-dimensional space that reveals how close the concepts are to one another. This answers the call for a clear rationale as to how the message concepts are similar to one another.

Finally, after having assessed how similar the message concepts are, we then assess how this is expected to impact research in cultivation. The research question for the empirical part of this book, therefore, asks how a bias between true and estimated message concepts affects the results from cultivation analysis. The validity and implications of the Postulates, Lemmas, and two-dimensional space are tested in a newly developed computational simulation. The simulation consists of a data generating framework in which the true state of the simulated world is defined, such as the way viewers behave and how messages are distributed. The four generated patterns, each guided by an according message concept, are then analyzed in a second step by a data analyzing framework. This ensures that data from each message concept is analyzed through the lens of each message concept. The results of the simulation are then discussed and practical implications for future research outlined. The book ends with a conclusion that summarizes the main theoretical developments, main findings, and discusses future research aims for cultivation scholar, and especially potentials for the use of the concept of subgenre messages in the future.

Chapter Two Cultivation Theory: Then and Now

Gerbner teed up a theoretical football that could be kicked in any number of ways.
Morgan et al., 2015, p. 683

A common way to explain cultivation theory briefly is the notion that the messages on television shape our respective beliefs and attitudes, i.e., heavy viewers perceive the reality more likely in ways that closely mirror the world portrayed on television. This effect—messages on television shape our conception of social reality—is labelled as the 'cultivation effect.' For example, in their pioneer study on cultivation, Gerbner and Gross (1976a) showed that an over-representation of the rates of violence and crime on television in comparison to reality, may leave heavy viewers with an exaggerated perception about the extent of danger and crime in the world while light viewers perceive the world more likely as-is; a cognitive bias in heavy viewers that was later coined by Gerbner, Gross, Morgan, and Signorielli (1980b) as the 'mean world syndrome' (p. 17).

This brief explanation of cultivation theory is nowadays almost regarded as commonsense to communication scholars and does capture some of the quintessence about the work Gerbner and his associates have done over the span of more than 50 years. Important for the reader, however, is the notion that it only captures *some* aspects of the initial conceptualization of cultivation theory, and none of its developments and refinements. To situate the above definition of cultivation theory, in this Chapter we are taking a look at its origins and developments. Because, compared to when it was originally conceived, cultivation theory has evolved greatly: Theoretical critiques and empirical results have advanced and refined the theory and research. For example, scholars linked cultivation to other theories and approaches, refined underlying premises such as selective viewing, made shifts from a sociological to a psychological level, and broadened the methodological and analytical toolkit for cultivation research. A research topic that is slowly gaining interest by cultivation scholars is the evolution of television, namely the trend towards SVOD services such as Netflix, Hulu, Disney+, or Amazon Video. After a short introduction to the origins of cultivation theory by Gerbner and his associates, we will therefore take a look at the role of online television in cultivation theory and research.

2.1 Origins of Cultivation

Oftentimes introductions to cultivation begin with the Cultural Indicators Project. While the program represents without a doubt a landmark in cultivation theory and research, its founder George Gerbner started drafting his idea about enculturation a few years earlier, partially as a reaction to the conventional academic discourse about the limitations of cultural implications of mass communication. The next Section shortly lays out Gerbner's groundwork and the historical context in which cultivation theory arose, before we take a closer look at the Cultural Indicators Project itself.

2.1.1 Prelude to Cultural Indicators Project

With television becoming increasingly available in American households in the late 1940s and 1950s, scholars were also becoming increasingly intrigued about its putative effects on the audience. Nowadays the study of television and media effects in general has expanded greatly and encompasses several dimensions such as duration (temporary or permanent), timing (immediate or lagged), immediacy (direct or indirect), change or stabilization, level (micro or macro), manifestation (observable or latent), type (beliefs, attitudes, behaviors, affect, physiological, cognitions), function (acquiring, triggering, altering, reinforcing), and so forth (for a systematic introduction to organizing dimensions of media effects see Potter, 2012). Naturally, more than fifty years ago communication studies was at an earlier stage of conceptualizing the definitions, types and mediators of media effects, and many mass communication scholars back then believed that a media effect is represented by a change in attitudes or behavior. This line of thinking implied that no change meant no effect (Katz & Lazarsfeld, 1955), and led to a concentration on studying the effects of single messages, advertisements, or programs, but less to an investigation of the overall patterns in mass media and how they form a recursive relationship with the audience. However, when television emerged, there were some exceptions to this rather narrow and very specific design of studying media effects: Some used historical experiments to learn more about the general impact of the new medium, while others investigated its effects in laboratory experiments (Shanahan & Morgan, 1999).

   In the historical experiments (sometimes also referred to as natural experiments), scholars were interested in the putative effects of television on people's attitudes and behaviors. In opposition to a laboratory experiment, the decision as to which participant would be in either the control or the experimental group was outside of the scholars' control, since the determining factor was which household (or community) has access to television (the experimental group) or has no access to television (control group; see for example the studies by Himmelweit, Oppenheim, & Vince, 1958; also Schramm, Lyle, & Parker, 1961). Thus, the participants were naturally allocated. For example, in one of the studies employing such a historical experimental setting, Schramm et al. (1961) investigated in a two-year research project the content of the programs on television, and several effects the programs may exert on children. More precisely, the scholars studied the general media and television use of children, their sought gratifications, as well as their reported affects and attitudes, and also tested their knowledge level via vocabulary tests. The findings were compared to children without access to television. Among other results, the project revealed an incidental learning effect from television, i.e., "learning that takes place when a viewer goes to television for entertainment and stores up certain items of information without seeking them" (Schramm et al., 1961, p. 75). Notably, the authors perceived the children as active agents with sought gratifications when they turn towards television—an idea that can be considered a trailblazer to the Uses-and-Gratifications approach in the 1970s by Katz, Gurevich, and Haas (1973). Although the results were of a short-term nature, it is also striking how the authors laid the groundwork for cultivation theory with their note on incidental learning. However, while the project was able to reveal valuable insights about the nature of adapting to a new medium, it was unable to explain what long-term effects television might exert on the society. The historical design of the study had the benefit of observing children in their natural environment. However, the design was also susceptible to historical changes: The rapid spreading of television changed the conditions and therefore hindered a replication of the study; and the increasingly shrinking number of households or communities without access to television also prevented a continuation of the study to investigate any long-term implications of television. Thus, the number of studies with a historical design—to approximate a before/after effect of television in the real world—was decreasing quickly, and left the question of potential long-term effects of television unanswered.

Other scholars investigated the effects of television on people's attitude from the start in artificial laboratory situations: The experiment by Albert Bandura (1965) about film sequences of people attacking so-called Bobo dolls is considered a pioneer study in that domain. Yet, while these experiments gave scholars from social psychology great insights about observational learning, they revealed less about the relationship of television and violence *per se*. As Shanahan and Morgan (1999) point out, "in most such studies, there is no need to know anything about the institution of television, or its status as a cultural object, or how people typically use it, to be able to interpret the results" (p. 9).

When George Gerbner then started to introduce to communication scholars his more general ideas about how television impacts society, his thinking emerged from a historical period in which the investigation of short-term effects of isolated messages prevailed. In its origins, cultivation can therefore be viewed as an attempt to change the common angle that scholars used to address societal implications of mass communication. While other scholars perceived communication research as a way to achieve an instant goal such as promoting a politician, selling TV's, or improving finances, for Gerbner it meant an investigation about cultural basics. In this line of thinking, media have their own agenda as any social institution does; and messages have a recursive relationship with the audience since their meaning is bound to the historical and social context, yet they also reconstitute this context. Even though Gerbner started to first make claims about these observations as early as in the 1950s and 1960s, the notions were either general models for mass communication effects (e.g., Gerbner, 1956) or specialized examples, e.g., about the depiction of teachers in mass media fiction and drama on television (e.g., Gerbner, 1966). In the late 1960s, however, Gerbner published one article (Gerbner, 1969a) and one book chapter (Gerbner, 1969b), both titled *Toward "Cultural Indicators": The Analysis of Mass Mediated Public Message Systems* which can be considered seminal efforts for the conceptualization of cultivation theory. Both publications take a closer look at the relationship between culture and mass media, specifically for television, and make several observations: Gerbner's first observation deals with the fact that television produces content for the general public, and that these mass-produced messages, as he noted earlier, "channel and cultivate the broadest common terms of image formation and social interaction in modern societies" (Gerbner, 1966, p. 215). Accordingly, these 'common terms' take the shape of messages and can be facts, values, and other contingencies of our human existence. Gerbner's second observation stems from the Chinese slogan of the 'Cultural Revolution:' Given the rise of television in the 1950s and 1960s, the economic goals for these messages have changed—they are mass-produced, rapidly distributed, and adapted to the change in the social bases. This change in the symbolic environment, as Gerbner (1969a)

35

coins it, leads to 'cultural indicators' which reflect the transformation in the media landscape and direct the public meaning and consciousness about elements in reality. Cultural indicators are thus equivalent to the concept of 'economic indicators' to guide policies in economics, or 'social indicators' to inform social policy making. From the very beginning, it is crucial to Gerbner to develop a theory that accounts for these cultural indicators which trace elements of the television world and shape the public consciousness through mass communication. These two observations formulate Gerbner's primary focus on the cultivation of shared messages on television that enables public interaction such as a public opinion (Gerbner, 1969a). The theory that he is then starting to conceptualize aims to answer one of the most general questions about collective concepts against the backdrop of mass-produced institutionalized message systems: "[W]hat general terms of collective cultivation about existence, priorities, values, and relationships are given in collectively shared public message systems [?]" (Gerbner, 1969a, p. 141). Already at this early stage of theoretical development, Gerbner is cautioning that claims such as 'Children believe in Santa Claus' cannot be interpreted as collectively shared and commonly-accepted unless the context is known to scholars such as the culture and timeline of occurrence, and whether the messages produced and distributed through the public mass system are inciting or pacifying this belief.

From its inception, Gerbner also insisted that the academic investigation of the public's cultivation through mass media should take a systematic rather than a normative approach: Judgments about quality, credibility, and style are considered orthogonal to the question of the social functions that messages fulfill in social life and collective memory. Thus, although a news story and a fable differ in terms of credibility, according to Gerbner (1969a) they both contain messages that are equally important. The messages address four specific questions whose answers lead to bigger picture presentations on (1) attention, (2) emphasis, (3) tendency, and (4) structure, namely "[1] what *is*, [2] what is *important*, [3] what is *right*, and [4] what is *related* to what" (p. 142). For example, consider a news story about a man assaulting a young girl by impersonating her grandmother, and the fable of Little Red Riding Hood. Even though the news story and the fable differ in their factual accuracy and credibility, both address lessons in power dynamics, gender roles, and crime, with the message that "big bad 'wolves' victimize old women and trick little girls" (Gerbner, 1999, p. ix). Thus, both the news story as well as the fable (1) direct the attention of the public on the respective lessons (attention); (2) emphasize more the elements conducive to the lessons on power, gender roles, and crime, and less the distracting elements such as 'taking a walk in the forest is good for your health' (emphasis); (3) highlight the sentiment that it is the 'little girls' who are innocent and the 'wolves' who are the 'bad guys' in order to ease the interpretation of goodness or badness (tendency); and (4) assert the logical association that a relationship between the elements 'wolves' and 'little girls' is a toxic one, a relationship that could not be revealed when the elements are viewed separately, but only in combination (structure). Table A.1 summarizes the definitions and explanations, as well as measure and analysis for these four functions of the public message system. How seminal these four distinct but related functions of messages is becomes visible forty years later, when Gerbner is still referring to the same functions of messages that "reveal how things work; [...] describe what things are; and [...] tell us what to do about them" (Gerbner, 1999, p. ix).

In summary, from the early stages of development onward Gerbner laid out several reasons detailing how his idea of cultivation differs from other theories and approaches of that time: First, cultivation stems specifically from the coming of television, which accelerated the production of content for the masses and the rapid distribution of it. These two aspects ease the reach of television (in general; more particular elements of television that Gerbner addresses in later notes are discussed in Section 2.2.1). Rather than being merely a new technical device, television is considered a social institution that has its own agenda. Second, the systematic change in the production and distribution of messages due to the emergence of television also represents a shift in the environment that the public turns towards in order to achieve guidance on the common terms on facts, values, and other important aspects of human existence. Herein, the idea of a 'cultural indicator' refers to elements in the messages in mass media that reflect our culture, basically a barometer of important cultural issues (Gerbner, 1969a, 1970). With the cultural indicators, Gerbner created a novel counterweight to the established economic or social indicators (Shanahan & Morgan, 1999). Third, cultivation also differs from other theories and approaches with respect to its focus on the cumulative impact rather than causes-and-effects since it asks which messages are collectively shared and what role television plays in inciting or pacifying the respective common terms (instead of merely employing television as an agent of social change; this notion is further discussed in Sections 2.1.2 and 2.2.1). This also implies that cultivation cannot be measured nor maintained by single message exposure but that the commonly and deeply held perspectives and beliefs in a culture are of a long-term nature (Gerbner, 1973). Fourth, cultivation is taking a systematic rather than a normative angle to include all questions of social functions that messages may fulfill in the community (Gerbner, 1969a).

One of the greatest distinctions of cultivation from other theories and approaches that target mass media effects might be that the theory targets the question "what public perspectives, conceptions and actions [the] different types of mass communication systems tend to cultivate" instead of "how to change ideas and behaviors" (Gerbner, 1966, p. 433). While Gerbner already called in the 1950s for alternative approaches and models that explain mass communication effects (see e.g., Gerbner, 1956), his notes a decade later are already targeting a specific idea about the role of television in the public's mindset and behavior. Gerbner's early critical appraisals serve as a stepping stone for the theoretical foundation for cultivation as a model of communication and as a way to investigate the systematic impact of mass media against the backdrop of institutional changes in his landmark Cultural Indicators Project.

2.1.2 Cultural Indicators Project

The 'Cultural Indicators Project' led by George Gerbner aimed to identify aspects of the television world and the conclusions they cultivate across the diverse television-viewing public. Herein, the paradigm 'cultural indicator' refers to elements in the messages that reflect our culture (Gerbner, 1969a). The project officially commenced in 1969 when it received funding by the U.S. Congress as part of the Surgeon General's Scientific Advisory Committee on Television and Social Behavior which funded 23 projects in total, including Cultural Indicators. As with many landmark projects, Gerbner's work on cultivation, however, started before the Cultural Indicators Project was officially commenced, both theoretically (as discussed above in Section 2.1.1) and empirically. For example, in 1968 the National Commission on the Causes and Prevention of Violence funded a content analysis of violence in prime-time television program which was under the direction of Gerbner at the Annenberg School for Communication. After the assassinations of Robert Francis 'Bobby' Kennedy and Martin Luther King, Jr., the U.S. faced a time of national turmoil, and was therefore increasingly interested in the examination of violence in society and on television (Morgan & Signorielli, 1990). The content analysis about the nature and degree of violence on television by Gerbner and his team is considered the first empirical step into what was later known as the Cultural Indicators Project (Shanahan & Morgan, 1999), and led to the development of the 'Violence Index,' a measurement that is discussed later.

2.1.2.1 Theoretical Implications of the Cultural Indicators Project

The Cultural Indicators Project focused on the implications of growing up and living with television, and was borne out of the need to know what "general terms of collective cultivation about existence, priorities, values, and relationships are given in collectively shared public message systems" (Gerbner, 1969a, p. 141) in order to quantify how television's message system impacts the public. The project consisted of three prongs to investigate the structure, content, and consequences of mass media: (1) the media institutions, (2) the media messages, and (3) the cultivating effect (Gerbner, 1970, 1973; Morgan et al., 2015). Analogous to these three interrelated prongs, the project asked three main questions: (1) "what are the processes, pressures, and constraints that influence and underlie the production of mass media content?"; (2) "what are the dominant aggregate patterns of images, messages, facts, values, and lessons expressed in media messages?"; And (3), "what is the independent contribution of these messages to audiences' conceptions of social reality?" (Shanahan & Morgan, 1999, p. 6). Thus, with the first prong, namely (1) media institutions, Gerbner directed scholars to investigate how messages in a media system are selected, produced, and distributed; to define the institutional, economic, and technological functions that govern these processes; and to identify the organization, controlling, and management of the mass-production of the messages (Gerbner, 1969b). This analysis of forces and changes in the mass production of media messages is coined 'institutional (process) analysis.' With the second prong, namely (2) media messages, Gerbner argued that scholars should look for the overarching common composition and structure of mass-mediated messages (Gerbner, 1969a). The form of analysis that he recommends is an on-going, systematic content analysis, coined as 'message system analysis,' of these widespread meanings across barriers of time and programs. Finally, with the third prong, namely (3) cultivating effect, scholars are directed to investigate how the cultivation of these messages in their respective institutional system shapes the public's conception of the real world (Gerbner, 1970). This type of analysis is coined 'cultivation analysis' and of a long-term nature: "The dynamics of continuities, rather than only of change, need to be considered in the examination of mass-produced message systems and their symbolic functions. Such examination is necessarily longitudinal and comparative in its analysis of the processes and consequences of institutionalized public acculturation" (Gerbner, 1973, p. 569). In its simplest form, the basic hypothesis for cultivation analysis is that heavy viewers of television are more likely to perceive social reality in ways that mirror closely the stable and dominant patterns of images and messages in the television world. Table 2.1 summarizes the questions, analytic approach, and aim of each prong in the Cultural Indicators Project.

Table 2.1 Prongs of the Cultural Indicators Project including question, analytic approach, and aim

Prongs of the Cultural Indicators Project			
Prong	Question	Analytic Approach	Aim
1. Media Institutions	What are the processes, pressures, and constraints that influence and underlie the production of mass media content?	Institutional Process Analysis	Investigation of selection, production, and distribution of media messages.
2. Media Messages	What are the dominant aggregate patterns of images, messages, facts, values, and lessons expressed in media messages?	Message System Analysis	Assessment of prevalence and nature of patterns, meaning, and messages in media content.
3. Cultivating Effect	What is the independent contribution of these messages to audiences' conceptions of social reality?	Cultivation Analysis	Study of television's contribution to conception of social reality by viewer.

Aggregated table from Gerbner (1970) and Shanahan and Morgan (1999)

Several key characteristics stem from these prongs: First, each of the prongs is investigated by a *distinct* methodological procedure, namely (1) institutional process analysis for the media institutions, (2) message system analysis for media messages, and (3) cultivation analysis for the cultivating effect. Second, an answer to any of the three questions has a significant impact on the other two. Institutions, messages, and implications are conceptualized as an *interrelated*, global framework, setting it apart from other theories and approaches that focus on a singular component, e.g., either institutions or content or effects. Thus, this global theoretical conceptualization goes beyond the classic causes-and-effects model. Third, media content is viewed as a *system* of messages. This part stems from earlier notions (as outlined in 2.1.1) about television being a systematic disseminator of cultural symbols. This means that cultivation research in the Cultural Indicators Project focuses on the overall stream of media messages, not on a single message or program. Fourth, the cultivation analysis investigates *long-term* acculturation. It is naturalistic as it does not manipulate messages in an experimental setting, but is interested in the long-term exposure of the public to what is naturally available to them on television.

Considered jointly, the three prongs define cultivation: Cultivation is about what stable, pervasive, repetitive, and ubiquitous patterns of images and messages the media system produces, and what implications they have on the audience. The emphasis is on implications, not effects. Cultivation research in the Cultural Indicators Project focuses on the stream of media messages *in toto*, and how these correlate to a *cumulative exposure* to these messages in total on television *over long periods of time*. For example, cultivation does *not* ask how viewers perceive the new commercial for the smartphone; it also does *not* investigate how voters perceive a political candidate after watching their newest ad campaign, whether they like them or find them unfit for the job; it does *not* study how aggressive viewers become after watching a horror movie; and cultivation is *not* about whether one specific channel such as HBO shows more explicit content than others. But cultivation *can* be about how common patterns in advertisement impact consumers over the years; it *can* investigate how we perceive the political system after being exposed to its dynamics over time; it *can* study how the exposure to thousands of violent images and messages over years and decades shapes our perception of crime in the real world; and cultivation *can* be about how demography, power dynamics, and gender roles are depicted in the stream of images and messages on television. Thus, cultivation "does not study direct effects from messages sent and received in the short term. The point is that cultivation's role is to examine broad patterns of relationships between the social consumption of media messages and stable, aggregate belief structures among large groups of people" (Shanahan & Morgan, 1999, p. 6). This line of inquiry analyses long-term consequences of cultural indicators depicted in television in a macrosystem approach, rather than specific attitudinal or behavioral effects from a single message in a microsystem perspective.

Thus, cultivation theory goes beyond a causes-and-effects theory, as it takes into consideration the implications of media institutions and messages in addition to the study of the effects of cultivation.

2.1.2.2 Some Empirical Assessment of the Cultural Indicators Project

In addition to the theoretical advancements in modelling mass-mediated communication as cultivation, the Cultural Indicators Project also consisted of empirical tests to investigate the prongs further. For the media messages, the analytic approach of "Message System Analysis focuses on the gross, unambiguous, and commonly understood facts of portrayal" (Gerbner, Gross, Jackson-Beeck, Jeffries-Fox, & Signorielli, 1978, p. 178). Message system analysis is discussed in greater detail in Section 2.1.3, but here we focus on its application in the Cultural Indicators Project specifically. Its first evidence stems from the study in 1967–1968 for the National Commission on the Causes and Prevention of Violence, in which Gerbner and his colleagues investigated the degree and nature of violence as portrayed on primetime American television. The study documented over time the extent to which crime and violence were shown; what the nature of the portrayals of crime and violence, victims and aggressors was; and developed the 'Violence Index' to capture the findings of these cultural indicators accordingly (see Gerbner's report to the National Commission on the Causes and Prevention of Violence, 1969, in Morgan & Signorielli, 1990). The Index was updated annually, and periodically, the results were published in a series named 'Violence Profile' (see Gerbner & Gross, 1976a; Gerbner, Gross, Eleey, et al., 1977; Gerbner et al., 1978; Gerbner, Gross, Signorielli, Morgan, & Jackson-Beeck, 1979; Gerbner, Gross, Morgan, & Signorielli, 1980b). The data from the message system analysis, thus, provided Gerbner and his team with information about the prevalence and nature of violence and crime on television, and enabled them to compare the findings directly to real world data about violence and crime. The goal was to determine how similar the data of television portrayals and the real world was. One major finding was that the rates of violence, crime, perpetrators, and victimization in the world on television were disproportionately higher than the rates as reported in the real world by the Census data (Shanahan & Morgan, 1999). For example, the message system analysis from 1970 showed that 58 percent of homicides were committed by strangers in the television world, whereas the rate in the real world was barely 20 percent as provided by the Census data. This means that the number of homicides committed by strangers in the television world was three times the percentage of the real world data. Moreover, the message system analysis revealed that characters in primetime drama had a likelihood ranging 1 to 2 out of 3 (i.e., 30–64 percent) of being involved in some act of violence. Compared to the Census data from 1970, the real world chance in this matter was below 1 percent—0.33 percent to be exact. This finding indicated a discrepancy between the crime rates on television and the rates in the real world: In general, the chances of being involved in a crime increased by 9,000 to 19,000 percent in the television world compared to the real world. These findings reported above were just two examples of the evidence gathered from their research.

As described in Section 2.1.2.1, message system analysis was just one prong of the Cultural Indicators Project: For the third prong, cultivation analysis, Gerbner and his associates investigated the independent contributions of television viewing to the viewers' social reality conceptions: "Once the 'television view' and the 'real world' or some other view of selected facts and aspects of social reality have been determined, we construct questions dealing with these facts and aspects of life. Each question has an inferred or objectively determined 'television response' reflecting the 'television view' of the facts and a 'non-television answer'" (Gerbner et al., 1978, p. 195). Simply put, the first publications on cultivation analysis were comparing the survey answers of the heavy viewers (e.g., those viewing television for four hours or more on average per day) with the answers from the light viewers (e.g., those viewing two hours or less a day on average). The results suggested that heavy viewers of television were more likely than light viewers to give answers that were closer to the reality as portrayed on television with regard to law enforcement and crime, victims and perpetrators, trust and danger (e.g., Gerbner & Gross, 1976a; Gerbner, Gross, Eleey, et al., 1977; Gerbner et al., 1978; Gerbner, Gross, Signorielli, Morgan, & Jackson-Beeck, 1979). For example, in their landmark study *Living With Television: The Violence Profile*, Gerbner and Gross (1976a) investigated how the discrepancies between the television world and the real world from their message system analysis are reflected in the viewers' estimations of the likelihood of occurrence of prevalence of crime and violence in reality and their respective attitudes. Are heavy viewers more likely than light viewers to believe that the real world was like the television world?

One finding in their study targeted the discrepancy of the number of working males in occupations such as law enforcement and crime detection, e.g., police officers, detectives, criminal lawyers, and judges. While the Census data showed that 1 percent of all working males had a job in this occupation domain, according to their message system analysis that figure was 12 percent in the world of television. Gerbner and Gross then tested whether heavy viewers were more likely to overestimate that specific number of working males in reality. The survey items consisted of two options: one response option reflected more closely the answer from the television world (the 'TV answer'), while the other option was closer to the number from the real world. Respondents were then asked whether the number of men working in the specified domain was closer to one percent (the real-world answer), or closer to five percent (the TV answer). Their results revealed that heavy and light viewers differed by 9 percentage points and that the heavy viewers' answers were more likely than chance to be closer to the TV answer. More precisely, 59 percent of the heavy viewers chose the 'five percent' option, compared to 50 percent of the light viewers. Moreover, as their study suggested heavy viewers were more likely to give the television answer with regard to their own chances of being involved in violence: 52 percent of heavy viewers but only 39 percent of light viewers believed that their chances of being involved in some type of violence is one in ten (the TV answer) instead of one in a hundred (the real world answer). These findings, among others, led to the development of the 'cultivation differential,' which is the "margin of heavy viewers over light viewers giving the 'television answers' within and across groups [which is] indicating conceptions about social reality that viewing tends to cultivate" after controlling for gender, age, education, and other sociodemographic characteristics (Gerbner & Gross, 1976a, p. 182). The cultivation differential is based on cross-tabulations between television viewing and the answers to the respective questions divided into real world and TV answers. In addition to the questions about occurrences of the facts presented in television and in the real world, Gerbner and his team also investigated the ways in which the exposure to these facts shaped the viewers' beliefs and attitudes. For example, in the aforementioned study, Gerbner and Gross (1976a) also asked respondents to indicate whether they believed that "you can't be too careful in dealing with people" or that "most people can be trusted." In comparison to light viewers, the heavy viewers were found to choose more often the first option that expressed greater caution in social interactions. Based on their first findings, by the end of the 1970s, Gerbner, Gross, Morgan, and Signorielli (1979, p. 196) summarized that "the most significant and recurring conclusion of our long-range study is that one correlate of television viewing is a heightened and unequal sense of danger and risk in a mean and selfish world." This finding, namely that television depicts the world as a scary and mean place, became one of the most commonly referred to message examples that is supposed to exert a cultivating effect, and is widely known as the 'mean world syndrome' (Gerbner, Gross, Morgan, & Signorielli, 1980b, p. 17).

The results reported above are just one example of the numerous studies and evidence of cultivation effects gathered by Gerbner and his colleagues, but also other cultivation scholars. For example, in the following years the Cultural Indicators Project team studied the degree to which television impacts the viewers' conceptions (and actions) for issues such as politics (Gerbner, Gross, Morgan, & Signorielli, 1982a, 1984), aging (Gerbner, Gross, Signorielli, & Morgan, 1980a), death (Gerbner, 1980a), health and medicine (Gerbner, Gross, Morgan, & Signorielli, 1981c, 1982b), science (Gerbner, Gross, Morgan, & Signorielli, 1981e), and law (Gerbner, 1980b), among many other realms. It is important to note that a complete discussion even of all Violence Profile reports, not to mention the mass of other studies, would fill more than one book: To date, more than 650 relevant studies have been published (Morgan et al., 2015), making cultivation according to an analysis of 16 journals between 1993 and 2005, *the* most-cited communication theory (Potter & Riddle, 2007). Thus, the Cultural Indicators Project, and other inspired research on cultivation by Gerbner and his team as well as from other scholars, proliferated remarkably over the decades.

However, it is striking that it has been mainly the third prong, namely cultivation analysis, that has been utilized most in empirical investigations on cultivation (Potter, 2014; L. Prince, 2018): "When we divide the cultivation literature into tests of claims for Gerbner's three components, we can see that the literature exhibits a heavy concentration in cultivation analysis while institutional analysis has been ignored. As for institutional analysis, there is no evidence that Gerbner or his team published any research" (Potter, 2014, p. 1024), despite their continuous acknowledgments of the importance of institutional analysis for cultivation research (see e.g., Morgan & Shanahan, 2010; Morgan et al., 2015; Shanahan & Morgan, 1999). Moreover, as Potter (2014) cautions, it is still unclear whether there are indeed widespread messages across all channels on television, since studies have mainly focused on mainstream commercial television, and rarely investigated other programs such as news or advertisement. Moreover, the literature from message system analysis is "fragmented because it continues to lack the synthesis needed to coordinate findings across genres, dayparts, channels, media, and cultures" (Potter, 2014, p. 1025). Aside from the empirical shortcomings regarding synthesizing the findings from studies on message system analysis in a systematic literature review or meta-analysis, even more troubling for the completeness of the study of media messages are the gaps in theory: To date, literature has yet to provide convincing arguments as to what the conceptual properties of cultivating messages are, and, given the theoretical advancement (discussed in further detail below), how the different kinds of cultivating message concepts differ from one another. Though unanswered, this call is still being made today (Morgan et al., 2015), and will be addressed later in this book.

Thus, while it is understandable that the question of cultivation analysis—how does television shape viewers' conceptions of social reality—exerts a pull on social scientists, it nonetheless marks a discrepancy from Gerbner's original idea of a trifold concept for cultivation. Since the emphasis of this book is on categorizations of concepts of messages in cultivation, next we will take a closer look at the analysis of the system of media messages, before taking a short glimpse at the critique, advancement and refinement of cultivation theory and research.

2.1.3 Message System Analysis

In general, cultivation scholars are interested in examining the relationship between the steady, slow and cumulative consumption of media messages and the stable, aggregate belief and attitude structures among large groups of people. Media messages, therefore, play a crucial role in the Cultural Indicators Project: For the first prong, namely media institutions, they are the result of the production of the institutions, and the object that is being investigated in the institutional process analysis is in terms of how they are selected, produced, and distributed; for the second prong, namely media messages, they are the subject of an analysis to track recurrent image and lesson patterns of demography, relationships, aspects of life, or actions in the media content, and investigated in a content analysis that is coined message system analysis; for the third prong, namely cultivation effects, media messages are expected to contribute to the audience conception of the real world, and usually serve as the predictor variable in the cultivation analysis. Thus, as Gerbner (1970) intended early on, media messages (and their analytic approach of message system analysis respectively) are highly intertwined with the other prongs. It seems therefore even more surprising that scholars, who undertake the important effort of aggregating conceptual foundations, methodologies and empirical findings in introduction books to cultivation, oftentimes devote only a single-page chapter to explain the role of media messages in cultivation, and are focusing otherwise on the third prong, i.e., cultivation analysis. Although the focus here is more on exploring ways to *categorize* cultivating messages—which will be discussed in Chapter 4 accordingly—rather than the nature of messages *per se*, below we nonetheless take a closer look at the definition and methodology of message system analysis in cultivation theory. We end the summary on message system analysis by walking briefly through a case study which outlines the steps that a cultivation scholar might take when performing a message system analysis in accordance with the Cultural Indicators Project.

Theoretically, the idea of message system analysis is—as discussed above in Section 2.1.2—that scholars investigate the common composition and structure of mass-mediated messages periodically in an analytic approach (Gerbner, 1969a; Gerbner et al., 1978). The nature of the analytic approach is that of an on-going and systematic content analysis of the widespread messages, images and lessons on television, independent of time, channels, or genres. Thus, instead of examining single messages, movies, or shows, Gerbner perceives them as a centrally produced and commercially supported *system* of messages. While in isolation the messages may vary on the surface, in the bigger picture the system of messages reveals common patterns of specific beliefs, images, values and ideologies that deal with "facts of life" (Gerbner, 1985, p. 17). As Gerbner (1990) argues in later writings, culture is a "system of stories and other artifacts—increasingly mass-produced—that mediates between existence and consciousness of existence, and thereby contributes to both" (p. 251). Thus, these uniform, repetitive, and pervasive patterns of images and messages that are examined in the message system analysis reach large and heterogeneous audiences who otherwise may have little in common despite the media messages they receive. This is the reason why message system analysis then focuses on the stream of messages across borders of time, channels, or programs, instead of the specific drops of messages here and there (Shanahan & Morgan, 1999).

2.1.3.1 Four Measures for Message System Analysis

To analyse which images, messages, and portrayals cut across most programs on television, cultivation scholars are directed either to examine existing content analysis or to conduct a content analysis (which is then coined message system analysis) themselves. As with any content analysis, so too does message system analysis begin with the selection of a representative sample, the development of a code book, and the training of coders. For the code book, the general idea is that the content analysis aims to identify the basic presentation of four dimensions that Gerbner (1985) labeled as (1) existence, (2) importance, (3) values, and (4) relationship. Those dimensions then yield measures for (1) attention, (2) emphasis, (3) tendency, and (4) structure, respectively (Gerbner, 1969a). Each element— and its relevant measure—aims to answer different questions, namely for (1) what *is*?; (2) what is *important*?; (3) what is *right or wrong*, good or bad?; and (4) what is *related* to what else? (Gerbner, 1969a, 1999; Shanahan & Morgan, 1999). In his chapter *Mass Media Discourse: Message System Analysis as a Component of Cultural Indicators*, Gerbner (1985) provides more information on the measurement of the four elements:

- Existence: What is?
  For (1) existence, Gerbner advises scholars to measure the distribution of the items, topics, themes, and so forth in the symbolic environment. For the content analysis, the scholar is directed to measure the frequency of these issues, e.g., by creating a list of themes and a typology of characters. These items in the code book then consist of an identifiable subject title or questions—such as 'Gender,' 'Occupation,' 'Age,' 'Does character succeed?', or 'Which weapon is used?'—and several answers. For example, Gerbner (1972b) investigated the representation of teachers, schools, and students in the mass media fiction; in another study, Gerbner et al. (1982b) reported the frequency of demographic features and images of physicians and health; and in another study, Gerbner, Gross, Signorielli, and Morgan (1980a) analyzed the number and image of old people in network drama on television. The practical measurement and results for some of these studies are discussed below.

- Importance: What is emphasized?
  To identify (2) importance, Gerbner directs scholars to use scaling to detect what is given priority, i.e., "emphasis is a measure of the relative importance of a unit of attention in the sample" (Gerbner, 1985, p. 22). The measure hews closely to attention since emphasis directs attention to some units but not others. While some units are emphasized by repetition, others receive attention by their size and placement such as a headline, the intensity of the mode of communication, the tone, loudness, order of presentation, number of details, and other textual or design characteristics. Therefore, while frequency might be a valid measure for emphasis by repetition, a ranking or scaling allows to estimate the importance of the other items. The measure of attention follows the measure of existence, since the scholar first needs to determine what

exists, before the scholar can rate their importance. By distinguishing 'existence' and 'importance,' the scholar gains further insight into discrepancies in the representation. For example, Gerbner and Signorielli (1979) found that even in the rare cases when the numbers of women and minorities on television are above their proportion of the real population ('existence'), they are more likely to take on supporting rather than leading roles ('importance').

- Values: What is the sentiment?
  For (3) values, Gerbner's advice is to measure differential tendency to determine evaluative or other qualitative characteristics that describe the themes, items, events, people, actions, and all other characteristics that were identified in the analysis of 'existence.' The scale may be defined by semantic differentials that express an evaluation or judgment such as 'good—bad,' 'positive—negative,' 'right—wrong,' 'strong —weak,' 'bright—dark,' 'smart—stupid,' or 'successful—unsuccessful.' The exact selection of the items for the scale depends on the interest of research. As Gerbner (1985) highlights, measuring the sentiment is important as it may have implications in the subsequent cultivation analysis, since "the frequency and prominence of good things certainly impresses us differently from the frequency and prominence of bad things" (p. 23). Moreover, tendency comes in useful in research projects that have a strong normative or ideological focus, e.g., investigating how the differing sentiment of news reports on crime cases shifts the light they appear in, even when shifts of attention and importance are considered equal (for a similar study see Gerbner, 1964).

- Relationship: What is related to what else?
  For (4) relationship, Gerbner emphasizes that scholars look for structures amongst the other three dimensions—namely existence, importance, and values—to reveal underlying relationships between them. Scholars may employ clustering to detect these proximal or logical associations of the messages. The main idea is that after determining what exists, how important it is, and what sentiment it entails, scholars then can make more general assumptions about what their stable representation is. For example, a movie may present a doctor as wise and authoritative, a mental patient as violent, and a politician as opportunistic. When taking all messages on television into consideration and the majority portrays doctors as omnipresent, politicians as corrupt, and mental patients as dangerous, then a structure unfolds that is dealing with certain stereotypes visible to heavy viewers, and that may cultivate a different view of the world than reality. Gerbner (1969a,

1999) was fond of exemplifying the importance of (4) relationship by referring to the fable of 'Little Red Riding Hood:' In the fable the toxic nature of the relationship between 'wolves' and 'little girls' only becomes visible when considered in combination, not when considered separately. Moreover, when viewed not as a single fable but as one message of many, the structure reveals lessons about gender roles, power dynamics, and violence: "You do not need to believe the 'facts' of Little Red Riding Hood to grasp the notion that big bad 'wolves' victimize old women and trick little girls" (Gerbner, 1999, p. ix).

Table A.1 summarizes the definitions and explanations, as well as measure and analysis for these four elements. All four elements are observed across three types of entities: The general program, the specific action in a specific program, and the characters appearing in the program. With regard to measuring violence on television, Gerbner and Gross (1976a) define these entities as follows: Program refers to "a single fictional story presented in dramatic form," e.g., a cartoon story, a movie, or a TV show (p. 184); action (here, violent action) refers to "a scene of some violence confined to the same parties" (p. 185); and characters means major or minor roles in the program that are either violent or not.

2.1.3.2 Analyses in Message System Analysis

The results from the aforementioned four elements—namely, existence, importance, values, and relationship—are re-aggregated into larger patterns in order to represent the "common elements of discourse such as thematic distribution, propositional context, characterization and action structure, social typing, fate (success, failure) of character types, and other reliably identifiable representations and configurations" (Gerbner, 1985, p. 17). Since the main goal of the message system analysis is to determine how issues and people are portrayed on television in order to facilitate cultivation analysis, an analytic procedure is necessary that allows a comparison of the data from the television world with the one from the real world. Gerbner and his team decided to compute statistical means, percentages, and indices for the television world data, and in a second step compared these generated insights with real-world data from the corresponding Census data in order to detect any discrepancies. To specify the measure of 'existence' further and to ease the categorization of the data in the analysis, Gerbner and his team differentiated three sub-measures: prevalence, rate, and role. For example, with respect to measuring the portrayal of violence on television, they computed the percentage of programs covering any violence (prevalence), the frequency and rate of violent episodes (rate), and the number of characters that are perpetrators and/or victims (role) (Gerbner & Gross, 1976a). Notably, the analyses are run with respect to the three different entity levels, namely program, action, and character, as described in Section 2.1.2.1. The results of the three measures of prevalence, rate, and role are usually reported separately, but in combination they also compose the so-called 'Violence Index.' The Violence Index was developed in the periodically published Violence Profile articles (e.g., Gerbner & Gross, 1976a; Gerbner, Gross, Eleey, et al., 1977; Gerbner et al., 1978; Gerbner, Gross, Signorielli, Morgan, & Jackson-Beeck, 1979; Gerbner, Gross, Morgan, & Signorielli, 1980b) and is probably the best-known index from message system analysis. The Violence Index is a multidimensional cultural indicator that expresses the overall level of violence on television in prime-time and weekend-daytime network television in any given year, across all genres and channels, and over time.The Violence Index is the sum of two other indices that the Cultural Indicators Project team invented, namely the 'Program Score' and 'Character Violence Score.' The former, the Program Score (PS), consists of the prevalence of violence in programs and the rates of violent actions, both per program and hour. Thus, the score is the percentage of all programs with any violence (%P) plus the rate of violent acts (R) per program (P) and per hour (H):

$$PS = \%P + 2\frac{R}{P} + 2\frac{R}{H} \tag{2.1}$$

The rates of violence per hour and per program are doubled "to raise their relatively low numerical value" (Gerbner & Gross, 1976a, p. 185), i.e., the coefficients are weighed because of their smaller arithmetic value compared to the others. This is justified by the results from a statistical comparison by Signorielli, Gross, and Morgan (1982) which revealed that this weighing manipulation enhanced the reliability by about.05 to the alpha, compared to a variety of other possible adjustments. The Character Violence Score (CS) is obtained by adding measures of characters involved in violence (V) and those involved in killing (K), both as percentages:

$$CS = \%V + \%K \tag{2.2}$$

The sum of PS and CS then creates the formula for the Violence Index (VI):

$$VI = \%P + 2\frac{R}{P} + 2\frac{R}{H} + \%V + \%K$$

respectively

$$VI = PS + CS \tag{2.3}$$

Thus, the Violence Index is a formula that adds measures of prevalence, rates, and roles in order to achieve a certain stability to reflect various aspects of portrayals of violence (Gerbner & Gross, 1976a; Signorielli et al., 1982). Since the absolute value of the index allows no intrinsic interpretation, its purpose is rather to examine and compare trends. In other words, rather than interpreting the index in its absolute terms, it is used in relative comparisons, e.g., comparing whether the Violence Index is higher or lower than the one from the previous year. Hence, "the index itself is not a statistical finding but serves as a convenient illustrator of trends and facilitates gross comparisons" (Gerbner & Gross, 1976a, p. 185). Despite this limitation, over time the Violence Index has become an important cornerstone to provide a quick overall assessment of the level of violence on television. Of course, generally speaking, the index could be renamed in accordance to the specific research object as it consists of a formula which is generalizable enough for any topic, not only violence. For example, a scholar investigating the patterns of lessons, images, and messages on television with regard to portrayals of science communication could coin the index 'Science Communication Index;' another scholar interested in portrayal of gender accordingly 'Gender Index;' and a scholar focusing on learning and school accordingly 'Education Index.' However, the emphasis is on 'Violence Index,' because it was the realm of 'violence' that Gerbner and his Cultural Indicators Project team mainly focused on; moreover, while the invention of the formula is indeed original, the naming of the index does not stem from Gerbner and his colleagues but from a call from several research consultants to the National Institute of Mental Health in the spring of 1972, who noted that the Violence Index should be further developed for the reports to the Surgeon General (Gerbner & Gross, 1976a). As described before the Cultural Indicators Project was to a large degree funded by the National Institute of Mental Health, therefore, it is only natural that the study of violence in the message system analysis was a continuing aspect, and that the terminology is consistent with wording from the funding Institute.

2.1.3.3 Example of Empirical Assessment

In order to track how issues and people are portrayed on television, Gerbner and his Cultural Indicators Project team conducted the message system analysis on a yearly basis beginning in 1967 as outlined before. The results from the message system analysis then facilitated the cultivation analysis. In the following, as a case study we briefly walk through the message system analysis as reported in the study by Gerbner and Gross (1976a), including additional information about the technique as reported elsewhere. In general, the study consists of a message system analysis about the portrayal of violence on television and a cultivation analysis about the impact of these portrayals on the public. While oftentimes in publications the focus is on summarizing the latter, here we focus on the former to understand Gerbner's typical procedure for conducting a message system analysis. Given that the information is by no means complete since it rather serves as a sort of a tutorial, the reader is advised to take a closer look at Gerbner and Gross (1976a), Gerbner, Gross, Eleey, et al. (1977), Gerbner et al. (1978), Gerbner, Gross, Signorielli, Morgan, and Jackson-Beeck (1979), Gerbner, Gross, Morgan, and Signorielli (1980b), as well as Signorielli et al. (1982), and Shanahan and Morgan (1999) for additional information.

Procedure. Beginning in 1967, Gerbner and his associates performed a systematic, quantitative content analysis—which is called message system analysis—on annual sample weeks of prime time and weekend daytime network dramatic programs. This analysis, covering content from 1967 to 1975, also constitutes the corpus for the study by Gerbner and Gross (1976a) with a focus on portrayals of various natures of violence in television.

Measures. The message system analysis measured many aspects of violence of television content. Violence was defined as "the overt expression of physical force against self or other, compelling action against one's will on pain of being hurt or killed, or actually hurting or killing" (Gerbner & Gross, 1976a, p. 184). It should be noted that the definition excluded violence to property and emotional/ psychological violence, while it included violence in a fantastic or humorous context, e.g., "if a 'pie in the face' does [inflict overt physical pain, hurting, or killing] it is considered violence and is recorded as such" (Signorielli et al., 1982, p. 164). All coding was recorded in accordance with three indicators: the program, each program's specific violent action (if applicable), and each character in the program. Program referred to "a single fictional story presented in dramatic form," e.g., a cartoon story, a movie, or a TV show (p. 184); violent action referred to "a scene of some violence confined to the same parties" (p. 185); and characters meant major or minor roles in the program that are either violent or not. Major roles were those essential to the storyline, whereas minor roles were considered all other speaking roles. The results reported in their study included major characters only. The specific measures for the indicators targeted the prevalence, rate, and characterizations, as well as the differential risks involved in violence. Hence, the measures hew closely to the four elements that describe the larger patterns on television, namely existence, importance, values, and relationship.

Sampling. The source material for the message system analysis was the content from the network dramatic programs shown in evening prime time, i.e., 8pm to 11pm daily, as well as network children's dramatic programs on Saturday and Sunday mornings, i.e., every weekend between 8am and 2pm. The exact hours for what is considered prime time and children's program before 1971 are slightly different due to shifting schedules by the networks, e.g., in 1967/68 the daily hours for prime time ranged from 7.30pm to 10pm. Relevant for the selection was therefore the defined prime time and children's dramatic program rather than the exact times. The message system analysis was carried out across a representative sample that was sampled based on four dimensions: network, program format, character type, and tone. The final sample corpus consisted of 924 programs which results in 630.2 program hours, and 2,649 major characters. This means that on average, every year 102.7 programs (min: 87, max: 121), 70 program hours (58.5 – 77.3), and 294 leading characters (196–364) were analyzed. Several sub-samples were created from this initial set, for example for violence measures for family hour only ($n_{programs}$: 294, $n_{program\ hours}$: 236.3, $n_{major\ characters}$: 911), for late night evening ($n_{programs}$: 260, $n_{program\ hours}$: 270.7, $n_{major\ characters}$: 841), for weekend children's program ($n_{programs}$: 370, $n_{program\ hours}$: 123.2, $n_{major\ characters}$: 897), or for risk ratios for all programs for characters' sociodemographic and other features (n_{male}: 2010, n_{female}: 605).

Coder Training. Between 12 to 18 coders were trained for the analysis of each program sample. The coders underwent a training unit of three weeks during which they analyzed the season's videotaped program sample. The coders worked in pairs and could view the content as often as necessary during both the training as well as data-collection periods. The double-coded data was finally tested for reliability.

Table 2.2 Reliability coefficients for study by Gerbner and Gross (1976a) and subsequent studies.

Reliability Coefficients				
Items (scale)	1967—1976	1977	1978	1979
Frequency of Violent Actions (interval)	.746	.860	.857	.862
Violence—Significance (ordinal)	.781	.740	.813	.765
Committing Violence (nominal)	.704	.734	.657	.717
Victimization (nominal)	.673	.691	.767	.668

As reported in Signorielli et al. (1982)

Signorielli et al. (1982) report and discuss the reliability coefficients for the study by Gerbner and Gross (1976a), and found varying, yet overall conditionally acceptable, reliability coefficients depending on the program indicator (see Table 2.2).

Analyses. Each indicator, i.e., program, violent action, and character, is first analysed separately and reported per annum. All measures (prevalence, rate, role) for the different hours of programs were presented in absolute numbers or in percent in crosstabs; line charts were used to show various trends over years in percent. The crosstab for risk ratios were not presented annually, but for all programs studied from 1967–75; the crosstab showed various sociodemographic characteristics (social age, marital status, class, nationality, race) and types (good, bad, ambivalent) with respect to the characters' gender. The three measures of prevalence, rate, and characterization (thus, excluding risk ratios) were further combined to form the Violence Index according to the formula 2.3, and presented in crosstabs and line charts as well (e.g., showing trends of the Violence Index for different hours by network, program, and so forth).

Presenting Results. The results revealed several trends of the portrayal of violence in television: For example, action programs such as crime, western, or adventure comprised more than 50 percent for the prime time and weekend children's programs. With regard to the first measure of prevalence, on average ($P =$)80 percent of all programs contained violence per year (min: 79.0, max: 83.5). For the second measure, rate, in total 4,694 episodes were found to be violent (yearly min: 394, max: 626), which results in ($R/H =$)7 violent episodes per hour on average (min: 6.7, max: 8.8), and ($R/P =$)5 violent episodes per program. For the third measure, roles, on average 45 percent of leading characters were violent, and 54 percent were victims, respectively. On average, $(V =)$63 percent of leading characters were involved in violence. With regard to fatal/ lethal violence, 8 percent of major characters were committing murder, and 4 percent of leading characters were killed. The study found that $(K =)$10 percent of leading characters had any involvement in killing. The coefficients were shown per year to allow interpretation of the annual trends. From the reported coefficients the Violence Index was computed according to formula 2.3, e.g., given $VI = \%P+2R/P +2R/H+\%V +\%K$ across all years the Violence Index is $(VI = 80 + 2(5) + 2(7) + 63 + 10 =)$ 177. Since the absolute value of VI cannot be interpreted, it is recommended to display the trend over years as in Figure 2.1.

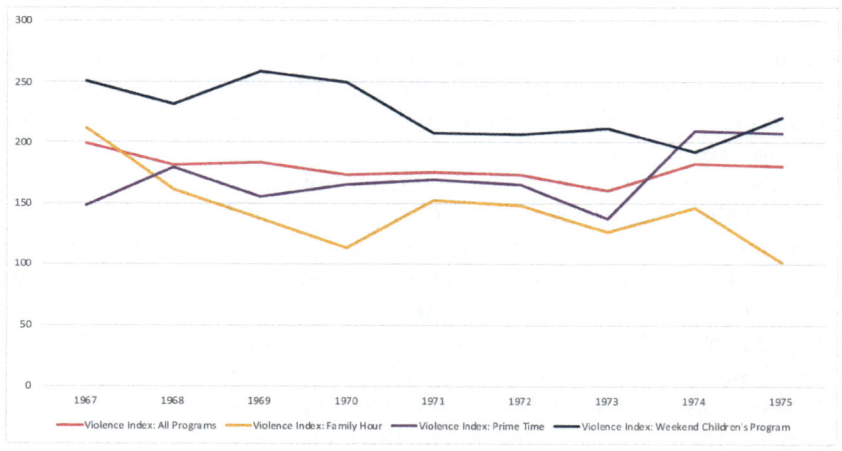

Figure 2.1 Trends of Violence Index 1967—1975 for various hours of program.
Figure re-creation from data by Gerbner and Gross, 1976a.

With regard to the risk ratios, for every violent male and female, the programs showed 1.19 male and 1.32 female victims. Most likely to get killed (rather than to experience injury) were married, old, poor, foreign, and nonwhite men. The killers were most likely to be the 'good guys' type. Among females, unmarried, lower class, foreign, and nonwhite women were more likely to be victimized. There were no cases in which old, poor, and black women were portrayed as killers. 'Good women' had no lethal power, while the actions from the 'bad women' were even more lethal (2.00) than the ones from the 'bad guys' (1.80). Of interest is again the trend, for example for victimization, which Gerbner and Gross (1976a) described as stable across years.

The results reported above are just one example of the various findings of the message system analyses. Rather than providing the reader with an exhaustive and complete summary of the findings—which would take up more space than can be granted—the focus here was rather on outlining the several steps such as procedure, measures, sampling, coder training, analyses, and presentation of results that Gerbner and his team took, and that should direct scholars when conducting a message system analysis themselves. Thus, the purpose was rather sort of a tutorial based on a case study. Nonetheless, the results outlined in the 'Presenting Results' Section overlap with the summary of the general findings from five decades of research according to the Cultural Indicators Project team:

> "We examined violence in prime-time network programs aired between 1967 and 2015. Violence, the research shows, has been a consistent and central part of programming even though it varies somewhat by genre. Two findings are especially noteworthy. First, there was a sharp reduction in the VI in the 1990s, due mostly to the greater prominence of two kinds of programs: sitcoms and procedurals. This was about a decade-long phenomenon. The second major finding is that violence is apparently making a serious comeback, with four of the index's five components reaching historically high levels in the 2010s. Only the percentage of characters involved in violence is lower than it was through the 1980s."
> — Signorielli, Morgan, and Shanahan (2019, p. 24)

2.1.4 Some Critique, Advancement, and Refinement

Although over the last 50 years cultivation theory has proven to be a popular approach to investigate media effects on beliefs and attitudes (Morgan et al., 2015, 2017), the theory and research is also notorious for semantic and methodological issues which have led at once to criticism and advancement. The levels of critique (or 'battles,' as Morgan and Signorielli, 1990 call it) are manifold and consumed hundreds of pages of book chapters and journal articles, even being addressed in popular media magazines such as *Time* magazine. Morgan and Signorielli (1990) evaluate the contribution of cultivation theory to the field of communication not despite, but because of, the challenges that the Cultural Indicators Project faced:

"In sum, these battles have been characterized as everything from 'healthy scholarly exchanges' to 'scathing exposees' to 'vicious and unprofessional spat.' They were challenging, unpleasant, and in some ways, fun. They attest to the importance of cultivation theory in the discipline and to the fact that cultivation analysis has not been a static research approach, but one that has evolved and developed in numerous ways, making it not only more complex and intricate but also more dynamic and intriguing"
— Morgan and Signorielli (1990, p. 25)

Below we walk through two major aspects—theoretical implications and methodology— and discuss selected arguments, counterarguments, and advances. It is not possible to review all the criticism and counterarguments here, but for a relatively complete account the reader is advised (preferably in the order listed) to take a closer look at:

- for terminology, completeness, qualitative approaches, and heuristic value: Newcomb (1978), Gerbner and Gross (1979), Potter (1993), Tapper (1995), Potter (2014),
- for replication issues: Wober (1978), Gerbner, Gross, Morgan, and Signorielli (1979), Wober (1979),
- for causality, spuriousness, and mainstreaming: Doob and Macdonald (1979), Hughes (1980), Gerbner, Gross, Morgan, and Signorielli (1980a, 1980b),
- for statistical evidence, controls, linearity, mainstreaming, and resonance: Hirsch (1980), Gerbner, Gross, Morgan, and Signorielli (1981a), Hirsch (1981), Gerbner, Gross, Morgan, and Signorielli (1981b), Potter (1981, 1994)
- for precision, shifts in focus and contextual forces: Hawkins and Pingree (1980, 1981a), J. Cohen and Weimann (2000), Shrum (2002), Morgan et al. (2012), Potter (2014), Morgan et al. (2015), L. Prince (2018),
- and for a more or less brief summary: Shanahan and Morgan (1999), Potter (2014), Morgan et al. (2015), Mosharafa (2015).

2.1.4.1 Some Critique on Theoretical Implications

Individual Differences. One of the first critiques of cultivation concerned, among other issues, the differences in definitional perspectives: Newcomb (1978) raised the concern that 'violence' has multiple meanings in U.S. history and society, and that some viewers may perceive the violence portrayed on television differently than others. The reason lies in the multi-generic status of the programs: According to Newcomb there is no program that can be boiled down to a single, invariant message that is perceived in the same way by all viewers. He concluded that this fact then prevents all programs, one of the main assumptions by Gerbner, to share a set of cultural indicators that is being distributed. Put simply, Newcomb doubted that viewers would understand the messages about violence on television in the same way that Gerbner and Gross (1976a) did in their study. To support his claim, an in-depth analysis of individual programs against the focus on aggregate patterns of the Cultural Indicators Project was conducted, and the results showed various differences in programs and, presumably, differences in viewers. In response to Newcomb, Gerbner and Gross (1979) argued that the focus of the Cultural Indicators Project was not on differences, but on the commonalities of messages and exposure. That is, they do not deny that the symbolic environment is complex and that "the layers of meanings we generate and construct as we interact with them are multiple, varied, unpredictable and slippery" (Shanahan & Morgan, 1999). The argument is rather that the technological and economic forces tend to shape a rather formulaic and uniform symbolic environment since the programs are market-driven and centrally produced (instead of uniquely crafted). Moreover, Gerbner and Gross (1979) point out that their definition of violence was on purpose minimal in order to be commonly understood and unambiguous as it "essentially entails hurting and/or killing, or forcing some action on pain of being hurt or killed" (p. 225). Three years later, Signorielli et al. (1982) provide a more exhaustive literature review in which they present definitions of violence by other scholars that are consistent to the one from the Cultural Indicators Project team. Finally, Gerbner and Gross (1979) argue that "Newcomb's big question, 'what does violence mean to the respondents' is not only irrelevant but distracting" (p. 227), since cultivation is not interested in individual interpretations of messages but in the contribution of television on the conceptions of social reality on an aggregate level. This line of reasoning traces back to the early stage of the project, when Gerbner (1969a) argued that cultivation focuses on the dominant patterns of media messages rather than individual differences in their interpretations: "Whether I accept its 'meaning' or not, like it or not, or agree or disagree is another problem. First I must attend to and grasp what it is about. Just how that occurs, how items of information are integrated into given frameworks of cognition, is also another problem" (p. 139).

Within the last two decades, however, there seems to be another increase in the number of critical voices of placing the—what Potter (2014) coins—'locus of meaning' in messages, and an increase in interest and advocacy for placing the locus in the viewers instead (e.g., Bilandzic & Busselle, 2008; Busselle, 2003; Nabi, 2009) or to investigate cognitive processes within the viewers during the cultivation process further (e.g., Shrum, 2002). Besides the shift from a societal to a psychological level of investigation, the acknowledgment of the viewers as individuals also allowed scholars to question the assumption of cultivation theory that viewers are rather nonselective in their viewing. As J. Cohen and Weimann (2000) point out, "viewers do not simply watch TV; they watch specific shows. They tend to prefer certain types of shows over others, and their choices of shows, or TV diets, often consist mainly of shows from a limited number of genres" (p. 102). Potter (1993) reasons that the assumption by the Cultural Indicators Project team may have been valid when there were only three channels available to the viewers, but with the steady increase of channels, the viewers were offered more choices and were able to be selective in their viewing. The critiques about the assumptions of uniformity of the system of messages and unselective viewing behavior are discussed in greater detail in Chapter 4.

Textual Differences. Newcomb's early concerns in 1978 about the uniform concept of messages may have also proliferated the research of cultivating messages within the boundaries of genres. That is, different genres may contain various messages which may exert differing cultivation effects (J. Cohen & Weimann, 2000; Potter, 1993, 2014). Like the aforementioned shift, this line of research also represents a movement from the macro to the micro level, but on a textual (instead of a psychological) level. Gerbner and his associates, however, maintained the assumption that the level of message system analysis should be on the totality of messages, hence, across genres, and cautioned that "the comparison of responses to those who claim to prefer or view this and that type of programming (one particular genre), instead of measures of total viewing, is likely to yield confusing, contradictory, and misleading results" (Gerbner, 1990, p. 257). To deal with messages as a system is a core element to cultivation as it represents an attempt to understand the symbolic environment comprehensively, generally, and systematically, and it is what distinguishes the message system analysis from other types of measurement (such as observation or commentary; Gerbner, 1985). Despite the disapproval for cultivation studies that investigate genre-specific messages since this type of investigation "goes against the basic tenets of cultivation theory"

(Morgan et al., 2015, p. 690), according to Potter (2014) there have been many scholars employing this micro level of testing: For example, Grabe and Drew (2007) showed that the magnitude of cultivation effects were stronger when tested genre-specifically rather than taking the total TV viewing as a predictor. Other studies focused on a specific show (instead of a genre) such as *Grey's Anatomy* (2005—; e.g., Quick, 2009) or a particular video game (e.g., Chong et al., 2012; Williams, 2006) to test cultivation effects. From a theoretical standpoint, proponents of the original idea of cultivation are still conflicted as to whether studies with this textual shift may be labeled cultivation or not (Morgan, Shanahan, & Signorielli, 2014, 2015; Shanahan & Morgan, 1999). The argument is that to date there is no "clear rationale for how they [genre-specific studies] are similar to or different from the more global concept of cultivation" (Morgan & Shanahan, 2010, p. 341). Though unanswered, this call for theoretical improvement is still being made today. An answer to this call, and to the implications of the concept of uniformity of messages and selectivity of viewers, will be addressed in Chapter 4 and Chapter 5 here.

2.1.4.2 Some Critique and Advances in Methodology

Violence Index. The methodology that the Cultural Indicators Project team employed has led to an abundance of critiques and advances. Until 1978, most of the criticism of the work on cultivation stemmed from the television industry directly and targeted the operationalization and measurement of violence and the calculation of the Violence Index, along with sample size, coding procedures, reliability, and validity. However, Shanahan and Morgan (1999) assume that the motivation for these critiques was driven less by a scientific interest, but rather by sales factors: "The industry had an obvious interest in discrediting the research, in wanting to declare that its estimates of the amount of violence on television were grossly overstated. So they focused on such issues as whether 'comic' violence and 'accidents' should be included" (p. 59). While the purpose of the Violence Index was initially to provide a quick and easy overall assessment of the level of violence on television over time, it increasingly was perceived as a direct and absolute measure and "many tended to see Gerbner as bean-counting 'numbers guru' for TV violence, solely interested in totting up how many times cartoon characters were bopping each other over the head" (Shanahan & Morgan, 1999, p. 52). With regard to the question whether or not violence in a humorous context should be included in the analysis, some scholars pointed out that there are violent incidents on television that differ in terms of intensity and goal from other portrayals, for example cartoons that ordinarily produce laughter and are not of a serious character; these portrayals should be disregarded. The Cultural Indicators Project team, however, counterargued that "a comic context is a highly effective form in which to convey serious lessons" and that it is doubtful that for example children will only adopt the 'good' messages in this humorous context (Signorielli et al., 1982, p. 162).

With regard to the formula, as explained before, the Violent Index is a combination of different measures—i.e., the percentage of programs containing violence, the frequency and rate of violent episodes per hour and per program, and the number of major characters involved in violence (either as victims or aggressors)—that provides an overall assessment of the level of violence on television in any given year and across a variety of categories. The main controversy centred on the calculation of the weighted items as the rates of violence per hour and per program are doubled in order "to raise their relatively low numerical value" (Gerbner & Gross, 1976a, p. 185). Despite the effort in weighing the items equally, in the end it is not a zero sum equation as Gunter (1981) points out: "While the number of violent scenes on television may decrease over a period of time, an increase in the number of characters involved in violent episodes during the same period could be sufficient to produce a higher overall violence score on the Violence Index" (p. 94). The doubts of the validity of the Violence Index led to a statistical comparison by Signorielli et al. (1982) which revealed that this weighting manipulation enhanced the reliability by about .05 to the alpha, compared to a variety of other possible adjustments. Moreover, the Cultural Indicators Project team pointed out that an index comes by nature with a reduction of information, and that the criticism raised for the Violence Index calculation would then also apply to established indices such as the Dow-Jones, GNP, or the Pollution Index. While this note certainly rings true, it may be worthwhile to offer additional Violence Sub-Indices that consider the details on the nature of violence, i.e., a Violence Index each for dramatic and humorous violence. This would also be in line with Gerbner's early research in which he disentangled programs with a comic or dramatic tone (e.g., Gerbner, 1969, as reported in Cumberbatch, Jones, & Lee, 1988).

Measuring Message Systems. A recent critique on the methodology of the message system analysis stems from Potter (2014): He compared the precision of overlap in theoretical statements of ideal methodology and practices in the test by the Cultural Indicators Project team. More precisely, the comparison refers to Gerbner's early notions that the message system analysis should be guided by analysing four dimensions (and their respective measure): existence (attention), importance (emphasis), values (tendency), and relationship (structure; Gerbner, 1969a, 1985; see Section 2.1.3 for further details). Potter then examines briefly whether the research by the Cultural Indicators Project team actually tested all four dimensions. As outlined above, Gerbner directed scholars to measure the frequency for answering the dimension of 'existence,' for 'importance' he recommends a rating exercise, for 'values' to use semantic differentials, and for 'relationships' a cluster analysis or similar in order to look for patterns across messages. Despite the call and instruction for carefully measuring all four dimensions, Potter (2014, p. 1029) states that "when we look at the cultivation team's annual profiles of television content, the reported findings are based solely on arguments about the frequency of certain manifested elements, without considering patterns of contextual factors." Thus, the practical tests of the message system analysis in the Violence Profiles focused heavily on the dimension of existence, with some tests for values through the risk ratios, but neglected the other two despite their importance. As a best practice example, Potter highlights the National Television Violence Study from 1999, in which 43 contextual variables were investigated and patterns between them extrapolated in order to make claims about broader patterns of the ways that violence was portrayed, thus, potentially addressing the dimension of relationships.

Measuring Cultivation. Soon after the first results from the cultivation analysis were published (Gerbner & Gross, 1976a), it became the focal point of criticism, advancement, and refinement alike. With regard to replicability, Wober (1978) contested the results from the initial study after failing to replicate the cultivation analysis in Great Britain. Wober's study led to an intellectual discourse between him, the Cultural Indicators Project team and other emerging cultivation scholars about cultural and structural differences between countries that may explain the lack of evidence (best read in the following order: Wober, 1978; Gerbner, Gross, Morgan, & Signorielli, 1979; Wober, 1979; Hawkins & Pingree, 1981a). For example, Hawkins and Pingree (1981b) pointed out that heavy viewers from Great Britain received less violence than the light viewers from the U.S. do; in numbers, the message system analysis identified merely 10 percent (38 out of 380) of the investigated shows in the British TV program as violent (Wober, 1978). That the rather low rate of portrayal of violence on television then has no significant effect on the viewers is consequentially not perceived as a negation of the idea of cultivation

(Shanahan & Morgan, 1999). Moreover, Gerbner and his colleagues challenged a direct comparison between the two studies since—even though Wober's aim was to replicate the findings—the study from Great Britain measured beliefs about fear and violence differently (in terms of scaling and operationalization), and covered up the purpose of research rather poorly (Gerbner, Gross, Morgan, & Signorielli, 1979). Van den Bulck (2012) has developed a contemporary typology for studying cultivation internationally that guides future scholars to avoid some of these replicability pitfalls.

There also has been a great debate about the optimal operationalization of the real world and TV answer in cultivation analysis, especially with regard to the forced-error-questions that Gerbner and his associates oftentimes employed, i.e., neither using the correct percentage for the real world and TV answer estimations that the respondents can choose from. Consequently, other scholars suggested alternative ways to operationalize the measurement of cultivation such as open-ended questions (as advocated by e.g., Potter, 1981, 1994), or closed questions but with multiple options. Since the scope here is not on cultivation analysis, but on messages, we refer the reader to take a closer look at Gerbner et al. (1981b), Shanahan and Morgan (1999) as well as Potter (1994) for a discussion of the merits and drawbacks of the various approaches. It is noteworthy, however, that in the empirical development of cultivation analysis, another important refinement emerged that distinguished between two different types of cultivation effects: Based on the ideas of Hawkins and colleagues (e.g., Hawkins & Pingree, 1980; Hawkins, Pingree, & Adler, 1987) the so-called 'first-order' and 'second-order' effects were introduced which define the measurement of social reality conceptions further. As exemplified by Gross and Aday (2003, p. 412), "first-order effects involve audiences adopting television's overestimation of the occurence of everything from the number of murders to the number of doctors in the real world; second-order effects are the ways in which television viewing shapes audiences'" real world beliefs and attitudes such as fear of victimization, or feelings of isolation.

Types of Cultivation. Another strand of critique targeted questions of spuriousness, controls and measuring artifacts: Doob and Macdonald (1979) reasoned that, perhaps, people who live in urban areas and/or high crime areas are more afraid of crime because of the area they live in—which leads to a greater amount of time they spent in their safe environment at home, where they then watch television. In other words, heavy viewers may be more fearful of violence and victimization because of the dangerous environment they are exposed to. In their empirical findings, Doob and Macdonald report that people who live in high-crime areas are indeed more afraid and that they also watched more television; and that the relationship between television exposure and fear of violence and victimization disappears when controlling for actual incidence of crime in their area. They conclude that "television may well act as a source of information with regard to questions of fact, whereas it does not change people's views of how afraid they should be" (p. 179). After being confronted with the claim that cultivation patterns may vary across subgroups, Gerbner, Gross, Morgan, and Signorielli (1980b) shortly introduced two major additions to the theory: mainstreaming and resonance. With regard to the former, they explain that "the 'mainstream' can be thought of as a relative commonality of outlooks that television tends to cultivate. By 'mainstreaming' we mean the sharing of that commonality among heavy viewers in those demographic groups whose light users hold divergent views. In other words, differences deriving from other factors and social forces may be diminished or even absent among heavy viewers" (p. 15). Thus, mainstreaming suggests that cultivation might only appear for some groups of people under some conditions. Resonance is defined as an amplification of messages stemming from real-world experiences and television alike and that are especially salient to certain groups of viewers: "When what people see on television is most congruent with everyday reality (or even perceived reality), the combination may result in a coherent and powerful 'double dose' of the television message and significantly boost cultivation. Thus, the congruence of the television world and real-life circumstances may 'resonate' and lead to markedly amplified cultivation patterns" (p. 15). For example, people living in dangerous areas watch a lot of television and receive a double dose of crime exposure, which results in a higher than average degree of cultivation. With these two additions of types of cultivation, Gerbner, Gross, Morgan, and Signorielli (1980b, p. 25) saw additional support for their previous findings and for their "theory of pervasive cultivation of mistrust, apprehension, danger, and exaggerated 'mean world' perceptions."

Distinction between Viewers. Another critique addresses the binary distinction in heavy and light viewers. Initially, the Cultural Indicators Project team identified light viewers as those viewing television for two hours or less a day on average; and heavy viewers as those viewing for four hours or more on average a day (Gerbner & Gross, 1976a; Gerbner et al., 1978). For a start, this kind of exposure measurement—which is the only distinctive feature for defining heavy and light viewers—does not consider exposure over time. This means that a 20 year old watching television for four hours/day on average is classified as a heavy viewer, whereas a 70 year old who had been watching television all of their life for two hours/day on average is classified in the light-viewers' group. Thus, any accumulation effects of viewing are neglected.

Secondly, the measurement of exposure makes an assumption of linearity, i.e., it is assumed that the more TV a person views, the more they are being cultivated. Of course, this assumption is hardly reflected in the actual binary measurement. And although Gerbner and his associates later changed their measurement from binary to three groups of viewers (light, medium, heavy), Hirsch (1980) reported that in an analysis of five groups (in addition to the other two: non-viewers and extreme viewers) the relationship was becoming curvilinear. More specifically, Hirsch found that the group of non-viewers were more fearful, alienated, and anomic than the light viewers, even though by definition they had zero exposure to television on average; the extreme viewers (those watching television for eight hours or more on average a day), on the other hand, were less fearful than the heavy viewers (who by definition had less exposure to television). The debate about the potential non-linearity of cultivation patterns stimulated a discourse that stretched over 20 years: Soon after Hirsch's publication of the non-linear relationship, Hawkins and Pingree (1982, p. 235) note that the sample sizes of the two extreme groups were so small and their idiosyncrasy "unusual enough that they probably differ from other groups on possibly relevant third variables" and that it seems unreasonable to perceive the results as a contradiction to cultivation. Moreover, Gerbner et al. (1981a, 1981d) cautioned that the classification in light, medium, and heavy viewers' group is a relative, not absolute ranking, and may vary across different samples. Thus, in some samples up to three hours a day defined a light viewer; similarly, different thresholds applied for children vs. adults. Thus, Gerbner and his associates "see self-reported viewing primarily as a useful ranking device and do not focus on specific hours of exposure" (Gerbner et al., 1981a, p. 46). Put simply, they "want to know if it's warm or cold, not if it's 68 degrees or 69 degrees" (Shanahan & Morgan, 1999, p. 78). As Potter (1981) points out, however, this argument only applies when the relationship between viewing and cultivation measures is indeed linear. To avoid the debate about linearity from their data categories, Gerbner et al. (1981a) increasingly started to use the viewing measurement as a continuous variable to bypass the problem completely.

Hence, several aspects of the Cultural Indicators Project were the subject of criticism, but also refinement and advancement. Next, we discuss critically the role of television in cultivation theory, what sets it apart from other mass media according to Gerbner and his associates, and compare the assumptions to today's new media environment. This aspect is important since some proponents of the original cultivation research are under the impression that today's era of online television has little impact on the tenets of cultivation theory.

2.2 Digitalization and Cultivation

Cultivation theory is more than a theory of cause-and-effect with television as an agent of social change. Rather, the approach of cultivation theory is the one of a cumulative impact, i.e., a theory that emphasizes the central role of television in the complex socialization process (Shanahan & Morgan, 1999). Thus, at its core, cultivation theory posits that television enculturates society by serving the function of society's storyteller. Gerbner (1999) emphasizes the role of television further: television "stories socialize us into roles of gender, age, class, vocation and lifestyle, and offer models of conformity or targets for rebellion. They weave the seamless web of the cultural environment that cultivates most of what we think, what we do, and how we conduct our affairs" (p. ix). Thus, from the perspective of cultivation theory, television plays a major role in shaping our conceptions of social reality, because it is this particular medium that we receive these very stories from. According to the cultivation perspective, "most of what we know, or think we know, we have never personally experienced" (Gerbner, 1999, p. ix), but learned from television. This assumption is based on the two propositions that television provides viewers with a "stream of messages" that cut across genres, networks and time; and that viewers are relatively non-selective in their viewing habits (Morgan et al., 2015, p. 667). Before we evaluate these two propositions further in Chapters 4 and 5, it is important to consider the circumstances of the times when they were developed and what has changed ever since.

When considering their historical origins, these propositions—along with of course cultivation theory in general—were initially developed during a time when three broadcast networks dominated much of television content. This is reflected in the notes by Gerbner and Gross (1976a), when they explained,

> "All major networks serving the same social system depend on the same markets and programming formulas. That may be one reason why, unlike other media, television is used non-selectively; it just

doesn't matter that much. With the exception of national events and some 'specials,' the total viewing audience is fairly stable regardless of what is on. Individual tastes and program preferences are less important in determining viewing patterns than is the time a program is on. The nearly universal, non-selective, and habitual use of television fits the ritualistic pattern of its programming."
— Gerbner and Gross (1976a, p. 177)

Consequently, the audience was confined by the linear and limited content available by the networks, with no technology allowing time shifting. This means that if viewers of yesteryear were going to watch television at 8pm, they would have three programs to choose from. And if they missed it, then there was no way of watching it at a later point of time.

Even as early as in the 1990s, however, there were already calls for taking into account the increasingly fragmented media landscape that resulted in a greater variety in content and greater control for the audience as well. Potter (1993), for example, pointed out that it may have been that previously,

"The small number of network programmers presented a narrow range of genres, and within each genre, there was a rigid formula. But this pattern has been breaking down for well over a decade, and it certainly is not the case in the 1990s when there is a much wider range of programs. During prime time, the range of messages still includes sitcoms and action/adventure shows, but it is also composed of music videos, sports, home shopping, headline news, in-depth documentaries, stand-up comedy, school board meetings, cartoons, low-budget science fiction, and fundamentalist preachers."
— Potter (1993, p. 573)

The Cultural Indicators Project team asserted, however, that a greater range of variety in programs, and even today's digitalized, new media environment did not challenge the basic assumptions of cultivation theory, since "although the way we now receive our 'stories' [...] has changed, along with the ways we consume them, [...] important aspects of their content arguably have not" (Morgan et al., 2015, p. 685). They argue that this is because more channels do not necessarily mean more "diversity in voice" (Shanahan & Morgan, 1999, p. 209). Below we take a glimpse at Gerbner's understanding of television and how this compares to formats that are considered an extension of television, starting from VHS and DVD to online television including SVOD services such as Netflix, Hulu, Amazon Video, or Disney+. The notions will be helpful in understanding the construct of cultivating messages, such as genre-specific messsages or metanarratives, and the novel type of cultivating message that we derive later in Chapter 4.

2.2.1 Gerbner's Idea of Television

Gerbner's assertion about television being "the central cultural arm of American society," was put forward decades ago, at a time when the number of channels and technical devices to receive the cultivating messages were more limited than today (Gerbner & Gross, 1976a, p. 175). The Cultural Indicators Project team was (and continues to be) convinced that television is the main source of a repetitive and stable symbolic environment that cultivates the common consciousness of the public. Thus, according to Gerbner and Gross (1976a), television is "a medium of the socialization of most people into standardized roles and behaviors," while it does not change, threaten, or weaken people's conceptions about social reality, but rather extends and maintains them; thus, its function is enculturation (p. 175). Defined briefly, enculturation is the process of maintenance of and socialization to salient values, ideas, and concepts of the norms of one's heritage culture (according to Herskovits, 1948, in Kim & Alamilla, 2007). While in general the process of producing and distributing messages became increasingly centralized and industrialized in mass media, it was neither radio or newspaper that became the focus of cultivation theory, but television: It was in particular the potential to create simultaneously a public experience of the same symbolic environment, spanning across otherwise diverse communities (e.g., differing in age, gender, race, or urbanity), that made television appealing as a research object. Thus, Gerbner and his associates believed that "television is essentially different from other media and that research on television requires a new approach" (Gerbner & Gross, 1976a, p. 174).

Gerbner and his associates assumed that television came with specific attributes and functions that distinguished it from other mass media. More precisely, amongst other publications, in his article *Television: The New State Religion?* Gerbner (1977) claims that television fills the void for a social symbolic environment that in pre-industrial times was to some degree left unattended by preceding media and rather filled by religions. The reason for the change, namely that television now provides the social symbolic environment, lies in six key characteristics that television consists of and that sets it apart from other mass media such as print or radio. While

Gerbner (1977) explains these characteristics in his article but does not label them, we suggest that they address the following realms,

- Time Consumption:

  Gerbner (1977) attests television to take up increasingly more time and attention than all the other mass media and any leisure time activities combined. The notion is supported by his claim that the average American home watches television for six hours and fifteen minutes a day.

- Omnipresence:

  Television is available directly at home and all the time. Hence, it requires no mobility such as going to a cinema, or a waiting period such as the daily newspaper: "Unlike the other media, you do not have to wait for, plan for, go out to, or seek out television" (Gerbner, 1977, p. 147). Moreover, television is not just another medium, but has become an integral part of the family, like a family member.

- Literacy:

  Television relies on images and sound, thus, it requires no literacy such as reading, writing, or using numeracy. This characteristic makes television a socially highly inclusive medium, since "it shows and tells about the world to the less educated and the non-reader—those who have never before shared the culture of the literate—with special authority and force" (Gerbner, 1977, p. 148). The way that television viewers are informed, however, is not through information but through entertainment. Thus, the inclusion comes with the danger that television "might dumb down the achievements of (in McLuhan's terms) the 'culture of the eye'" (Morgan et al., 2015, p. 677). However, Gerbner (1977) also argues that while the two genres of information and entertainment were sharply distinguished in the print era (news vs. drama), in television these lines are getting blurred.

- Totality:

  The increasingly blurred differentiations between genres in television are according to Gerbner (1977) to some degree trifling, since "viewers typically select not programs but hours of the day and watch whatever is on during those hours" (Gerbner, 1977, p. 148). Thus, if the viewer turns on the television after work, they can select their program from a small set of channels. And since the content for the channels is produced on the assembly line, the message formula is consistent and repetitive across all channels. Hence, the reason for the assumption that the audience is unselective in their viewing habits, rests in the assumption that the production of television content is institutionalized and mainstreamed: "All types of programming within the program structure complement and reinforce one another. It makes no sense to study the content or impact of one type of program in isolation from the others. The same viewers watch them all; the total system as a whole is absorbed into the mainstream of common consciousness" (Gerbner, 1977, p. 148).

- Reach:
Unlike other mass media, television has the ability to reach various social groups. It encompasses young and older age groups likewise, making it a "cradle-to-grave experience" (Gerbner, 1977, p. 148). Moreover, for the younger generation, television will have consumed more time by the time that they enter school than they would spend in a classroom in college; and for the older generation, television represents a gateway to experience regular (but mediated) human contact and engagement with the rest of the world. Television is also experienced together as a family, no matter the age differences.

- Autonomous Publics:
Gerbner (1977) assumes that television reaches formerly heterogeneous audience groups, i.e., despite their age, gender, race, economic status, and other interest groups. The danger, however, is that the viewers are receiving all the same stable and repetitive messages on cultural indicators. Since the content is produced by and for the majority this means that minorities are forced to view their own images through the lens of the majority. Hence, as the church once shaped the images of minorities by the dominant interests of the majority, now television is shaping their images with its monolithic and stable structure. In the end, this may lead to "the dissolution of the concept of autonomous publics and of any authentic group or class consciousness" (Gerbner, 1977, p. 149).

The first three characteristics—high time consumption, omnipresence, and low requirements of literacy—also shape the concept of television further, namely as providing a "ubiquitous, unified, and undifferentiated 'stream' of messages" (Morgan et al., 2015, p. 677). For the individual, television is highly time consuming, it is omnipresent, and available to everyone as it requires no literacy. For the public, everyone receives the same monolithic and stable patterns of images (totality), regardless of their age or their race (reach), shaping the portrayals of minorities through the hand and lens of the public's majority (dissolving autonomous publics). Thus, while printing as the first industrial product enabled novel approaches in endless accumulation of information, since it "made it possible for the newly differentiated consciousness to spread beyond the limiting confines of face-to-face communication," it also requires a greater literacy, is exclusive as it is only available to the literate, and needs to be sought out each time (Gerbner, 1977, p. 146). Therefore, print media such as books or newspaper are different from television with regard to the characteristics of omnipresence, literacy, totality, reach, and variety in portrayals. Since print media is competing with (and losing to) television in terms of time devoted to it, it can also be argued that it differs with regard to the characteristic of time consumption.

However, arguably the media landscape has changed substantially since the 1970s. With the emergence of VHS, DVD, and SVOD services such as Netflix or Disney+, corresponding shifts occurred in the technological and economic forces that affect the audience recursively. Before we assess how Gerbner's idea and characteristics of television compare to today, we first take a look at the current concept and understanding of television.

2.2.2 Television Today: What Is Online Television?

There has been a considerable shift in the components of television as a medium ever since its first introduction in the broadcast era (1930s-70s). The strictly linear television experience got shaken first with the introduction of VHS tapes and DVDs, which allowed the viewers to time shift in their viewing habits. This means that the viewers could watch any content at any time; and if they missed a movie on television, they could watch the VHS tape or buy the DVD to catch up on it at their convenience. While in the 1990s the internet was still perceived as a separate medium from television since it came with its own forms of content (e.g., websites and blogs), this sharp distinction changed around 2010: Suddenly, the internet served as a means of facilitating the access and delivery of television programs and other audiovisual content. The increased ubiquity and use of the internet was proliferated by advances in the technological infrastructure (such as 4G and superfast broadband), the development of technological media that enabled such formats (e.g., tablets or smartphones), and the increased acceptance and adoption by the audience of the respective media that had internet connection (e.g., smartphones or internet-connected television sets; Johnson, 2019). For example, superfast broadband and 4G paved the way for the possibility to stream and to download audiovisual content outside of one's home. The increasing numbers of ownership of smartphones and tablets enabled people to consume content on the go, and while television was initially a medium for the family, the new technology also individualized the access and use of audiovisual (amongst other) content. Moreover, the new technology not only enabled access to a greater degree of mobility but also situated watching television as another form of mediated activity, i.e., users can easily switch between different forms of activities such as reading, communicating, or watching audiovisual content. The changes in the media landscape and society also prompted semantic questions for the definition of television today: For example, Johnson (2019, p. 3) points out that "as the internet simultaneously intertwines with and competes with television as a means of providing viewing experiences, it becomes harder to conceptualise television as a medium distinct from the internet."

Thus, online television—also coined TVIV by Jenner (2016)—as introduced in the 2010s belongs to a different era than the one from earlier broadcast (TVI), cable/satellite (TVII), but also the digital era from the 1990s (TVIII). For example, the simple question 'Did you watch television yesterday?' would have evoked a different reaction in each era: From a definite answer, to a request for precision, to a shrug with many question marks on the other person's face. It is therefore crucial to understand television not merely as a technology for delivering audiovisual content to viewers, e.g., as a screen to watch a movie, but also with regard to its textual features, industrial practices, cultural memory and understanding, and audience behaviors (Lotz, 2017a, 2017b). Hence, television is a concept (not merely a technology) that comes with its own components and set of propositions. In order to provide a concise definition for television regardless of the era, according to a recent publication by Johnson (2019, p. 4), in general television can be defined as a medium "made of different technological, cultural, industrial, organisation and experiential components." These five components—namely, technology, culture, industry, organisation, and user experience—shape the concept of television in each era accordingly. That is because the underlying forces for each component are susceptible to change, and accordingly challenge the definition of television as a medium for each era, respectively. As Uricchio (2014) explains,

"Television's ongoing change seems endless—from tubes, to transistors, to chips; from cathode ray displays, to plasma, to projection; from broadcast, to cable, to Internet streaming; from dial-up, to remote control, to algorithmic recommendation; from mass audiences, to niche audiences, to individuals."
— Uricchio (2014, p. 275)

Thus, television as a medium transforms in accordance to the changes in the forces. But defining television as a medium consisting of the aforementioned five components enables scholars to distinguish it further from internet writ large, let alone other television eras. For example, the television as we experience it today is to a large degree so-called 'online television.' The aforementioned components (technology, culture, industry, organisation, and user experience) set online television apart from television from the broadcast, cable/satellite, and digital eras. More precisely, as outlined by Johnson (2019, p. 8) the five components of online television consist of the following properties:

- **Technology**: digital infrastructure (including terrestrial, satellite, and cable), broadband, 4G, and cloud computing; viewing is enabled on TV sets, smart TV, desktop, laptop, tablets, and smartphones; several add-ons are possible such as game consoles or DVD players,
- **Cultural Form**: several services available such as mass and niche channels, pay-per-view, video on demand, peer-to-peer; frames are according to a linear schedule, electronic program guide, interfaces, or algorithms; content varies from professional to amateur programs,
- **Industry**: funding options vary from state/license fee, over advertising, and subscription, to transaction,
- **Organisational structures**: from national, regional and local broadcasters, to global conglomerates, to a deregulated structure,
- and **User experience**: various activities with different agency levels possible such as viewing, surfing, buying, playing, curating, sharing, up- and downloading, or engaging (such as linking, commenting, rating).

For a direct comparison of the various eras and their characteristics of the components see Table A.2. In a nutshell, online television is defined as "services that facilitate the viewing of editorially selected audiovisual content through internet-connected devices and infrastructure" (Johnson, 2019, p. 167). With the updated definition of television as online television, however, the question occurs, whether (and how) it impacts cultivation's theoretical assumptions that are based on a specific idea of television.

2.2.3 Consequences of Online Television for Cultural Indicators Project

The Cultural Indicators Project consists of three interrelated prongs: the media institutions (institutional analysis), the media messages (message system analysis), and the cultivating effect (cultivation analysis; Gerbner and Gross, 1976a). At its core, cultivation is about what stable, pervasive, repetitive, and ubiquitous patterns of messages the media system produces, and what implications these have for the audience. The focus is on the system of messages from television since television is the central arm of society and superimposed upon other mass media. Since the three prongs of the Cultural Indicators Project are interrelated, it is needless to say that a change in one of the prongs causes a shift in the others. Hence, given that television plays a central role to institutional analysis, a shift in the components and set of propositions of television naturally causes changes to both the media messages and the cultivating effect as well. For example, Pelzer and Raemy (2020) argue that the technological and economic changes in the journalism and entertainment industries (institutional analysis) have given rise to infotaining formats (media system analysis), causing changes to the definition of infotainment, what its constitutive properties are, and how its cultivation effects may differ from other formats (cultivation analysis).

Proponents of the initial Cultural Indicators Project, however, argue even in recent publications that television's ongoing change is more or less only a technological change that is independent from the formulaic pattern of the messages that are being produced and distributed through television. As Morgan et al. (2015) argue,

> "'Mere' technological change need not mean much for cultivation; whether a program is received on a tablet or a giant wall-screen (or some device we can't even imagine yet) is at most a secondary consideration for the cultivation theorist. But we need to know if today's (and tomorrow's) new media are offering more meaningfully different and diverse messages than did yesterday's new media in terms of their underlying lessons about life and society. If not, then the primary question for cultivation will still be whether massive, long-term, common exposure is occurring, and what consequences that has for viewers' beliefs about social reality. If the messages they provide have not changed fundamentally, then cultivation, as an explanatory model, will be as relevant today—and tomorrow—as it was 50 years ago."
> — Morgan et al. (2015, p. 687)

On the contrary, scholars studying the changes of television as an institution argue that it is invalid to conceptualize television merely as a technology: Instead television must be conceptualized in terms of its technological, cultural, industrial, organisational and experiential components (Johnson, 2019; Lotz, 2017a, 2017b). For example, broadcast television—which shaped much of Gerbner's assumptions about television—and today's on-line television— which should shape the recent work in the Cultural Indicators Project—are not only distinct with regard to the sheer number of screens that the viewers can watch the content on, but also with regard to implications on mobility, availability, content fragmentation, individu-ality, engagement levels, and algorithmic recommendation systems. Today, the viewer can watch anything wherever and whenever they want; they can watch the content by themselves, co-view with their family and friends, or co-view various content simultaneously; not only can they watch TV shows, but play, like, comment or rate them; they can write a message to their friends whilst watching; and receive the recommendation of which movie to watch not from a printed TV guide but from the algorithmic recommendation system that is offered by the video on demand services. Nonetheless, Morgan et al. (2015, p. 678) argue that "new technologies should mainly be seen as new 'delivery vehicles' for 'more of the same' content, especially for heavy viewers." The claim is more than troubling; after all, airplanes were also not just another vehicle compared to horse carriages to travel from A to B, but changed people's global understanding of connectivity and mobility, among others. Thus, when it is argued that "although the way we now receive our 'stories' [...] has changed, along with the ways we consume them, [...] important aspects of their content arguably have not" (Morgan et al., 2015, p. 685) and that therefore, cul-tivation theory is not impacted by the new era of television, then one main assumption of Gerbner is being violated: In fact, if changes in the institutions were to have no impact on the other two prongs, then the three prongs would no longer be interrelated.

Through the lens of Gerbner's characteristics of television from 1977, it becomes clear that some characteristics of the broadcast television era overlap with online television, while in other respects online television differs considerably: With regard to time consumption, online television remains the mass medium that requires most time and attention of its audience (e.g., Total Audience Reports by Nielsen, 2018, Q3); with regard to omnipresence, online television is even more easily accessible than ever before; and with regard to reach and literacy, online television can also be used by children by simple swiping or pushing buttons. With regard to totality, however, the viewers have the options to be highly selective in their viewing habits, and the algorithms that recommend the next best movie or show to watch based on previous behaviors support this selective behavior (Lobato, 2018). As Jenner (2016) points out Netflix, for example, is building on individualised and self-scheduled viewing practices; and as the quarterly Total Audience Report by Nielsen (2018, Q3) reveals, algorithmic recommendations are a main influence on video streaming. This shift in Gerbner's outlined characteristics then also questions the presumed dissolution of the autonomous public, when media institutions are actually now incentivized to produce fragmented content for any minority in order to secure their attention and click or subscription rates, respectively. This new approach of online television—namely, the production and presentation of content in a hyper-targeted way (Jenner, 2016)—may have led to "VOD service offer[ing] none of the more 'traditional' television genres, such as news, game shows, sporting events or other programmes associated with TV's live aesthetics" (p. 261). Thus, the shift towards a hyper-targeted production and presentation, and arguably also selection, of content in online television reveals the recursive relationship of the media institutions and the audience: On the production side, formerly distinct genres are nowadays being casually intermixed, resulting in hyper-targeting sub- and even microgenres such as 'romantic horror' or 'mockumentary;' on the audience side, the viewer remains in this hyper-targeting content bubble since their viewing habits feed the algorithm which determines the recommended show system further, an effect known as lock-in effect (Lobato, 2018; Napoli, 2016; Smith-Rowsey, 2016). Thus, genres play an increasingly important role in the production, distribution and selection of content in online television—and accordingly stress the question of what role genres play in cultivation theory today. This aspect is further discussed in Chapter 4.

In summary, online television differs greatly from the initial idea of television by the Cultural Indicators Project team. Online television is not just another technological screen to watch more of the same, but with the changes in its technological, cultural, industrial, organisational and experiential components, it also impacts the formerly conceptualized message system and the cultivation analysis. With regard to message system, the novel systematic boundaries of online television (in which the production system and the audience operate) might have changed the assumptions that viewers are unselective in their viewing behaviors and that they are exposed to a uniform stream of messages, regardless of genre. Quite the contrary: Online television may have elevated the role and importance of genres in cultivation. Naturally the questions occur: Are the initial genre concepts which scholars refer to in theoretical and empirical advancement still valid today? And how would a shift in the definition of genres affect a theory such as cultivation theory that relies on a coherent concept of messages that mirrors the *zeitgeist* in technology and viewing habits?

Next, we take a look at how messages and genres can be defined. Since narratives play an increasingly pivotal role in communication studies, and also cultivation, we also explore how narratives can be defined. These elaborations set the stage for discussing in Chapter 4 how message systems can be categorized in cultivation theory, referring back to the implications of online television and the importance of genres.

Chapter Three Defining Genre, Narrative, & Message

The clock has struck thirteen; we had best call in the theoreticians.
Altman, 1984, p. 6

This Chapter gives the reader a short general overview of the perspectives that can be applied to define messages, genres, and narratives. Although it might appear at first as an excursion, it is actually essential to understand these concepts in a general way before moving on to disentangling the various concepts of cultivating messages in Chapter 4. There is a theoretical and empirical reason underlying this step which will be outlined first, before defining genre, narrative, and message through a variety of perspectives.

3.1 Why to Consider Genre, Narrative, & Message

There is a theoretical as well as an empirical reason for why it is important to consider genres, narratives, and messages as concepts in general when discussing cultivating messages: First, from a theoretical standpoint, the three existing concepts of cultivating messages—which will be discussed in Chapter 4—refer in their terminology to messages, genres, or narratives in general. For example, 'uniform messages' refers to messages, 'genre-specific messages' to genres and messages, and 'metanarratives' to narratives. Thus, when the goal is to collect and advance the defining elements of cultivating message concepts further, it seems indispensable to take a closer look at their etymological origins. At best, the original concept lines up with the one from cultivating messages and deepens our understanding of it; at worst, the original concept appears to have little in common with the concept from cultivating messages except for the terminological loan, thus, resulting in a clear distinction that is helpful to future scholars of either research object.

The second reason for taking a closer look at messages, genres, and narratives stems from converging empirical evidence that 'genres' and 'narratives' are increasingly discussed alongside 'messages' in the articles recently published by Gerbner's associates including Michael Morgan, James Shanahan, and Nancy Signorielli. This is surprising, insofar as the systematic literature review (SLR) that we conducted (as reported below) suggests that Gerbner devoted by far more space in his articles to talk about 'messages' than about 'genres' and 'narratives' combined. The systematic literature review aimed to quantify how often Gerbner and his associates mention 'messages' in contrast to 'genres' and 'narratives' in their peer-reviewed journal articles on cultivation published between 1966 and 2001. The search was conducted (13/03/2020) on EBSCO's Communication & Mass Media Complete and complemented with a search on the George Gerbner Archive by the Annenberg School for Communication Library Archives (1955–2006) using the following search parameters: AU = George Gerbner; Publication Type = Academic Journal; Document Type = Article; Language = English. The search was restricted to peer-reviewed journal articles that mention 'cultivation' at least once in the main text in an attempt to focus the analysis on those articles for which the concept of 'messages' and its ancillaries was central to the Cultural Indicators Project. Because the goal was to observe how often Gerbner actually used the specific terms, we did not impose any exclusion criteria relating to the use of the term or any related concepts in the articles. In total, this procedure yielded a corpus of 37 articles. Each article's main text (excluding title, abstract, keywords, and literature) was coded by counting how often each of the following terms appeared: message*; narrativ*; genre*; story* OR stories. Table A.3 lists the respective articles and the findings.

In summary, the results reveal that between 1966 and 2001, Gerbner mentioned 'messages' eleven times per year on average across all journal publications, while 'narratives' and 'genres' were mentioned almost never. 'Story,' on the other hand, was mentioned on average five times per year. Figure 3.1 shows the trend over years on average for the four terms. In total numbers, 'messages' appeared 298 times, 'narratives' five times, 'genres' seven times, and 'story' 166 times. This means that 63 percent of all mentions were devoted to 'messages,' another 35 percent to 'story,' leaving 'narratives' and 'genres' at one percent. Figure A.2 shows the overall mentions of the respective terms in the articles per year.

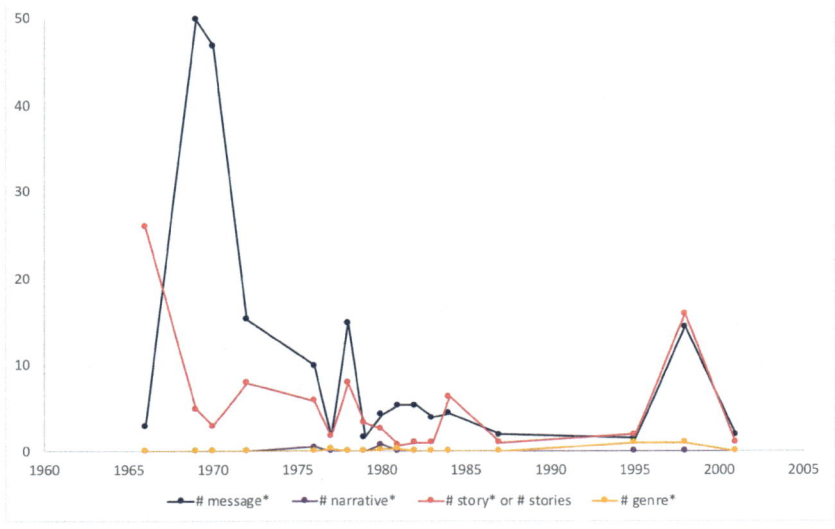

Figure 3.1 Number of times 'message,' 'narrative,' 'story,' and 'genre' was men-
tioned in an article by Gerbner et al. between 1966 and 2001 per
year on average

Thus, 'narratives' and 'genres' were rarely addressed by Gerbner et al.,
while an abundant number of articles mentioned 'messages,' and less
often, 'stories.' Given the dominance of 'messages' in the coded articles,
of which in 35 cases out of 37 Gerbner was first-author, it is therefore surprising that his close associates then continued his work by devoting more
space to 'narratives' and 'genres.' The difference becomes visible by taking
into consideration five of the most-recent and most-cited peer-reviewed
articles published by at least two out of Gerbner's three closest associates,
namely Michael Morgan, James Shanahan, and Nancy Signorielli (Morgan & Shanahan, 1997, 2010; Morgan et al., 2015; Morgan & Shanahan,
2017; Signorielli et al., 2019). Note that there is no overlap between the
aforementioned, previous articles with Gerbner as (co-) author and this
set of articles by his colleagues. Between 1997 and 2019 they mentioned
'messages' 117 times (equal to 40 % of all mentions), 'genres' 69 times
(24 %), 'stories' 63 times (22 %), and 'narratives' 40 times (14 %). Figure
3.2 shows the absolute number of times that the respective terms were
mentioned in the five articles.

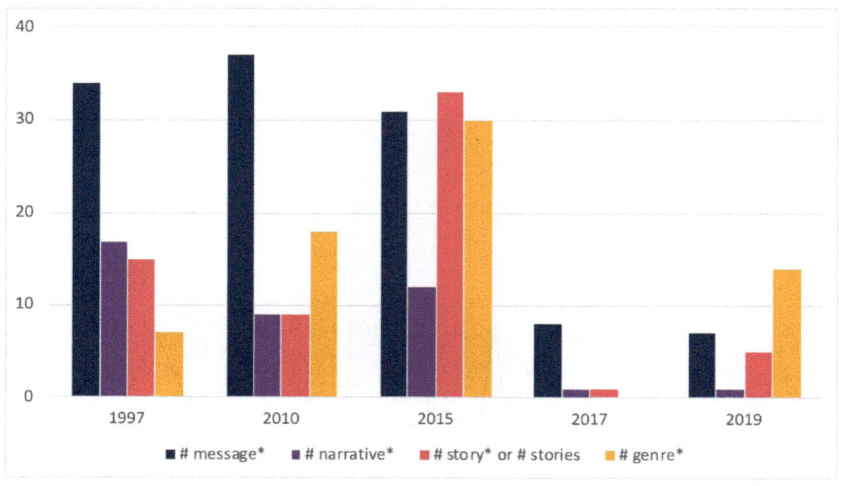

Figure 3.2 Overall number of times 'message,' 'narrative,' 'story,' and 'genre' was mentioned in five articles by Morgan, Shanahan and/or Signorielli between 1997 and 2019

Even though the selection procedure for these five articles by Morgan, Shanahan and/or Signorielli was not systematic, it still provides converging evidence that Gerbner's closest associates have begun to address other concepts than 'messages' in cultivation. Whether it may be for the purpose of integrating these concepts in cultivation theory or critically discussing how they are unfit to be integrated—devoting percentage-wise this much more space to these concepts shows how they have made an entrance in cultivation theory one way or another.

Thus, given the theoretical and empirical reasoning outlined above, it seems indispensable to take a closer look at how 'genres,' 'narratives,' and 'messages' can be defined, drawing from various perspectives. As the notions in narratives from a semiotic perspectives reveal, stories and narratives have a long intertwined history in their conceptualization; Section 3.3 therefore also addresses what a story is, and how it relates to narratives.

3.2 Four Perspectives to Define Genres

As outlined above, today's era of online television and subsequently the rise of SVOD has the potential to lead to an ever-more-diverse array of genres. In order to maximize their profit by reaching a larger audience, media institutions are nowadays incentivized to offer not only more but also a mixture of formerly distinct genres. This explains for example the rise of 'infotaining' formats, a hybridization of 'information' and 'entertainment' with a variance in news values (Pelzer & Raemy, 2020). The notion of genre is also gaining importance in cultivation theory with regard to the concept of genre-specific messages which we shall discuss more in Chapter 4; briefly, the idea of genre-specific messages assumes that messages are not uniformly distributed across television, but that various genres carry different messages, and that this distinguishes one genre from another one. Consequently, proponents of genre-specific messages in cultivation assume that heavy viewers of one genre differ in their cultivation effects from heavy viewers of another genre. As the reader will notice further below in Chapter 5, genres are not only central to define the assumptions of genre-specific messages, but also to disentangle the various concepts of cultivating messages. Despite the importance of genre in today's online television era as well as in contemporary cultivation research, unfortunately, 'What is a genre' and 'How do we know to which genre a movie or show belongs' are fundamental questions that are almost never asked, let alone answered in cultivation theory and much of communication studies in general. Instead "genres were always [and continue to be] treated as if they spring full-blown from the head of Zeus" (Altman, 1984, p. 7). Rather than developing comprehensive definitions, the few cultivation scholars who have tried to define genres often refer to rather descriptive statements and examples. While descriptive statements and examples are a gateway to introduce less-experienced scholars to the topic, they are also limited in their precision and generalizability. For example, J. Cohen and Weimann (2000) note,

> "Genres identify classes of programs that follow a similar formula in terms of production and plot development (Feuer, 1987). Genres also include norms about content, so that shows are generally produced as comedy, drama, or horror shows. Though genres, and TV genres especially, may lack clearly articulated borders, genre theory posits that they are nonetheless meaningful categories for understanding literature, theater, art, film and television (Rose, 1985). TV genres are formulas for producing shows and include norms about whether content is real or fictional, sad, funny or suspenseful, filmed on location or indoors, the range of production costs, etc."
> — J. Cohen and Weimann (2000, p. 102)

While their definition of genres does contain some relevant elements, it is also imprecise since different perspectives from psychology (whether genres are 'sad, funny or suspenseful'), semiotics ('plot development'), and economics ('production costs') are being casually intermixed. Moreover, the definitional criteria according to setting (e.g., western), actions (e.g., crime shows), audience effects (e.g., comedy), and narrative structure (e.g., mysteries) remain unclear. To proceed with a definition of genre, it is important to disentangle how a genre is formed (by e.g., social or economic forces) from how it can be identified (e.g., by a scholar or a viewer). A genre is a 'category' or 'class,' or 'corpus' or 'grouping,' or 'formulaic' (Neale, 2015, p. 3) that reveals the *relationship between a specific production system and a given audience* (Altman, 1984, 2000; Cobley, 2001; Mittell, 2001). Following the trail blazed by the essay by Gehrau (2003) on how genres decrease uncertainty, it is proposed that there are four perspectives on the constitution of this dialogical relationship and the resulting conceptualization of genre: the linguistic, economic, sociological, and psychological approach. Each perspective shapes the aforementioned definition of a genre differently according to their intrinsic force, which is outlined for each perspective below. By distilling one moderating factor from each perspective that shapes the definition of genres further and comparing the accordingly four factors in an interdisciplinary way, we will later be able to reveal from which perspectives the criticism of genre-specific messages in cultivation theory stems from. Next, we walk through the linguistic, economic, sociological, and psychological perspective on genres, and distill one moderating factor at the end of each Section accordingly.

3.2.1 History and Genre from the Linguistic Perspective

The linguistic approach provides the dominant theoretical model in textual as well as cinematic analysis and categorization, even though it may no longer be the only show in town. However, it still shapes much of the vocabulary for approaches in psychoanalysis, critical theory, cultural studies, and economics (Stam, Burgoyne, & Flitterman-Lewis, 2005). The (structural) linguistic perspective focuses on a specific object, for example a movie, and examines stable commonalities to other objects, clustering and labeling those with generic titles into genres. Typically, the linguist distinguishes between two approaches to categorize film genres: the semantic and the syntactic approach (Altman, 1984, 2000). The semantic approach stresses the genre's building blocks such as characters, shots, locations, sets, and the like, whereas the syntactic approach privileges the structures in which these blocks are arranged. For example, based on Marc Vernet's remarks (in 1976) on the genre 'western', the general atmosphere ("emphasis on basic elements such as earth, dust, water and leather") as well as stock characters ("the tough/soft cowboy, the lonely sheriff, the faithful or treacherous Indian, and the strong but tender woman") follow the semantic model; whereas the syntactic approach is outlined by Jim Kitses (in 1969) that the genre western grows out of a dialectic between the West as Garden and Desert, i.e., the dialectic "between culture and nature, community and individual, future and past" (Altman, 1984, p. 10). Both approaches have merits and drawbacks: The semantic approach is easily applied, but rather descriptive and has little explanatory power; the syntactic approach, on the other hand, surrenders broad applicability in exchange for extracting a genre's specific meaning-bearing structures (Altman, 1984, 2000). The main problem with the two approaches, however, is their use in isolation, i.e., applying one approach in ignorance of the other, which might result in generic encyclopedias and scholars sticking religiously to either an inclusive list or an exclusive pantheon. The inclusive list refers to genre definitions that are broadly applicable, but also tautological, such as 'a *music*al is a movie with *music*' or 'a *west*ern is a movie that takes place in the *West*.' The exclusive pantheon refers to scholars creating a narrow range of movies that are mentioned over and over again as a stand-in for the genre. The problem with such a narrow list of movies for a genre is that the overall meaning or syntactic structure of a genre is left wide open, which makes it impossible to add other, for example more recent or rather niche movies and TV shows. The main issue, however, may be that the sets of genre corpora that are created with the two approaches could be competing. This means that a movie is simultaneously included and excluded from the same genre based on the different approaches (Altman, 1984, 2000).

Indeed, Altman (1984) argues that the most promising approach lies in a combination of the semantic and syntactic approach. When applying the so-called 'semantic/syntactic approach,' the scholar would look for both the building blocks (semantic approach) and for the way that they are arranged (syntactic approach). Thus, the complementary semantic/syntactic approach is preferable to account for differing levels of generality. As Altman (1984) outlines, the semantic/syntactic approach also solves the contradiction of a split genre corpus as outlined above. Notably, the approach reveals patterns of the production system as it investigates the interrelations of objects. A genre, however, is not solely defined by the production system, but by the relationship between the production system and an audience. In order to forge the link between the production system and an audience, we suggest that the semantic/syntactic approach is broadened to the Bakhtinian translinguistic social semiotic movement (Bakhtin, 1981; Bakhtin & Medvedev, 1985). The Bakhtinian approach elaborates the notion by Altman (1984, p. 12) that "no major genre remains unchanged over the many decades of its existence." Hence, it takes into account how genre categories operate outside of their textual boundaries, i.e., it considers the cultural inflections of the 'life of signs in society.' Coined as *chronotope*—literally space-time—Bakhtin (1981) suggests that time and place are key elements in the dialogue between film and viewers that are expressed artistically (Bakhtin & Medvedev, 1985). The *chronotope* asserts that genres are not stable, solely inter-textually related entities, but instead fluid over time. For instance, the genre 'musical' initially employed music to convey "sorrow of death or parting" in a melodramatic syntax. While the semantic building blocks such as characters or locations remained similar, some years later (and still nowadays), however, 'musical' changed the direction of this syntax and incorporated music to express the "joy of coupling, the strength of the community, and the pleasures of entertainment" (Altman, 1984, p. 13). Thus, the genre 'musical' started off with a relatively stable semantic list, but over time began to borrow syntactic structures established by other genres.

It becomes clear that any genre definition and corpus only produces reliable and valid outcomes if the semantic/syntactic approach is coupled with the consideration of historic changes. This joined approach does not require a genre to abruptly be dissolved or swallowed up by another genre, when a relatively new, stable set of semantics is developed through syntactic experimentation (or vice versa, the existing syntax of a genre has adopted over time a new set of semantic elements). Instead, the historical component allows a genre categorization to be fluid over time while still remaining coherent at any given moment (Cobley, 2001; Mittell, 2001). Hence, according to the linguistic perspective, the relationship between the semantic/syntactic structures of an object and a given audience is influenced by *history*.

3.2.2 Financial Forces and Genre from the Economic Perspective

Before semiotics came along, generic genre categorizations were largely borrowed from the industry itself (Altman, 1984). From a media economic perspective it is convincing that the movie industry promotes multiple genres around any single film and TV show to maximize audience appeals and reach (Lobato & Ryan, 2011; Lobato, 2018; Smith-Rowsey, 2016). For example, consider the Internet Movie Database (IMDb) which is owned by a subsidiary of the economically-driven company Amazon.com Inc.: While it is perfectly possible to search the database based on a single genre such as comedy or adventure, each movie and TV show is associated with not one but three genres in the database. This maximizes the likelihood of visibility, which in turn creates greater click rates for each movie and TV show. For example, the movie *Star Wars: Episode IX — The Rise of Skywalker* (2019) is associated with three genres, namely action, adventure, and fantasy; the children's movie *Frozen II* (2019) is categorized into three genres of animation, adventure, and comedy; and the TV show *Game of Thrones* (2011—2019) is linked to the genres action, adventure, and drama. Thus, *Star Wars: Episode IX — The Rise of Skywalker*, *Frozen II*, and *Game of Thrones* are categorized, among other genres, in the same genre of adventure—despite their differences that would be revealed in, for example, the semantic/syntactic approach.

Hence, this approach of attaching several genres to a single movie or TV show stresses the expected relationship between a specific production system—here the media organization—and a given audience, asking the extent to which economic and financial forces affect the kind of content that is produced in the media, while considering the implications of various factors for culture, politics and society as a whole (McQuail, 2010; Picard, 2003). Although this perspective takes the audience into account, it links the production system and the receiver in "a 'calculative' rather than a normative or social [... or] communication relationship" (McQuail, 2010, p. 401). Therefore, the audience is seen in terms of socioeconomic criteria of consumption and less in terms of internal relations amongst the viewers involved (McQuail, 2010). This is the reason why, in the economic perspective, the audience is referred to as 'consumers.' The media content then is produced in terms of profitability, which increases with market share. Since media content is a cultural product *per se*, its production exhibits a high risk of failure (Van Cuilenburg, 2000). Therefore, companies try to produce various media products based on previous (successful) productions to maximize the return on investment. This refers to physical objects (for instance reusing costumes, sets or properties in different movies; Altman, 2000), as well as to recycling popular basal ideas in storylines.

Thus, on the one hand, these economic and financial forces shape a genre standardization in order to minimize their costs; on the other hand, they tend toward heterogeneous genres each organized around one single media product in order to maximize their consumer reach (such as the IMDb, but also SVOD services like Netflix as we will discuss in Section 4.4). Nowadays, this negotiation between the production system and the consumer is especially visible in genre labels which address various potential interests of the consumers, e.g., by combining romance and comedy into 'romantic comedy,' a documentary with drama into 'docu drama,' or satire and documentary into 'mockumentary.' The economic perspective, hence, balances the examination of commonalities and differences among genre categorization by taking into account *economic and financial forces* that shape the relationship between the production system and consumers.

3.2.3 Reality Observation and Genre from the Sociological Perspective

The sociological perspective sheds light on the categorization of genres resulting from attributing meaning, or symbolic generalizations, to the communicative themes. A reasonable approach to investigate the relationship between mass media and the audience is offered by the system theory of Niklas Luhmann (2000): In general, from the functional-structural system theory it can be argued that social reality is constructed through mass media, and that the concept of 'reality-observation level' offers a framework to further cluster genres into other categories such as sub-programs and programs.

Briefly, in system theory, the mass media constitute one of the functional systems of society, alongside the political system, the legal system, the economic system, and so forth. Mass media are an operationally closed and autopoietic system, i.e., they produce all their elements within themselves to fulfill their social function. Communication reduces complexity on the internal side of the mass media system, and creates order out of noise by attributing meaning to the communicative information. The reality-observation level refers to the specific relationship each program has with reality due to the communication. There are three programs according to Luhmann—namely news, advertising, and entertainment—which serve as gateways to observe and describe our social reality. While there are several ways to observe reality, here we focus on first- and second-order reality in order to describe the way genres are formed in Luhmannian terms: The first-order reality is "an indicator of successful tests for consistency in the system" (Luhmann, 2000, p. 11). Put simply: the first-order reality refers to our reality. The second-order reality refers to an as-if world that is created by the programs. Furthermore, each program uses some sort of tool ('medium' in Luhmannian terminology) which consists of different forms such as objects, symbols, or signs. These provide more fine-tuned ways to observe and describe the world.

With regard to genres, Luhmann's way to observe reality offers a framework to cluster genres into broader categories: Applying both ways of observing reality, i.e., first- and second-order reality, it becomes clear that the program 'news' refers to the first-order reality as it is held accountable to report the truth. 'Entertainment,' on the other hand, provides some kind of doubling of reality, such that while watching the program for a given time a fictional second reality arises (Luhmann, 2000). Hence, 'entertainment' is held accountable with regard to second-order reality, i.e., the as-if world. How can a scholar decide if a genre is further clustered into either the program 'news' or 'entertainment'? Instead of dividing genres due to their inter-textual topics, settings or audience effects, the system theoretical perspective shifts the focus on the relationship that the objects, symbols, and signs (i.e., the forms) in the program have with reality. This relationship can be described by truth, credibility, or verisimilitude. As outlined before, news is held accountable with regard to reporting the truth, hence, the relationship between the forms in news and reality is defined by truth. Any genre that is obliged to report the truth, therefore, is clustered into the 'news' program. This could for example apply to the genre 'documentary.'

In comparison, for entertainment the two key factors are credibility and verisimilitude. This results in the creation of two distinct sub-programs of 'entertainment,' namely 'fictional entertainment' and 'performative reality.' Their difference is that the sub-program 'fictional entertainment' is expected to be neither true or credible, but verisimilar within the second-order reality. For example, TV shows such as *Game of Thrones* (2011–2019) or movies such as *Frozen II* (2019) create a second-world and this world is expected to be faithful and consistent to its own rules (the second-order reality), but not with regard to the rules from our reality which is the first-order reality. In contrast, the sub-program 'performative reality' is obliged to credibility with reference to first-order reality. This refers to any agents appearing in any staged actions, such as reality TV shows, talk shows, docu soaps, and the like. For example, the reality TV show *I'm a Celebrity... Get Me Out of Here!* (2002–) is credible with regard to the rules of reality.

In summary, the sociological perspective offers a framework to cluster genres into broader categories, namely 'news' and 'entertainment,' with the latter consisting of two sub-programs which are 'fictional entertainment' and 'performative reality.' While for the other perspectives, history or financial forces shaped the relationship between a production system and the audience and accordingly refined the definition of a genre, from the system theoretical perspective it is the *level of reality-observation* that shapes the relationship between the mass media and the audience and results in a broader framework to cluster genres.

3.2.4 Knowledge Structures and Genre from the Psychological Perspective

From a media psychological perspective, one might argue that the definition of each genre is shaped by individual viewers and, respectively, their cognitive processing and comprehension of a movie or TV show and its characteristics. In this context, mental representations subsume different cognitive constructs such as memories, concepts, scripts, attitudes, schema, or mental models (Bodenhausen, Macrae, & Hugenberg, 2003; Schneider, 2012; Smith & Queller, 2001). With regard to genres, attitude and schema theory have received special attention. By considering schema "more as a description of a function that can be performed by a learned knowledge representation... than a description of an actual entity inside our heads" (Smith & Queller, 2001, p. 127), this then means that genre schema are relevant knowledge structures for movie or TV show comprehension (Schneider, 2012). Thus, schematic representations focus on the summation and storage of past experiences, which are organized in independent knowledge structures (Bartlett, 1932), and are useful for describing how cinematic knowledge is acquired and criteria thereof developed (Bordwell, 1989).

It follows that the same schema can influence the evaluations of an object differently. Put simply, the labels for genres depend on the individual knowledge structure. For example, Potter, Pashupati, Pekurny, Hoffman, and Davis (2002) conducted a study in which they exposed participants to an episode of the television show *Walker, Texas Ranger* (1993–2001) in which a combination of violence, intimidation, and murder are depicted. The results show that some of the participants rated the explicitness of violence in the TV show episode as low, while others perceived it as high. Subsequently, participants who perceived low explicitness concluded that there is low violence, whereas participants who perceived the explicitness of violence as high concluded that the episode depicts a great amount of violence. Hence, the results revealed that the viewers relied more on their personal schema than on the content they were exposed to in order to construct an interpretation of violence. This means that even though viewers rate a movie or a TV show with the same criteria, they arrive at different judgments due to individual differences in their schema of violence. With regard to genre categories this implies that one viewer might categorize a TV show or movie as 'gore' because they rate the violence as high, whereas another viewer labels the same TV show or movie with the genre 'action' because they perceive the overall rate of violence as low.

Hence, the dividing factor that leads to the different genre labels is the individually perceived level of various show reactions such as excitement, humor, explicitness, graphicness, and so forth. The psychological perspective on genre categorization, thus, requires an evaluation of the *knowledge structures* and attitudes on an individual level.

3.2.5 Implications of the Four Moderating Factors

In order to make common progress in theory and research that is based on genres, including parts of cultivation theory, it is important for scholars to define clearly what a genre is and how they sorted a movie or TV show into a certain genre. As noted, genres can be defined as a corpus, category or class that reveals the relationship between a production system and a given audience. Hence, the widely accepted genres such as romance, comedy, crime, drama, or fantasy, are based on the association that the media institutions have with the audience. This relationship, however, is influenced by different factors that stem from different perspectives. As outlined, from a linguistic perspective, the relationship between the audience and the semantic/syntactic aspects of the movie or TV show are moderated by history. The economic perspective focuses rather on the financial forces that shape the relationship between the movie or TV show and the consumers. The sociological perspective employs the reality observation level to cluster genres further into programs. And the psychological perspective explains genres as schema, shifting the focus towards individuals' knowledge structures and attitudes as moderating the relationship. Thus, while there is a certain degree of understanding in academia and industry that there is a set of genres (such as romance, comedy, drama, or fantasy), the sorting decision—which movie and TV show belongs to which genre exactly—depends on these factors. For example, a movie may be included in the genre 'western' due to its content characteristics, its broader implications, and its similarity to former movies from that genre (linguistic perspective). But since western movies are not as popular anymore as they once were, financial forces label the movie as 'adventure' to increase its monetary value (economic perspective). Some viewers, however, label the movie as 'action' due to its gun scenes (psychological perspective). Meanwhile, some scholars avoid the genre labelling altogether and sort the movie into the program 'entertainment' that encompasses several genres. Hence, the same movie ended up in four different genres/programs depending on the perspective that is applied. In order to facilitate comparisons of theoretical advances and empirical research on genres, this calls for scholars to clearly outline what perspective they are taking when labeling a movie or TV show with a certain genre label.

This aspect is even more glaring given the trends in the economic perspective to attach several genres to a single movie or TV show: Some scholars sort movies or TV shows into genres by an economic perspective, e.g., using the IMDb. However, in order to ease the interpretation of the results, they choose only one of the several labels when sorting their data set of TV shows or movies. The problem with this approach is that if scholars do not outline the concrete criteria for their decision-making process, this may lead to at best confusing, and at worst invalid, results when movies and TV shows are sorted into the same genre, but actually have little in common. For example, as described above, based on the IMDb *Star Wars*, *Frozen II*, and *Game of Thrones* could be lumped together in the genre 'adventure.'

This contradiction can be solved by scholars (1) acknowledging and being aware of the impact the different perspectives have, and by scholars (2) clearly stating which perspective they are taking and what adjustments they made to it. The sociological perspective then offers another framework to cluster genres further, i.e., into formats of performative reality or fictional entertainment. Thus, this perspective abstracts the common labels for genres further. It also becomes clear by the system theoretical perspective that entertainment, news, and advertisement are programs that differ with regard to their reality-observation level. This is important for example for scholars who study how effects from public service announcements (PSA) differ when they either report statistics or personal testimonials, but struggle to identify the mechanisms of why these types of PSA should differ. For example, one reason why the magnitude of cultivation effects from information and entertainment differs might lie in the assumption that the audience holds information accountable with regard to truth, while entertainment is expected to be credible or verisimilar (Pelzer & Raemy, 2020). Hence, all four perspectives offer a promising approach to sort movies and TV shows into genres, and to cluster genres further, but they also stress the importance of clearly outlining the perspective scholars are employing. Especially in a field such as communication that draws from various perspectives, it is necessary for scholars to define how they derived their genre definition and explain how they decided which movie and TV show belongs to which genre, accordingly. This then also addresses the worry that "viewers may not define genres in the same way as do researchers" (Morgan & Shanahan, 1997). Here, we brought together four different perspectives that are usually viewed separately, and, through synthesizing, were able to distill one moderating factor for each perspective that explains the definition of a genre further. This original interdisciplinary focus can be expanded by future scholars when they take more perspectives into account.

3.3 What's in a Narrative?

Since there is a pull towards narratives by cultivation scholars as the literature review revealed, next we explore narratives further. The notions about narratives are also important since narratives may be connected to the concept of metanarratives as an alternative concept of cultivating messages (this is explored in Chapter 4). Thus, in the following, we walk through the use of narratives in communication in general and how narratives may be defined drawing from communication as well as from a discipline that studies narratives since centuries, namely semiotics.

3.3.1 Narrative Turn Across Fields

Over the past several decades there has been a 'narrative turn' (Hyvärinen, 2010) unfolding across several fields, ranging from semiotics, psychology, behavioral medicine, and communication studies. Even in fields such as music theory and mathematics there is a burgeoning interest in narratives. In general, the pull towards narratives across several fields indicates a shift towards legitimizing stories as an important source for empirical knowledge (Hyvärinen, 2010). For example, the medical field is developing the method of 'narrative therapy,' in which patients tell their own life story as part of their psychological treatment (Brown & Augusta-Scott, 2006). In mathematics education, teachers use narratives to present their teaching or learning experiences and to weave descriptions with regard to their thinking, emotions, beliefs and attitudes that are essential to understanding the experiences in the stories (Chapman, 2008). Hence, in mathematics education, narratives—as in written or oral self-authored stories—are employed as an educational tool to increase the motivation for the field (Hannula, 2006). And in music theory, narratives play a crucial role in techniques such as Schenkerian analysis, which examines the underlying structure of a tonal piece (Tarasti, 2004). Musical narratives then are characterized as a lifelike *leitmotif* since "[i]t is not that music does anything as crude as to tell a story, but rather that as one chunk or phrase or event is followed by or transformed into the next, a sense of narrative develops which in its own musical terms is coherent and directed (by the composer or performer or both, in collaboration with the listener)" (Leech-Wilkinson, 2017, p. 363). Likewise scholars from health communication and public relations show an increasing interest in narratives due to their ascribed persuasive quality when (implicit) arguments about topics or actors are integrated into a fictional, entertaining narrative (Kreuter et al., 2007; Green & Brock, 2000; Quintero-Johnson & Sangalang, 2017; Marsen, 2014). Indeed, a meta-analysis by Shen, Sheer, and Li (2015) on the impact of narratives on persuasion in health communication revealed that while exposure to health narratives seems to be ineffective in encouraging people to quit risky or harmful behaviors (e.g., smoking or drinking), it appeared to be modestly effective in persuading individuals to adopt detection or preventive behaviors. For example, after being exposed to health narratives about mammography, skin exam, or Pap test, the likelihood increased to adopt detection measures; likewise, being exposed to narratives about steps to avoid breast cancer, colorectal cancer, skin cancer, depression, HPV, or osteoporosis increased the likelihood of prevention behavior.

In general, within the field of communication the interest in narratives is rapidly growing: Within two decades, the number of articles with the term 'narrative' in their title has increased by nearly 8,900 percent, more precisely from 15 titles in 1993 to 1,346 titles in 2013 (Braddock & Dillard, 2016). The general pull towards narratives in communication is understandable, considering that narratives are expected to shape both the individual and society: The former, because narratives are considered a "fundamental structure of human experience" (Connelly & Clandinin, 1990, p. 2), and the latter, because narratives and culture reify one another reciprocally (see e.g., Tamborini, Weber, Eden, Bowman, & Grizzard, 2010). Thus, it is only natural that a multifaceted discipline such as communication that investigates micro- as well as macro-level effects is drawn towards a concept that has the potential to address both.

3.3.2 Narratives in Communication

Narratives have emerged as a powerful concept for a variety of fields such as semiotics, psychology, behavioral medicine, and communication studies. For communication scholars, narratives are generally not of interest in and of themselves, but rather because of the way they are used by communicators, or their putative effects. As a meta-analysis of 74 studies by Braddock and Dillard (2016) reveals, the exposure to a narrative is positively related to narrative-consistent beliefs, attitudes, intentions, and behaviors. For example, scholars have found narratives to affect related beliefs and attitudes with regard to organ donation, the salience of moral intuitions, and empathy for stigmatized groups (Eden et al., 2014; Oliver, Dillard, Bae, & Tamul, 2012). Likewise, narratives have been shown to affect behavior, for example of user-character dialog, or in road safety education (Endrass, Klimmt, Mehlmann, Andre, & Roth, 2014; Oschatz & Klimmt, 2016). Additionally, in the realm of climate change communication, narrative analysis along with frequency analysis and framing analysis has emerged as one of the most frequently used analytical techniques to construct meaning from the content (Metag, 2016). Moreover, research has prospered on the putative processes underlying narrative effects, such as the extended elaboration likelihood model (E-ELM; Slater & Rouner, 2002), the role of transportation (Bezdek & Gerrig, 2017; Busselle et al., 2004; Green & Brock, 2013, 2000) and absorption (Hakemulder, Kuijpers, Tan, Bàlint, & Doicaru, 2017), as well as moderating effects from, for example, perceived realism (Busselle & Bilandzic, 2008). Slowly, scholars are also increasingly interested in components of narratives—such as the point of view or presence of a narrator—that may "enhance or inhibit narrative potency" (Braddock & Dillard, 2016, p. 463).

Narratology scholars from other disciplines, however, urge caution regarding the state of understanding and use of narratives in communication studies altogether: Because whereas "literary scholars have an ongoing debate regarding the proper definition of narrative, [...] only a few social scientists have pondered the issue. The argument [...] is not at all that social scientists have a wrong definition of narrative [but rather] about the lack of theorizing and self-consciousness about the theoretical aspects of narrativity itself" (Hyvärinen, 2010, p. 78). Especially in a field with multidisciplinary roots such as communication (Craig, 1999), any concept that is used across a variety of subfields (such as journalism, mass communication, human-computer interaction, and so forth) stands a good chance of being understood differently in each of the subfields. Of course, trailblazers such as Melanie C. Green and Helena Bilandzic, among others, have added considerably to the knowledge base of narrative effects, and have provided definitions of what they consider to comprise a narrative. However, the question is how consistently these definitions are used across subfields, and how well they resonate with the conceptual development regarding narratives from the field of narratology, which has a long-standing interest in defining narratives, as well as in narratives *per se*. For example, in communication a narrative is sometimes considered "a representation of connected events and characters that has an identifiable structure, is bounded in space and time, and contains implicit or explicit messages about the topic being addressed" (Kreuter et al., 2007, p. 222); in other places, a narrative is defined simply as a form that contains "representations of events and/or inner states of characters" (see Bilandzic and Busselle, 2017, p. 24; also Bilandzic and Busselle, 2012b); and less generally, a narrative "requires a story that raises unanswered questions, presents unresolved conflicts, or depicts not yet completed activity; characters may encounter and then resolve a crisis or crises. A story line, with a beginning, middle, and end, is identifiable" (Green & Brock, 2000, p. 701).

Already, with only these three examples, two issues can be raised with the conceptualization of narratives: First, some differences in the conceptualization of narratives are evident. For example, some definitions require the presence of characters and additionally a certain order of events, whereas in others it seems optional or not important. However, a common agreement on the definition of narratives in communication seems important because only then will theoretical development be enabled, and the results of narrative effects synthesized for example in meta-analyses. Alternatively, several strands to define a narrative may be called into existence, but at a minimum this requires awareness of the differences between the definitions that currently exist. And second, while the definitions indeed allow the investigation or use of great literature and fictional movies and TV shows, they may also include many examples from advertisement, sporting events, courtroom testimony, or song lyrics. Even the game 'peek-a-boo,' short texts like 'The boy sneezed,' or recipes would be included in those definitions. For example, a recipe for a cake represents connected actions ('separate the eggs') and happenings ('bake until crust is slightly brown'), connects an identifiable beginning, middle and end, has baking ingredients as characters, and is bounded in time and the space of one's kitchen. Of course, communication scholar are not in general interested in recipes and the like, thus, the question remains how narratives can be defined in order to be more exclusive. Next, we take a look at the way narratives are conceptualized in semiotics in order to arrive at a more exclusive definition that fits the research objects studied in communication.

3.3.3 Narratives in Semiotics

The field of semiotics has a long history of research on narratives—coined 'narratology'—and an ongoing debate about the definitions of narration, story, and narrative discourse. Taking a peek at our discipline, semioticians even give valuable advice: "David Herman suggested [...] that perhaps the most important thing that social scientists could learn from narratology is the key distinction between story [...] and narrative discourse" (Hyvärinen, 2010, p. 78). In direct comparison, 'story' refers to the inferred sequence of events which explains the *what* of the narrative, whereas 'narrative discourse' refers to *how* it is delivered by drawing on elements such as distance, voice, or point of view (or in semiotic terms, focalisation). Before disentangling other concepts of narrative and narrative components further through the lens of semiotics, it is important to note that to speak of *the* semiotic view on narratives is invalid, as there are several fully differentiated strands, each with their own intrinsic assumptions. The most common way to categorize the various strands in narratology is the binary distinction into classical and post-classical eras as proposed by David Herman (1997). Both classical and post-classical narratology ask the same questions such as:

- What is a narrative (compared to a non-narrative)?
- What are the possible kinds of narratives?
- What affects the degree and nature of narratives?

In addition, post-classical narratology explores what the function of a narrative is, what impact narratives have as a process (not only as a product), how the context shapes the effects of narratives, and how narratives interact with real world knowledge (G. Prince, 2008).

Next, we go through the way that the strands from classical and post-classical narratology have shaped the idea of narratives further. In general, semioticians from various strands have agreed on a minimal definition on narratives, which is coined 'minimal narrative.' The minimal narrative definition conceptualizes a narrative "as the representation of at least one event, one change in a state of affairs" (G. Prince, 1999, p. 43), and that the nature of narrative comprises both story and narrative discourse. As outlined above, a "story is an event or sequence of events (the action); and narrative discourse is those events as represented" (Abbott, 2008, p. 19).

The definition of the minimal narrative is further shaped by the elements each strand focuses on and/or the micro- or macro-perspective they are applying.

In order to enable scholars to differentiate the various strands, here we offer a brief synthesis of the major trends in semiotics on the study of narratives. The goal is to enable scholars to differentiate the strands and the key elements they are adding to the minimal definition of narratives; to familiarize scholars with main representatives of each strand; and to introduce some merits and drawbacks of each strand with regard to their specific changes to the minimal narrative definition. For example, let's assume that the reader encounters a journal article from communication that uses a definition of narratives by Algirdas Julien Greimas. After reading the next two Sections, the reader should be able to identify that Greimas is a proponent from the structuralism strand in classical narratology; the reader should know that structuralists tried to abstract away from single narratives to broader patterns and frameworks such as a general list of characters in a narrative or a typical structure; and the reader should be cautious about the use of that definition since structuralists drew their conclusions from (amongst others) Russian Formalists, who based their work on oral instead of written examples—thus, the drawback of the structuralist strand is the lack of generalizability. The reader could then consider how an approach informed by post-classical narratologists could have influenced the article they are reading and (possibly) improved it.

Next, we first outline the focus of three strands from classical narratology (namely, rhetorical strand, Russian Formalists, structuralism), before we synthesize some of the works by post-classical narratology.

3.3.3.1 Classical Narratology

Rhetorical Strand. With regard to classical narratology, the first strand on narratives we will consider is the rhetorical strand, represented by scholars such as James Phelan, Gerald Prince, or Wayne C. Booth. As we will see, the rhetorical strand assumes that a narrative takes over many characteristics of a living thing. To define narratives, the rhetorical strand builds on Aristotle's work *Poetics* and the distinction it makes between *physis* and *techne*, and how they become explicative models of one another (Davis, 2012). *Physis* represents nature or everything outside of human control. Given the properties of *physis*, all activities of things in nature move towards an end, which is coined *telos*. For example, the *telos* of a flower is its death. On the other hand, *techne* is everything that has been crafted or exists because of humans' know-how and their product-making. For example, a stool is a product that only exists because of humans, and the same goes for the production of a movie. Of course, one could argue that so too do products crafted by humans come to an end, as does everything outside of human control: A piece of wood turns into a stool, or frames of pictures are put together in a sequence to result in a movie. Nonetheless both concepts are distinct, since only *techne* is subject to human control, and comes to an end solely by the agency of the human. For example the piece of wood does not inevitably need to turn into a stool. *Physis* and *techne* are the building blocks for understanding Aristotle's concept of narratives further: According to Aristotle the structure of parts of narratives are connected in an orderly way. Nowadays scholars oftentimes describe this as the narrative structure of a beginning, a middle, and an end (Davis, 2012). While a movie is considered a *techne*, the end (thus, the *telos*) that a narrative inevitably moves towards, resembles the characteristic of a living being. Thus, a narrative employs parts of *physis*. Based on this argument, there are several more conditions of living beings that apply to a narrative: Living things come with an appropriate order and magnitude—that is, they are neither too minuscule nor too large. For example, there is no animal that is a thousand miles long (Davis, 2012). Applying this characteristic to narratives, this explains the (1) spatial and temporal restrictions, (2) the arrangement of the sequence of events, and (3) the effects on the audience further: The created world in narratives must have (1) an appropriate space and time set-up that is holistically comprehensible to the audience; (2) the parts must be ordered in a causal chain to allow for a coherent perception; and (3) to enable the audience to interpret something meaningful from the story, it needs to be coherently remembered—thus, eliminating media entities that have an inappropriate magnitude for the audience, e.g., a movie that lasts 200 hours. The latter refers to what is sometimes called reportability or tellability by semioticians, and indicates what makes a narrative worth telling, interesting, or appealing to the audience. Moreover, Aristotle argued that narratives such as a tragedy have a soul or *psuche*: The plot of the narrative that represents the soul aspect is the main principle guiding it by imitating action and life (coined *mimesis praxeos kai biou* by Aristotle; see Davis, 2012). In summary, the rhetorical strand assumes that a narrative such as a tragedy takes over many characteristics of a living thing, including a recognizable structure of parts (a beginning, a middle, and an end standing in orderly connection), a holistic appearance, and an imitation not of persons but of action and life (instead of an array of facts; Davis, 2012). Aside from the independent contribution to an understanding of narrativity, the rhetorical strand, and especially Aristotle's *Poetics*, also influenced to a great extent the conceptualizations of narratives in the subsequent strands.

Russian Formalism. The second strand we will consider that is categorized as belonging to the classical era comes from the Russian Formalists. The Russian Formalists can be dated back to the 1920s, and include scholars such as Boris Tomashevskii, Viktor Shklovskii, or Vladimir Propp. In general, in comparison to the rhetorical strand, the Russian Formalists started to shift the focus more towards the actants, which are the characters, in defining a narrative. While characters were in the rhetorical strand only secondary, they play a major role for the Russian Formalists, and allowed them to expand their ideas to other topics. For example, Tomashevskii (in 1925) started to distinguish between 'bound' (or plot-relevant) and 'free' (non-plot-relevant) motifs in a narrative. When altering the 'bound' elements, one will no longer have the same story; whereas, when altering the 'free' elements, one will have the same story but told in a different way (Herman, 2009). Another example that refers directly to actants, stems from Propp's *Morphology of the Folktale* (first English translation in 1958): Based on his analysis of Russian folktales, Propp argued that character actions were defined with regard to their importance for the plot. In total, Propp abstracted 31 character actions or functions (called 'spheres of action') defined by their significance for the plot development (Herman, 2009). The spheres of action includes actions such as 'villainy' (e.g., the villain causes harm or injury), 'departure' (e.g., the hero leaves home), 'struggle' (e.g., the hero and the villain join in direct combat), or 'punishment' (e.g., the villain is punished). Propp concludes from this observation that the number of character actions or functions is limited (to 31 in fact), and that one function follows another with logical necessity (Dogra, 2017). The work on narratology by the Russian Formalists served as foundations for structuralists later on, starting in the 1960s. For example, Tomashevskii's distinction between 'bound' and 'free' motifs provided the foundation for Roland Barthes' 'nuclei' and 'catalyzers,' terms he coined in 1966 referring to core and peripheral elements in a narrative (Herman, 2009). Likewise, the idea (published in 1929) of plot as a structuring device by Viktor Shklovskii initiated the *fabula/sjuzhet* or story/discourse distinction in structuralist narratology. In the same tradition, structuralist A.J. Greimas (writing in 1966) created a typology of narrative actors (such as subject, object, sender, receiver, helper, opponent) that extrapolated from Propp's *Morphology of the Folktale* (Herman, 2009).

While the Russian Formalists introduced the importance of the characters to define narratives and developed taxonomies to identify the characters' functions and plot elements further, they disregarded the receiver of the narrative (such as a reader or viewer), and excluded historical and contextual features (Dogra, 2017).

Structuralism. The third and final strand from within classical narratology we consider is structuralism, which subsumes several legacies such as cognitive narratology (represented by e.g., Roland Barthes, Gérard Genette, Alison Bechdel, or Judith F. Duchan) or feminist and postcolonial narratologies (represented by e.g., Susan Lanser, or Robyn Warhol, but also latter-day Gerald Prince and Alison Bechdel). Besides borrowing from the Russian Formalists as outlined above, structuralism also construed the distinction between *la langue* (language as system, i.e., grammar) and *la parole* (commonly spoken language) by linguist Ferdinand de Saussure: Inspired by this distinction, the structuralists like Barthes and Greimas perceived "particular stories as individual narrative messages supported by a shared semiotic system" (Herman, 2009, p. 28). And similar to Saussure's assumption that grammar with its structural constituents and combinatory principles (la langue) succeeds the spoken language (la parole), the structuralists privileged a framework of studying narratives in general over the isolated analysis of single narratives. Hence, instead of focusing on developing a taxonomy of narrative elements like the Russian Formalists, the structuralists rather sought to understand how elements, themes and patterns are arranged in general in narratives. For example, from Propp's taxonomy of characters' actions, Greimas abstracted six actants to which all characters could be reduced: subject, object, sender, receiver, helper, and opponent. Barthes, on the other hand, focused more on the "elements of the supra- or transtextual code" (Herman, 2009, p. 28) in order to enable scholars to identify the narrative discourse. The narrative discourse is one of the grounding assumptions established by the structuralists that targets the investigation of how a narrative is being told (in contrast to what is being told). The structuralists coined this distinction narrative discourse/story. More precisely, 'story' refers to the inferred sequence of events which explain what is being told in the storyworld, whereas 'narrative discourse' refers to how it is delivered by drawing on cues such as distance, voice, or point of view (in semiotic terms, 'focalization'). And Genette borrowed from the linguists when he established the concepts of temporal sequence, manipulations or viewpoint, or modes of narration in structuralist narratology, which are rooted in traditional grammar concepts such as tense, mood, or voice (Herman, 2009). In summary, the structuralists aimed to abstract from the individual narratives to a broader concept and framework for the constituents of narratives. To this end, they built on the observations by the Russian Formalists and linguists, but abstracted further away. The issue that arises with such an approach, however, is the lack of desired generalizability: Several structuralists such as Barthes, Genette, Todorov, or Greimas based their work about literary (i.e., primarily *written*) narratives on Propp's categorization of spheres of action. This taxonomy, however, was rooted in *oral* traditions and used a restricted corpus of folktales. As a consequence, structuralism is "an approach that championed the study of narratives of all sorts, irrespective of origin, medium, theme, reputation, or genre, but lacked the conceptual and methodological resources to substantiate its own claims to generalizability" (Herman, 2009, p. 33).

3.3.3.2 Post-Classical Narratology

Post-classical narratology, which emerged in the 1980s, can be viewed as an extension of classical narratology, because its proponents believe that "the concepts devised by classical narratology have not lost their relevance. On the contrary, they are open to a fruitful development and supplementation and can be adapted to recent approaches" (Alber & Fludernik, 2010, p. 16). In order to enable progress, the post-classical narratologists apply novel methods and measures that were unavailable to Russian Formalists or structuralists—such as computational linguistics, sociolinguistics, and psycholinguistics—in order to combine classical narratology with recent perspectives on the forms and functions of narratives stemming from, for instance, gender theory, post-Saussurean linguistics, and cognitive sciences (Herman, 2009; G. Prince, 2008). Post-classical narratology subsumes various legacies such as socionarratology (represented by e.g., David Herman), computer-mediated narratives (e.g., Marie-Laure Ryan, Jörg Helbig, or Werner Wolf), or the distinction of natural/unnatural narratology (e.g., Monika Fludernik, Stefan Iversen, or Jan Alber).

It is beyond the scope to review the full range of post-classical legacies, but this book provides at least a brief sketch of some approaches and trends. For an excellent introduction, the reader is advised to consider the edited book *Postclassical Narratology. Approaches and Analyses* by Alber and Fludernik (2010); also consider the blog *The Living Handbook of Narratology* by Hühn and et al. (n.d.) that is updated regularly. Moreover, Nünning (2003) summarizes some of the legacies, sorting them by their degree of theoretical elaboration (see Figure A.4). In general, the various legacies in post-classical narratology employ one of the following two approaches to advance classical narratology: either a refinement and extension of classical approaches by adding new distinctions, questioning presuppositions, and sometimes radically revising traditional frameworks and concepts; or an extension of the corpus by adding a variety of media and new themes by integrating work from other disciplines.

Refinement of classical approaches. This approach in post-classical narratology aims to refine the constituents of narratives and the frameworks as developed by the Russian Formalists or structuralists against the backdrop of the ways narratives are constructed, produced, and distributed nowadays. This work is advanced by scholars such as Michael Toolan, Richard Walsh, or H. Porter Abbott, and concerns aspects of narratives such as story and plot, space and time, point of view/ focalization, character, and dialogue. For example, Walsh (2010) combines the insights from the rhetorical strand with a semiotic model of communication, and reconsiders the conceptualizations of points of view or voices by distinguishing them into three broader patterns of first-person situation, authorial situation, and figural situation in order to sort concrete elements such as internal perspective, a teller-character, a reflector-character, an omniscient perspective and so forth. He also finds that narrative and non-fiction are not exclusive since "it is possible in non-fiction for a narrating instance to be transmitted within a framing instance (for example when a historian quotes an eye-witness account, or when a literary biography quotes from the work of its subject)" (Walsh, 2010, p. 48). Another emerging trend in post-classical narratology is the study of unnatural narratives: these refer to narratives that violate mimetic conventions by implementing improbable or impossible events that are not simply unrealistic but antirealistic (Richardson, 2012). Anti-mimetic narratives challenge our real-world understanding of crucial elements such as time, space, or identity by presenting events that are impossible in the real world. For example, Alber (n.d.) explains "the island in Daniel Defoe's *Robinson Crusoe* (1719), for example, is fictional, but such an island could exist in the actual world: it is based on 'natural' parameters. The flying island of Laputa in Jonathan Swift's *Gulliver's Travels* (1726/1735), on the other hand, could clearly not exist in the real world; it therefore constitutes an unnatural phenomenon." Unnatural narratology, to a certain degree, is linked to cognitive narratology which is explained below.

Extension by transdisciplinarity. The second approach aims to expand the corpus of relevant themes, formats and media, as well as incorporating the insights from other disciplines. This approach broadens the themes to the feminism or more recently queer perspective, extends the formats to autobiography or non-literal ones such as medical interviews, and augments media to include e.g. visual narration. Oftentimes, these corpora are merged with the work from other disciplines: For example, issues of gender are combined with modes of psychoanalyses, or visual narratives are linked with cognitive effects (Alber & Fludernik, 2010). In the cognitive approach to narratology (which is coined 'cognitive narratology'), rather than investigating written work and conceptualizing the functions of its narrative elements, this merged approach uses narrative as a mode of mental access and theorizes about the mind and its functions in light of narratives. This may include work on the perception of narratives, the cognitive processes while reading, the prospect of shared mental experiences, or the types and functions of you- and we-narratives. The focus therefore moves more towards the recipient and their experience of the narrative instead of constraining the theorizing and analyses to textual properties (Olsen, 2011). Proponents of cognitive narratology such as Monika Fludernik, David Herman, Manfred Jahn or Lisa Zunshine, for example, show that recipients use their individual schemata on their real-world knowledge to project fictional worlds (Alber & Fludernik, 2010). This means that the recipients make sense of narratives in a similar way as they make sense of the world, its events and people. For example, a main component that stems from cognitive narratology is the Deictic Shift Theory/ Deixis (Segal, 1995) which indicates temporal, spatial, and person components of a story world, such as 'here,' 'now,' or 'you,' and assumes that during the reception of a narrative the recipient is relocated to these specific space-time coordinates (Herman, 2002, 2009; Duchan, Bruder, & Hewitt, 1995). Hence, "Cognitive narratology can thus be argued to affect the status of categories of narratological analysis; it shifts the emphasis from an essentialist, universal, and static understanding of narratological concepts to seeing them as fluid, context-determined, prototypical, and recipient-constituted" (Alber & Fludernik, 2010, p. 12).

In transmedial approaches which deal with for example computer-mediated narratives, concepts and methods from classical narratology are applied to new media (Olsen, 2011). Cognitive and transmedial narratology are highly intertwined since they both focus on the process and the effects of constituting narrativity (an aspect that is coined 'narrativization' by Fludernik, 1996). The transmedial approach then deals with the investigation of non-verbal narratives such as music, ballet or paintings which despite their lack of textual properties still evoke a storytelling structure to the audience. The transmedial narratologists investigate how images can suggest time, how gestures can imply causality, what meaning a graphic layout entails (M.-L. Ryan, n.d.). While classical narratology was limited to novels, proponents of transmedial narratology investigate poems, cartoons, movies, video clips, new stories, and narrative modes in medical or legal contexts (Alber & Fludernik, 2010). Transgenerically, the approach also studies non-literary work such as scientific prose which aims to reach a larger audience: For example "TV documentaries on wildlife, too, frequently fictionalize and narrativize their topic by presenting, say, the life of a bear family or a group of elephants in terms of human life experience, turning their instinct-driven actions and wanderings into story matter" (Olsen, 2011, p. 6). Hence, the transmedial narratology approach investigates properties and dimensions of narratives (such as space and time) and how they are shaped by media: They can be temporal and dynamic (e.g., music, radio), or temporal and static (e.g., written word), or purely spatial (e.g., photography), or spatio-temporal (e.g., comics), or even kinetic spatio-temporal (e.g., movie, gestures; M.-L. Ryan, n.d.). Moreover, the transmedial approach deals with the reception of the narrative, hence, linking the properties of narratives as outlined by classical narratologists with modes of perception and processing.

3.3.4 Implications from Semiotics for Communication

As the brief introduction to classical and post-classical narratology has revealed, there are several ways how the minimal narrative definition is refined and advanced. According to the consensus of semioticians from various strands, a minimal narrative defines a narrative as the representation of at least one event, which is one change in the state of affairs (G. Prince, 1999). For example, the first and the third event are considered stative (e.g., the beginning and the end) while the second event is active. The definition of minimal narratives, however, is not the absolute definition that semioticians have arrived at but represents the starting point for refinement in accordance to each strand. For example, the rhetorical strand attributed to narratives the characteristics of a living thing, such as a recognizable structure of parts in an orderly connection, a holistic appearance, and an imitation of action. The Russian Formalists investigated single narratives such as oral fairy tales, and focused on the characters' actions. The structuralists took a look at the bigger picture of the structure, character types, temporal sequences, viewpoints, and so forth that in their point of view were applicable to all kinds of narratives. Nowadays, the post-classical narratologists are adding to the minimal narrative definition new methods, measurements, and theories from other disciplines.

With the background knowledge of the various strands from classical and post-classical narratology, it is now possible to situate the three definitions of narratives that shape much of the communication research body on narratives: When Kreuter et al. (2007, p. 222) state that a narrative is "a representation of connected events and characters that has an identifiable structure, is bounded in space and time, and contains implicit or explicit messages about the topic being addressed" one can assume that they refer back to the strand of rhetorical narratology (e.g., the identifiable structure) and to the structuralists given the emphasis on characters. Also, Green and Brock (2000) arguable hark back to these two strands, when they define that a narrative "requires a story that raises unanswered questions, presents unresolved conflicts, or depicts not yet completed activity; characters may encounter and then resolve a crisis or crises. A story line, with a beginning, middle, and end, is identifiable" (p. 701). Especially the mention of story, which is reminiscent of the story/discourse distinction by the structuralists, the focus on characters and the structure (structuralism), and the beginning, middle and end (rhetorical strand) are identifiable elements from these two strands. On the other hand, the short definition of narratives as "representations of events and/or inner states of characters" by Bilandzic and Busselle (2017, p. 24) does not seem to fit either strand (or any of the others), given that it is not explained how the 'events' relate to one another, for instance in an orderly connection.

Several implications can be drawn from this: First, communication scholars refer to concepts from semioticians who aim to refine the minimal narrative definition. This is applaudable since semioticians have a long history in the study of narratives. However, communication scholars oftentimes refer just implicitly to semioticians, i.e., they neither name the specific strand nor the semiotician from whom the reference stems. This sets the condition for a considerable amount of confusion for scholars who are less experienced with the various strands from semiotics, and may lead to literature reviews and meta-analyses that lump together various strands since they assume a homogeneous understanding of narratives. This is not the case: Each strand comes with its own presuppositions and assumptions of narratives. In order to facilitate the understanding of narrative terminology in semiotics, a glossary (Appendix B) is offered of the most important narrative terms in semiotics and (if possible) their equivalents from communication studies. This may bridge the gap between the fields further, and raise the awareness of the distinctions between the various strands in semiotics which is also notable in their vocabulary.

Second, while communication scholars seem to be (more or less) aware of the work by classical narratologists, it seems that they are somewhat unaware of the legacies in post-classical narratology: Hyvärinen (2010) concluded from a survey of several handbooks, articles, and encyclopedias on narrative theory and research in psychology and the social sciences that there is "almost no interest at all in what is now called 'post-classical narratology'" (p. 79). This is surprising since communication scholars have an increasing interest in the putative effects from narratives, which would seem to align well with the focus of post-classical narratology on offering a deeper understanding not only what narratives are, but how they 'work.' Instead of having one definition for narratives, and a separate hypothesis for the effect on the recipient, in post-classical narratology the narrative and the recipient are considered jointly in one single definition. For example, drawing on contemporary post-classical narratology, using the transmedial narratology definition by M.-L. Ryan (2004, 2007) and implications from cognitive narratology by Herman (2009) as a foundation, a narrative could be defined as follows:

1. In the beginning, a narrative creates a world.
    1.1. A limited temporal and spatial dimension underlies the created world.
    1.2. The world referred to is populated with characters and objects.
    1.3. The characters in the created world are interpretive agents, i.e.with mental awareness, and psychological states and traits.
    1.4. The agents have the power to influence some of the events on purpose.
    1.5. The sequence of events is connected in an orderly way.
2. In the middle, the world undergoes a change of state.
    2.1. The transformation is caused by random physical events, i.e., accidents, or deliberative human actions.
3. In the end, the transformation forms a new world.
    3.1. Some events were more meaningful than others in shaping the new world.
    3.2. The audience interprets the sequence of events as something meaningful.

As the definition above demonstrates, is it perfectly possible to include the audience in the definition of a narrative and its properties with the new developments in post-classical narratology. The definition furthermore puts more constraints on the definition of a minimal narrative in order to exclude entities such as recipes or the game 'peek-a-boo' from a narrative. The definition may be visualized as in Figure 3.3 to ease the parsing when scholars undertake the effort to investigate how great the degree of narrativity is of an entity.

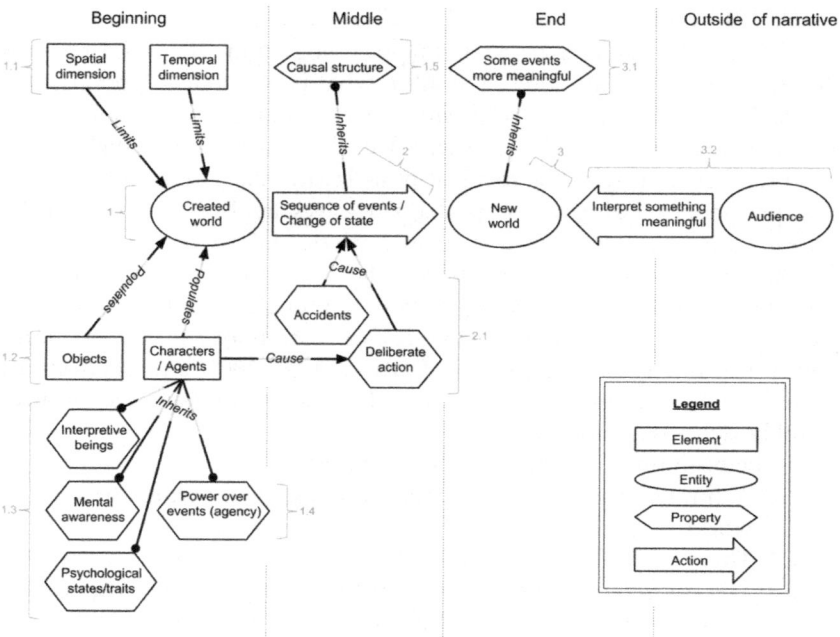

Figure 3.3 Defining narratives by the degree of narrativity

In summary, it is indispensable for scholars to clearly articulate which is the strand *within* a discipline upon which they are drawing when defining a narrative, because each has its own intrinsic assumptions and focus of study. Moreover, post-classical narratology appears to hold substantial promise for communication scholars, as this strand combines classical narratology with a range of disciplines and methods that reveal similarity to communication studies. Therefore, communication scholars are advised to take a closer look at contemporary work in semiotics that addresses similar questions to those raised by our own discipline.

3.4 What Is a Message?

3.4.1 Defining Messages in Cultivation

Similarly to narratives, messages are a central research object in communication and other disciplines. In communication, the interest is less on the definition of messages in general, but rather on the putative effects that messages might exert (Danesi, 2004): For example, scholars investigate the effects of messages from a certain domain such as health messages or entertaining messages; they study elements of messages that may enhance its effectiveness such as message credibility or message framing; or they explore the individual perception of messages such as cognitive processing of messages. In cultivation theory, television messages play a prevalent role since cultivation scholars are interested in investigating the relationship between the steady, slow and cumulative consumption of media messages and the stable, aggregate belief and attitude structures among large groups of people. As Gerbner (1998) describes, "Cultivation analysis begins with message system analysis identifying the most recurrent, stable, and over-arching patterns of television content. These are the consistent images, portrayals, and values that cut across most types of programs and are virtually inescapable for regular (and especially the heavy) viewers. They are the *aggregate messages* embedded in television as a system rather than in specific programs, types, or genres" (p. 181; emphasis added).

While the importance of messages in cultivation is repeatedly reiterated over the fifty years of research, what actually constitutes messages remains to a large degree unanswered. Rather, cultivation scholars refer to potentially tautological synonyms, describe the properties of the categorization of messages, or what messages do (e.g., create a symbolic environment; Gerbner, 1970), but less what messages *are*. For example, sometimes it is implied that 'message' is superior to and subsumes concepts such as 'images,' 'portrayals,' and 'values' (e.g., Gerbner, 1998, p. 181). On other occasions, however, it is noted that "Even though there are ever more channels to watch, it is now even more important to look at the common messages *and* lessons that permeate these images" (Morgan et al., 2015, p. 693; emphasis added). Here, 'messages' is mentioned side by side as an equal concept to other concepts, in this case: 'lessons.' Based on this notion one would assume that 'messages' is a distinct concept from 'lesson' and other concepts, a distinction that is also implicit in earlier writings by Gerbner and Gross (1976a, p. 177). Then again, on other occasions, 'messages' is exchanged for 'meanings' or 'lessons' altogether, as when it is stated that "television provides an organically related synthetic symbolic structure which once again presents a total world of *meanings* for all" (Gerbner, 1977, p. 149; emphasis added).

Despite the uncertainty in later writings with regard to a concise and comprehensive definition of messages that distinguishes it from other forms, there are two early notes by Gerbner (1958, 1970) that reveal his understanding of 'messages' and the strand he draws from a bit further: In 1970, Gerbner defines that "Messages are specialized events (or aspects of events) that signify other things in enormously varied and creative ways unique to human culture" (p. 72). To understand the definition, one must take a brief glimpse at Gerbner's general model of communication as introduced in 1956, and which follows almost a Lasswellian formula, namely:

1. Someone
2. perceives an event
3. and reacts
4. in a situation
5. through some means
6. to make available materials
7. in some form
8. and context
9. conveying content
10. with some consequence.

The formula is also visualized as a figure (see Figure A.3) and elaborated in more detail below: Gerbner's general model of communication starts with an act of perception by a communicating agent (M in Figure A.3) who can be a human being or a machine such as a thermostat. What is perceived is coined an event (E) and the act of perception of the event by the communicating agent is E'. The event can be anything from a news article to just reality (Gerbner, 1958; McQuail & Windahl, 1981). What the agent perceives is determined by their way of selecting, the context of the event, and the degree of availability of this event in contrast to others. The next step then assumes that the agent wants to communicate about the perceived event, and therefore produces a message which is a statement about the event (SE) in a certain shape/form and with a certain content. The shape of the message (such as its syntactic patterns) never stands by itself but is always coupled with the content, unless it signifies noise. The message may then in turn be perceived by another agent (M2), and activates a similar pattern of communication (Gerbner, 1958). For example, condensation of moisture in the air is an event (E), which is perceived by the child (M) as rain (E'), and leads to the message 'It's raining' (SE), which then is received by the mother (M2) as 'It's raining.' Likewise, with regard to mass media, the model may answer questions such as 'How good is the correspondence between reality and the stories (between E and SE) about reality given by television (M)?' or 'How well is television content (SE) understood by the viewers (M2)?' (McQuail & Windahl, 1981). As Gerbner (1958) highlights,

> "The investigation of content focuses attention on SE, the communication product. It proceeds as a relational analysis on two levels. Both 'formal' and 'content' aspects of the communication product are studied with respect to all other elements of the communication sequence of which SE is a part. Study of the formal continuities traces the flow or configurations of conventional ('arbitrary') systems of signs and symbols through classification and measurement. It relates the state of specific signal-systems to that of others for comparison, or to intentions, desires, behaviors of the source, or to the 'effectiveness' of the responses they elicit, or to technical use of communicative means."
> — Gerbner (1958, p. 94)

Thus, according to Gerbner (1958) 'messages' are arbitrary, consisting of a form and a content: The formal, conventional part refers to a "form or code" consisting of "denotative and connotative associations" (p. 86); the other part, content, is underlying the formal part and creates the basis for inference about specific relations between the agent and the events and any consequences. This idea of conceptualizing a message in a dyadic (or triadic) way shows resemblance of the work by semioticians and their theories about the way that signs (such as a message) can transfer information and how they are interpreted.

3.4.2 Messages in Semiotics

"Semiotics pays [...] attention to what messages mean, and on how they have been put together with signs" (Danesi, 2004, p. 10). In semiotics (Greek: sēmiōtikḗ epistḗmē)—which is etymologically the science (epistḗmē) of signs (sēmêíon, sēma)—a sign can be anything that conveys a meaning that is not the sign itself, and communicate this meaning to an interpreter (Posner, 2004). There are two major theories both describing the way that signs entail information and how they are interpreted: One theory by Ferdinand de Saussure assumes that the nature of the signs is dyadic; the other theory was posited by Charles Sanders Peirce and conceptualizes signs as triadic.

For Ferdinand de Saussure (1857–1913), a sign consists of a form (the 'signifier') and its meaning (the 'signified'), for example a large object with a trunk and leaves in a park is associated with the meaning 'tree' (note that the acceptance of a physical form of the sign is accepted by post-Saussurean proponents). Signifier and signified are highly entangled and cannot be conceptualized as separate entities: This means that it is impossible to encounter a meaningless signifier (unless it is noise) or a completely formless signified. Thus, the relation is dyadic. Moreover, the relationship between signifier and signified is arbitrary, i.e., random. For example, there is nothing about the physical quality of 'television' that requires the denotation as such; and likewise there is nothing about the word 'open' (signifier) that indicates that the store is open for business today (signified). While signifier and signified are terms that belong to the essential toolkit for any scholar from the humanities, they can also be viewed simply as X and Y that a sign consists of. Part X of a sign can be rather small such as a number, a musical note or a word; or it can be much larger such as a mathematic equation, a melody or a letter. Thus, part X of the sign can take any form or size, as long as it moves within the possible boundaries of paradigmatic and syntagmatic structure, and assumes signification in some way. The latter refers to the relationship between X and Y which is described as $X := Y$. Thus, Y in this relationship is the other part of the sign that interprets what X is standing for. For example, the equation $a^2 + b^2 = c^2$ (part X) stands for the Pythagorean Theorem ('the square on the hypotenuse of a right-angled triangle is equal to the sum of the squares of the other two sides'; part Y). The $X := Y$ structure also occurs when communication scholars ask participants what the health campaign (part X) they watched was about (part Y). It is, however, important to view both parts (X and Y) jointly, since a meaning would not exist without an object that conveys it, and likewise, an object can't exist without a meaning—only in the cases of mere noise.

At around the same time that de Saussure proposed his structuralist, dyadic model of signs that bracketed any communicating agent such as a receiver of a sign, an alternative pragmatic, triadic sign theory was proposed. For Charles Sanders Peirce (1839–1914), "nothing is a sign unless it is interpreted as a sign;" thus, signs are triadic since they consist of a "triple connection of sign [in the form of a representanem], thing signified [an object], cognition produced in the mind [the interpretant]" (Peirce, 1993[1884–1886], p. 245). The representanem is the form which the sign takes (similar to signifier in Saussurian terminology); the thing signified is an object to which the sign refers; and the interpretant is *not* a human interpreter but the sense that they make of the sign. For example, when reading the word 'Friends' on the screen at the intro of the sitcom *Friends* (1994–2004), in Peirce's triadic model, the pixels on the screen are the representanem; the object is what the representanem represents, in this case the word 'Friends' stands for a certain, original meaning about the relationship between people; and the understanding or experiences of friendship in an interpreter's mind forms the interpretant (Herzig & Assmann, 2014). This interaction between representanem, object, and interpretant is coined by Peirce as semiosis.

Despite the differences between de Saussure's and Peirce's model—a discussion which would go beyond the scope of the short introduction here—both theories have in common that messages are not synonymous with 'meaning.' First, a single message can entail more than one meaning, and several messages can entail the same meaning. For example, the phrase 'Nice day, today!' encodes a simple message, yet the meaning of the message could be literal (the sun is shining) or ironic (it is actually raining). Similarly, the word 'open' can refer to an open shop or an indication where to open an envelope, a box, a door, and so forth. Each combination constitutes a different sign. Second, semioticians believe that there are 23 different meanings of the word 'meaning' (by Ogden and Richardson in 1923, see Danesi, 2004): For example meaning could stand for intention ('She means to stop binge-watching'), or indication ('A green light means go'), or purpose ('What is the meaning of life?'), or importance ('Love means happiness;' Danesi, 2004). Thus, a meaning hews closely on the context of interpretation, and a concrete definition of meaning faces at a certain point the problem of looping patterns or tautology that surfaces with all definitions. While it is possible to understand the concept of messages better by exploring the concepts of signs, for meanings Danesi (2004) concludes that "like the axioms of arithmetic or geometry, the notion of meaning is best left undefined" (p. 12).

3.5 Interim Conclusion

Genres, narratives, and messages are imperative to much research in communication. In general the three concepts are not of interest in and of themselves, but rather because of the way they are used by communicators, the effects they can putatively cause, or the ways of clustering they enable to facilitate the research. This Chapter gave an introduction to current conceptualizations of genre, narrative, and message. By aggregating definitions and considerations from a variety of disciplines, a synthesis for each concept emerged that in its totality is more complex than the single pieces: With regard to genre, it was found that genre is defined as a class that reveals the relationship between a specific production system and an audience. By comparing the perspectives from linguistics, economics, sociology, and psychology on defining that relationship, for each perspective a moderating factor emerged: History shapes the relationship between the production system and an audience further from the linguistic perspective, for economy it is the financial forces, and for psychology it is the individual's knowledge structures. It was moreover shown that the sorting decision of movies and TV shows depends on the dominance of the factors for the scholar. Put simply: Which genre label a movie or TV show receives, varies.

With regard to narratives, the Chapter outlined the main strands and legacies in semiotics and their presuppositions accordingly. The synthesis of classical and post-classical narratology revealed that there are several ways how the minimal narrative definition is refined and advanced. A minimal narrative was defined as the representation of at least one event, which is one change in the state of affairs. It was also outlined how the minimal definition of narratives necessarily requires a refinement/ advancement since it is otherwise too inclusive. Accordingly, for each strand in classical narratology it was outlined how the minimal narrative is shaped further. The goal of the Section was to enable the readers to differentiate the strands in semiotics and the key elements each strand is adding to the minimal definition of narratives, to familiarize the readers with the trailblazers of each strand, and to introduce some merits and drawbacks of each strand. Moreover, the cursory overview of the legacies from post-classical narratology revealed that the interests of post-classical narratologists represent the greatest overlap with communication scholars because they increasingly incorporate the recipient in their study of narratives. Future communication scholars are therefore advised to take a closer look at the work by post-classical narratologists. To facilitate the understanding of narrative terms in semiotics, a glossary of the most important narrative terms was furthermore offered.

With regard to messages, it was found that Gerbner conceptualized messages as arbitrary and consisting of a form and a content. This dyadic conceptualization of messages shows some similarities to the concept of signs by de Saussure from semiotics: A sign consists of a form (the signifier) and its meaning (the signified). As outlined, the two components are highly entangled and arbitrary. Since this conceptualization is excluding a recipient, another dominant conceptualization of signs was introduced, namely the triadic model by Peirce. From both models it was found that messages are not analogous to meanings, since a single message can entail more than one meaning, and several messages can entail the same meaning. Rather, it was found that meaning may be one part of messages, aside from the form.

In summary, it was found that the concepts and understanding of genre, narrative, and message is advanced by integrating the insights from other perspectives. Especially semiotics has a long history in the study of these entities. The goal was to integrate the different perspectives and synthesize them. In this effort, there are several advances that arose for each of the concepts. By integrating and synthesizing (rather than merely aggregating) all perspectives together, it enabled development in each domain separately. Thus, it is important for future common progress to clearly outline the perspective or strand they are drawing from. With the background knowledge to better understand the concepts of genre, narrative, and message, in the next Chapter we take a look at common ways to categorize them in cultivation theory and research.

Chapter Four Ways to Categorize Cultivating Messages

Does the fish in the ocean know that it is swimming in salt water?
Gerbner, 2001, p. 186

Messages are central to cultivation theory and research as they permeate all three prongs that the Cultural Indicators Project consists of: Messages are the result of the production of media institutions and the research object in the institutional analysis in terms of how messages are selected, produced and distributed; messages are also the research object in message system analysis; and they are the predictor variable in cultivation analysis since they are expected to impact people's conception of social reality. Rather than examining the contribution of single messages, for Gerbner and his associates it was the system of messages on television that has the potential for enculturation. Thus, while in isolation the messages may differ, viewed from afar the system of messages reveals common patterns of specific meanings that deal with social reality (Gerbner, 1985). Hence, the message system analysis looks deeper at the "underlying *uniformity* of the basic 'building blocks' of the television world: thematic structure, interaction patterns, social typing and fate" (Gerbner, 1990, p. 255; emphasis added). Inspired by Hawkins and Pingree (1981a), this type of categorizing the cultivating messages on television is oftentimes referred to as 'uniform messages.' The basic assumption of categorizing messages in a uniform way is that across all genres, channels, and times, there is a similar set of cultivating messages. As early as the 1980s, however, several scholars questioned this assumption, for example Hughes (1980) notes,

> "While it may be very useful to know what total television watching is related to, some of the more subtle effects might be more apparent only if we knew precisely *what* people watched and were able to control for predetermined personality and other characteristics which are related to the *selection* of certain kinds of programs"
> — Hughes (1980, p. 300; emphasis added)

Likewise Hawkins and Pingree (1981a), among others, challenged the assumption of uniform messages and the habitual rather than the selective use of television empirically, and conducted a study that differentiates between various program types in the cultivation effect. Their results revealed that discarding the initial assumptions strengthened rather than weakened the cultivation hypothesis. Based on the findings, an abundance of studies followed which focused on the cultivation effect from single genres or even single shows. In this line of research, it is argued that messages do in fact vary across genres, thus, the label 'genre-specific messages.' Proponents of the original idea of cultivation, however, argue that studying genre-specific cultivation messages "goes against the basic tenets of cultivation theory" (Morgan et al., 2015, p. 690) and question whether research with genre-specific messages in fact deserves to be labeled as 'cultivation.' On the one hand, the argument is understandable given that Gerbner and the Cultural Indicators Project team emphasized that it is about the aggregate system of messages and not about the isolated contribution of a specific genre or TV show. On the other hand, rather than rejecting the idea of genre-specific messages altogether based on a violation of Gerbner's initial assumption, it is helpful to assess in what ways the categorizations actually differ, and then to determine how great the degree of similarity is between them. This seems to be in line with the call for "a clear rationale for how they [genre-specific studies] are similar to or different from the more global concept of cultivation" (Morgan & Shanahan, 2010, p. 341) that remained heretofore unanswered. The need for a broader framework for categorizing cultivating messages seems especially glaring given the recent development of another categorization, namely 'metanarratives.'

Hence, in this Chapter, we consider current ways to categorize messages, from uniform messages, to genre-specific messages and metanarratives. From the notions about online television, another way of categorization arises which we coin 'subgenre messages.' Chapter 5 then distills everything into two Postulates and a number of Lemmas that describe the different conceptualizations of cultivating messages, and reveal in a two-dimensional space how close the concepts are to one another.

4.1 Uniform Messages

Cultivation as outlined by Gerbner and his associates is not interested in the impact of single messages or isolated TV shows, but in the stream of messages that is presented. More precisely, the Cultural Indicators Project operates under the assumption that we are constantly presented with a fundamental pattern of messages that is present through all television channels and times. As Gerbner et al. (1978, p. 2) explain, "the message system composing that world presents coherent images of life and society."

In general, there are two main assumptions underlying the research on cultural indicators:

> "One is that commercial television, unlike other media, presents an organically composed total world of interrelated stories (both drama and news) produced to the same set of market specification. Second, television audiences (unlike those for other media) view largely non-selectively and by the clock rather than by the program. Television viewing is a ritual, almost like religion, except that it is attended to more regularly."
> — Gerbner, Gross, Signorielli, Morgan, and Jackson-Beeck (1979, p. 180)

Hawkins and Pingree (1981a) were the first to suggest that the two assumptions from above can actually be broken into three presuppositions: First, the idea that television sends out a set of monolithic messages which they coin the "uniformity of messages" (p. 292). A uniform message could be, for example, that the world is a dangerous and mean place. Second, the notion that the total world is organically composed implies that the television messages are interrelated by nature. Hence, rather than the single incidents it is the totality of messages that matters and the fact that the messages hang together as a system instead of being unrelated facts. In the words of Shanahan and Morgan (1999): Cultivation deals with the bucket, not the individual drops. Third, even if there were differences in the system of messages on television, television viewing is presumed to happen habitually and unselectively, "thus, all viewers get the same symbolic messages, and the only variable is the *amount* of exposure to these message" (Hawkins & Pingree, 1981a, p. 292). Several scholars have critiqued the assumptions of uniform messages and unselective viewing by Gerbner and his associates: For example, content-wise they questioned whether there are no differences across shows or genres (Potter, 1993), and audience-wise they cautioned that viewing behavior might be selective (Hawkins & Pingree, 1981a), especially given the increased number of network channels (Potter, 1993).

However, none have assessed what philosophical strand or 'super-theory' may underlie these presuppositions of cultivation before voicing their critiques. The argument is not that the former critiques are wrong, but rather that their criticisms may rest upon a different perspective than the initial theory. This then explains why the proponents of the original idea of uniform messages hold onto the concept to this date, despite the critiques. Thus, understanding the underlying super-theory—which aims at universal applicability, encompassing several disciplines and domain-specific theories—enables a different level of fundamental understanding of the roots of Gerbner's assumptions, which in turn enables an assessment as to how coherently the assumptions fit into the super-theoretical framework.

4.1.1 Critical Theory and Uniform Messages

Over the decades, Gerbner and his associates reiterated the importance of the Cultural Indicators Project for communication and its assumptions about the interrelation of media institutions, media messages, and cultivation of society, while publishing a number of groundbreaking studies on cultivation effects. However, what super-theory actually underlies the study of cultivation, and in particular the assumption of uniform messages, is rarely addressed. In fact to the author's knowledge there is only one article that mentions the root for cultivation theory: In one of his last writings in 2001, Gerbner specifies that the work by the political economist Herbert 'Herb' Schiller had an influence on the presuppositions of the Cultural Indicators Project. Gerbner states that

> "Herb Schiller, as an economist and polemicist, basically ignored media effects theories [...]. His intellectual stance was perhaps closest to my cultivation theory, which focuses on monopoly media, especially television, as a centralized system of story-telling—a structure that brings a relatively coherent system of images and messages into every home, and thereby cultivates from infancy our predispositions, preferences, and world views."
> — Gerbner (2001, p. 189)

In his work, Schiller focused on a critical observation of economic and cultural systems in the United States. For example, Schiller (2000) observed that companies penetrate nearly every aspect of society ranging from fast moving consumer goods such as our daily diet and toiletries to the clothes we wear to much greater meanings such as the way we communicate with each other. Critically, he states that "throughout life, from infancy on, Americans, like all others, absorb the images and messages of the prevailing social order. These make up their frame of reference and perception. With few exceptions, it is this framework which insulates most from ever imagining an alternative social reality" (p. 183). While Schiller did not identify himself as a Marxist or with any other super-theory, other scholars (e.g., Murdock, 2006; Jin, 2020) locate his observations aside from radical populism in the realm of critical theory. Briefly, from the perspective of critical theory, mass media is a form of culture industry that is shaped by the industrialization and commercialization of culture under capitalist relations of production. Critical theory is a super-theory that can be traced back to the Frankfurt School in Germany and the sociologists Max Horkheimer and Theodor Adorno, two of its main representatives. Schiller probably developed his critique of the corporate influence on culture and society while Horkheimer and Adorno, both directly threatened by the violence of National Socialism in Germany, were living in exile in the U.S. (Murdock, 2006). As Murdock (2006) points out, Schiller's critical assessment of the commercial cultural industries being drivers of the deception of society shows great similarity to Horkheimer and Adorno's analysis that "the basis on which technology acquires power over society is the power of those whose economic hold over society is greatest" (Horkheimer & Adorno, 1973, p. 121) and that "progress in the culture industry [...] mask[s] a skeleton which has changed just as little as the profit motive itself since the time it first gained its predominance over culture" (Adorno, 1991[1972—1981], p. 87). While critical theorists from the Frankfurt School focused on ideology critique for historical reasons —i.e., based on the consequences of Nazi ideology—Schiller's approach of political economy was based on the fight against fascism. Despite the initial reason for ideology critique, both Horkheimer and Adorno and Schiller have in common that they voiced great concern about fascism (Fuchs, 2014).

Given the connection between George Gerbner and Herbert Schiller and likewise between Herbert Schiller and the Frankfurt School, naturally there are similarities in the trains of thought between Gerbner and Horkheimer and Adorno as well, even though they are implicit. For instance, in their criticism on the culture industry as "infecting everything with sameness", Horkheimer and Adorno (1993[1944]) observed that "films and radio no longer need to present themselves with art [..., indeed] the truth that they are nothing but business is used as an ideology to legitimize the trash they intentionally produce" (p. 95). By this, they point out that the economic-driven commodification of culture such as mass media is the commodification of human life, thereby eradicating autonomous thinking. Similarly Gerbner (2001) argues that "Today children are born into a commercial media (mostly television) environment that defines their world and their role in it. Lacking an alternative for comparison and judgment, the media-dominated cultural environment seems natural, inevitable, and unalterable" (p. 186). Thus, both argue that mass media have taken over reality as the filter through which people experience reality, to the point that their lives are shaped and conditioned by mass media's products such as film, radio and magazines, but especially television. According to Gerbner,

"Television is the chief creator of synthetic cultural patterns (entertainment and information) for the most heterogeneous mass publics in history, including large groups that have never before shared in any common public message systems. The repetitive pattern of television's mass-produced messages and images forms the mainstream of the common symbolic environment that cultivates the most widely shared conceptions of reality. We live in terms of the stories we tell—stories about what things exist, stories about how things work, and stories about what to do—and television tells them all through news, drama, and advertising to almost everybody most of the time."
— Gerbner et al. (1978, p. 178)

Similarly, Horkheimer and Adorno (1973) argue that television will become the prototypical artifact of commercialized and industrialized culture, given that it is "exclusive to none but shared by all" (p. 127). Thus, Gerbner et al. as well as Horkheimer and Adorno caution the emergence of market stratification. The dominance of television over other mass media and the magnitude of impact it has on society happened to such a degree that "no national achievement, celebration, or mourning seems real until it is confirmed and shared on television" as Gerbner and Gross (1976a, p. 176) assess. This means that although all movies and shows on television appear to be different, they follow in fact the same recycled standardized formula, a trend labeled as *same-same, but different*. This explains why Gerbner and associates assume that the messages are uniform in nature. Due to this fundamental pattern that permeates all programs on television, the uniformity is less visible and therefore more pervasive (Schiller, 2000). Television is like salty water in the ocean that goes unnoticed by the fish that swims in it (Gerbner, 2001). As early as in the 1940s and 1950s, Horkheimer and Adorno argue that the shows on television are highly formulaic and reproduce conformity and adjustment, criticising the portrayal of stereotypes on television as producing pseudo-realism. They also call for an alternative assessment for studying the impact of television given that

"The effect of television cannot be adequately expressed in terms of success or failure, likes or dislikes, approval or disapproval. Rather, an attempt should be made, with the aid of depth-psychological cat-

egories and previous knowledge of mass media, to crystallize a number of theoretical concepts by which the potential effect of television—its impact upon various layers of the spectator's personality—could be studied. It seems timely to investigate systematically socio-psychological stimuli typical of televised material both on a descriptive and psychodynamic level, to analyze their presuppositions as well as their total pattern, and to evaluate the effect they are likely to produce."
— Adorno (1991[1972—1981], p. 136)

While the idea that scholars should assess the effects of television specifically through psychoanalytic and ideological readings does not show much similarity to the approach in cultivation, in general also Gerbner called for an alternative measurement of television effects (see e.g., Gerbner & Gross, 1976a). Moreover, the idea that there are hidden meanings on television by Adorno (1991[1972—1981]) is similar to the notion by the Cultural Indicators Project team that television presents the audience with a unified stream of messages which are "recurrent, stable, and overarching patterns of television content. These are the consistent images, portrayals, and values that cut across most types of programs and are virtually inescapable for regular (and especially the heavy) viewers" (see e.g., Gerbner, 1998, p. 181). In summary, the reasoning and deliberations from the Cultural Indicators Project team and the proponents of critical theory show a great overlap. Also the link between Gerbner and Herbert Schiller, and likewise Herbert Schiller and the Frankfurt School gives support to the assertion that critical theory underlies the presuppositions of uniform messages. Given the similar arguments by Gerbner et al. and Horkheimer and Adorno, the line of reasoning for uniform messages in cultivation theory appears concise and logical according to the tenets of critical theory.

4.1.2 Precision of Uniform Messages

According to Potter (2014), precision refers to the level of clarity with which a theory articulates its assumptions and propositions so that scholars can understand its explanation and so that they can design adequate tests. In isolation, the precision of the presuppositions of the Cultural Indicators Project, namely the assumption of uniform messages and unselective viewing behavior, are an easy target for criticism: In the past, scholars have argued that with the fragmentation of broadcast channels, viewers can be more selective in their viewing behavior, and that the program may in fact differ according to channel, times, or genres. For example, Hawkins and Pingree (1981a) argue,

> "If viewing behavior reflects selectivity as well as ritual, then not all viewers will see the same thing. If viewing differences exist, then the relevant patterns of action for symbolic messages lie not in the sum of what is presented, but in the sum of what is viewed. And if differences in patterns of action do exist between types of programs, and if these mesh with any patterns of viewing, then quite different cultivations can occur within a single population, and total television viewed is not the only independent variable."
> — Hawkins and Pingree (1981a, p. 292)

Likewise, Potter (1993) argues that the rigid formula of television content has been breaking down with the introduction of a much wider range of programs on television. Hence, the uniformity of messages across the wide range of genres is in question. And J. Cohen and Weimann (2000) add that "viewers do not simply watch TV; they watch specific shows" or genres (p. 101). Thus, they argue that the audience is not as unselective in their viewing behavior as the presuppositions of the Cultural Indicators Project suggests.

While the precision of uniform messages appears ambiguous, outdated and inconsistent when viewed in isolation, the assessment outcome changes when the precision of uniform messages is compared to its fit with critical theory: The argument that there is a pervasive pattern of messages across television that follows a rigid formula is in line with the assumption from critical theory that mass media are commercial products that infect everything with sameness. Moreover, the assumption that the behavior of viewers is rather unselective and that the same viewer watches all, alludes to the assumption by critical theorists that television is shared by everyone and eradicates autonomous thinking. Even the special position of television in society in comparison to other mass media is shared by both George Gerbner and the Frankfurt School.

Thus, the tenets of a system of uniform messages and unselective viewing appear to be rather precise with regard to the underlying super-theory, namely critical theory. From this it follows that the critiques about uniform messages' precision are based on a different super-theory or come from a different perspective that is applied: First, the argument that there is a greater fragmentation of television content, which questions the uniformity across genres, is not consistent with critical theory. It rather seems to be an argument stemming from an economic perspective in which a greater fragmentation of channels, genres, and content is desirable as it maximizes the audience reach. Second, also the argument that the audience is rather selective in their viewing behavior which goes against the assumption of unselective viewing in uniform messages, has little in common with the assumptions of critical theory. Rather, this argument is made based on a psychological perspective which focuses on the microlevel of viewers, taking for example into account their sought gratifications when they conceptualize viewing behavior. In summary, the precision of uniform messages appears high when compared to the assumptions of critical theory, but low when compared to other perspectives such as the economic or psychological filter.

4.2 Genre-Specific Messages

4.2.1 Tenets and Critiques of Genre-Specific Messages

Based on the skepticism—supported by empirical proof—about whether people watch television unselectively, and likewise, whether there is a fundamental message present across all television, an alternative way of categorizing cultivating messages emerged: The concept of genre-specific messages (Bilandzic & Rössler, 2004; J. Cohen & Weimann, 2000; Potter, 1993; Potter & Chang, 1990). Genre-specific cultivation deals with the long-term contribution of viewing particular genres to viewers' conception of social reality (Bilandzic & Busselle, 2012a). This means that the more viewers watch a certain genre, the more the genre-specific messages are internalized in their worldviews. The basic assumption for genre-specific messages is that various genres carry different messages and that viewers are watching specific genres instead of TV in general. Murder, for example, is a core element of crime shows but virtually absent in sitcoms; and a positive attitude about love may be associated with heavier romantic comedy viewing (Bilandzic & Busselle, 2012a). Moreover, genre-specific messages in cultivation hews closely to the idea that heavy users of a certain genre differ in the extent and form of their cultivation effects from heavy users of another genre. For example, some scholars argue that the cultivated belief in a mean and dangerous world should be associated with exposure to genres with a high level of violence rather than with total television exposure. In accordance, their empirical results suggest this expectation since exposures to crime drama were found to be stronger predictors of fear of crime and other indicators of fearful perceptions than general TV exposure (see e.g., Eschholz, Chiricos, & Gertz, 2003; Hawkins & Pingree, 1980; Holbert, Shah, & Kwak, 2004). Similarly, gender stereotypes and expectations with reference to marriage and romance may reveal divergent associations with exposure to specific genres in comparison to the total amount of television viewing (see e.g., Segrin & Nabi, 2002; Ward, Merryweather, & Caruthers, 2006).

Scholars also studied cultivation effects relating to certain programs or single TV shows or movies, and labelled them as genre-specific messages as well. For example, Grabe and Drew (2007) tested how the cultivation effects differ with regard to portrayals stemming from either news, reality TV shows, or fictional shows such as crime drama. Their study showed little evidence of cultivation effects associated with crime drama, but some evidence for non-fictional programs. Comparing the programs, they concluded that this "provide[s] evidence that nonfiction TV might be more effective than fiction in cultivating perceptions of crime, fears, and potentially defensive behavior" (p. 152). Other scholars have tested cultivation effects from a single TV show such as *Grey's Anatomy* (2005–) under the label of genre-specific cultivation effects as well (e.g., Quick, 2009). In order to distinguish between genres or programs, scholars assume that each genre or program has its own set of depicted symbols, myths and references to reality (J. Cohen & Weimann, 2000; Grabe & Drew, 2007). They are distinct because these elements do not overlap between genres; this assumption is oftentimes described as *tertium non datur* (literally translates 'third is not given,' meaning 'it can be either A or B, but not both').

Hence, 'genre-specific messages' serves as an umbrella concept, which encompasses messages that are specific to either genres, programs, or single shows or movies. The latter, however, probably serve as a stand-in for the typical message in a specific genre. For instance, studying the messages from the TV show *Grey's Anatomy* (2005–) serves as a gateway to assess the genre-specific messages of the genre 'medical drama' in general. It goes beyond the scope of this book to summarize all the findings of genre-specific cultivation effects, but for an overview, consider for example Bilandzic and Rössler (2004) who offer a comprehensive list of cultivation studies on crime drama in comparison to overall television viewing or other genres; also consider Morgan and Shanahan (2010) for a comparison of findings from cultivation studies with either the assumption of genre-specific or uniform messages.

The categorization of genre-specific messages was mainly criticised by proponents of the original global idea of television messages, but other scholars also voiced concerns. For example, Newhagen and Lewenstein

(1992) cautioned that viewers may not define genres in the same way as scholars do. A disconnect between the genre labels by the audience and scholars may then lead to bizarre and nonsensical associations. Others have pointed out that the study of genre-specific messages may lead to "pointlessly reductionist studies of, for example, the influence of the Golf Channel on attitudes about golf" (Morgan et al., 2015, p. 690), or "trivial and irrelevant, though potentially true, conclusions, as 'Heavy viewing of the Home and Garden Channel 'cultivates' awareness of when to plant different bulbs'" (Morgan & Shanahan, 1997, p. 6). Hence, they argue that the study of genre-specific messages may be tautological in nature or irrelevant. Moreover, it is argued,

> "Too often, studies look at the impact of watching some genre on some attitude and assume they are observing the independent contribution of exposure to that genre, but most viewers still watch more than one genre. Although viewers may learn a lot about doctors from medical dramas, messages about doctors (perhaps contrary, perhaps congruent) also appear in sitcoms, police shows, reality shows, and many other genres."
> — Morgan et al. (2015, p. 691)

Thus, Morgan et al. (2015) caution that an isolated measurement of genre-specific cultivation effects (especially in an experimental setting) is not consistent with people's overall use of and exposure to television, and the portrayals that cut across genres. In addition, critiques questioned whether the categorization of genre-specific messages belongs to the Cultural Indicators Project altogether, because it goes against the basic tenets of cultivation as presenting the viewers with a coherent, ubiquitous, and uniform stream of messages (Morgan et al., 2014, 2015).

4.2.2 Precision and Relevance of Genre-Specific Messages

In order to assess the value of these critiques, the concept of genre-specific messages can be evaluated according to its precision and relevance. In the Section 3.2 'Four Perspectives to Define Genres,' we noted the general lack of progress in addressing basic questions about how to conceptualize genres. Unfortunately, this is also true in the more confined domain of genre-specific messages. An exception to this is the work by Bilandzic and Busselle (2012a) who point out that "the quality of genre-specific cultivation research depends on our ability to conceptualize and articulate the content of a genre" (p. 262). The authors developed a framework to define the cultivating messages of genres that serves as an excellent practical guide for conducting the genre-specific content analysis. However, it is important to note that their approach is focusing solely on the linguistic perspective. Taking other perspectives into account, however, allows one to address some of the aforementioned critiques of genre-specific messages in cultivation theory.

Thus, to increase precision for genre-specific messages, we consider again the notion of how genres could be conceptualized from four perspectives as outlined in detail in Section 3.2. As a brief reminder, a genre is a corpus, category or class that reveals the relationship between a production system and a given audience. This relationship is further shaped by different factors associated with each perspective. According to the linguistic perspective, history shapes the relationship between the production system and the audience; from an economic perspective, it is the financial forces; and from a psychological perspective, the relationship is further shaped by the viewer's knowledge structures. System theory offers a framework to cluster genres further into programs such as news and entertainment, or respectively subprograms such as fictional entertainment or reality TV, each with reference to the level of reality observation. While there is a certain consensus about a set of genres (such as romance, comedy, drama, and so forth), the decision of which movie or TV show is sorted in which genre exactly varies with respect to the perspective that is applied. Thus, the precision of the categorization of genre-specific messages is increased when a particular perspective is applied. The precision, however, decreases when scholars undertake the important efforts of comparing in systematic literature reviews or in meta-analyses the effects from genre-specific messages but fail to account for their specific perspective.

The linguistic, economic, sociological, and psychological perspectives on the definition of genres allow an evaluation of the critiques of genre-specific messages from afar: First, the worry about a dissonance between viewers and scholars with regard to their definition of genres, hews closely to the psychological perspective. From this perspective, the individual knowledge structures of a viewer may lead to a different genre label than the label that the scholar anticipated. Moreover, from this perspective, different viewers may assign different genres to the same movie or TV show: For one viewer, the movie *The Hitchhiker's Guide to the Galaxy* (2005) may be science fiction, while for another viewer that movie belongs to the genre comedy. Hence, this criticism may be resolved when the respective perspective is accounted for, e.g., by including items in the survey that address the allocation of genres for certain TV shows, or open-ended questions to define the core elements that define a certain genre. Second, the criticism that studying genre-specific messages may be tautological refers to the linguistic perspective in which the issue of a split-genre corpus is addressed: The linguistic perspective tries to solve tautological definitions for genres, e.g., a western = takes place in the West. Applying a semantic/syntactic approach to assess the building blocks and broader implications of a genre, while allowing and assessing any historical changes, is the recommended approach from this perspective. Thus, from a linguistic point of view, genre-specific messages that are tautological (e.g., Golf shows entail messages about golfing) would not be considered as belonging to the study of genre-specific messages, and would therefore be dismissed. Third, the argument that genre-specific messages are invalid because there is a system of messages that cut across genres could be rephrased as the worry that genres are not distinct. This criticism alludes to the economic perspective: From the economic perspective, the production system tries to label a single movie or TV show with several genres in order to maximize its audience reach. Hence, the financial forces incentivize the ambiguous association of movies and TV shows with genres in order to increase their sales. The argument may be dissolved by applying a different perspective that does not allow for a multi-generic status.

In summary, the first step to address the critiques is to being aware of the specific perspective that is applied. This then enables the scholar to take appropriate measures as outlined in the examples above. However, the worry that genre-specific messages mark a departure from the basic tenets of cultivation theory, as it rejects the initial assumption of uniform messages, cannot be addressed by the aforementioned perspectives. Rather, this calls for a greater framework to situate genre-specific messages along with uniform messages in order to assess in what ways they exactly differ. Such a framework (provided in Chapter 5) also increases the precision of genre-specific messages.

Aside from precision, another dimension that assesses the heuristic value of genre-specific messages is relevance. In today's online television environment, "viewers can now be heavily exposed to very specific, and very diverse, genres of their choice" (p. 690) given that nowadays "subscription video-on-demand services such as Netflix provide easy access to both entire seasons of television programs and a vast library of theatrical films, and the amount of original online programming being produced by Netflix, Amazon, YouTube, Hulu Plus, and many others is exploding: We now have TV shows that are not even 'on TV'" (Morgan et al., 2015, p. 685).

Thus, the technological and economic forces have led to a greater fragmentation of genres and accessibility to the content. As outlined in Section 2.2, the new era of online television has shaped implications on mobility, availability, content fragmentation, individuality, engagement levels, and algorithmic recommendation systems. Genres play an increasingly important role in the production, distribution, and selection of messages in online television. Thus, genre-specific messages in cultivation may reflect to a greater degree the changes from broadcast to online television, and therefore mark their relevance.

4.3 Metanarratives

In addition to genre-specific messages, the skepticism about uniform messages and whether people watch television unselectively also gave rise to the concept of metanarratives. Introduced by Potter (1993) and fostered by Bilandzic and Busselle (2012a), according to this concept of cultivating messages, a set of primary values lies at the base of the actual story and permeates all types of genres and programs: "Rather than single features of the program, such as violent acts or demographic characteristics of television persons, meta-narratives represent complex semantic structures" (Bilandzic & Rössler, 2004, p. 319). Hence, metanarratives are often conceptualized as general topics or lessons about life in terms of morality such as 'truth wins out' or 'hard work is rewarded' (Potter, 1990, 1993), or more banal ideas about what the world is like. For example, the shows *Bob the Builder* (1998–2011) and *Home Improvement* (1991–1999) may belong to different genres, but they both entail the metanarrative that builders are friendly people. Similarly, from the perspectives of metanarratives, messages about physicians are not constrained to medical drama, but they also appear in soap operas, sitcoms, cartoons, and so forth. Thus, metanarratives "are not confined to a certain show or a certain genre, but cross genre borders liberally" (Bilandzic & Rössler, 2004, p. 309). Metanarratives can be found at any level of abstraction of the story. Similar to the conceptualizations of uniform messages and genre-specific messages, metanarratives assume that people learn general messages from (online) television rather than singular facts. However, in contrast to genre-specific messages, metanarratives assume that the exposure effect is due to great commonalities which cross genre-specific borders on television (Bilandzic & Busselle, 2012a). In contrast to uniform messages, metanarratives do not address television in general, but rather small, local meanings. Thus, while the fundamental assumption of cultivation theory as expressed by Gerbner and associates is that there are messages that are widespread across all television, the idea of metanarratives is that there are certain messages that only appear in some of the content on television. However, before we assess the precision of metanarratives, and given the clear etymological reference within metanarratives to narratives, in the next Section we explore whether metanarratives are a concept that exists distinctly in narratology as well.

4.3.1 Postmodernism and Narratology on Metanarratives

Metanarratives are a research object in postmodernism as well as in narratology, and addressed by the synonyms of 'metadiscourse,' 'grand narrative,' or, especially nowadays, 'master narrative.' In general, the prefix 'meta'—meaning beyond or about—in the term metanarratives emphasizes that this concept addresses the overarching narratives that explain the smaller narratives (for a discussion of the definition of narratives, see Section 3.3). The definition and critical evaluation of metanarratives differs between the two strands: The first strand, postmodernism, perceives metanarratives as sociocultural forms of interpretation, because they "refer to totalizing social theories or philosophies of history which, appealing to notions of transcendental and universal truth, purport to offer a comprehensive account of knowledge and experience" (Russell, 2010, p. 1). Based on the work *The Postmodern Condition* by French philosopher Jean-François Lyotard (in 1984[1979]), there were two great metanarratives in modernity: 'Enlightenment,' which is the metanarrative of infinite progress and liberty, and 'Science,' which is the metanarrative about the triumph of pure knowledge. However, in postmodernism these two metanarratives that offered stability, universal claim, and legitimization have come to an end: They are either extended to all sorts of legitimization strategies to preserve the status quo of suppression, or they are being replaced by smaller narratives that do not offer any universal claim (Hutcheon, 1989; Russell, 2010). This is why postmodern thinkers express some sort of antipathy towards metanarratives, given that they distrust the extension of universal theories and philosophies that they perceive as either being repressive or ignorant of important social discourse elements (such as difference, diversity and rebellion); this leads to an oppression of all which does not fit the initial model of the universal theory or philosophy. For example, from a postmodern perspective, a metanarrative could be the patriarchy, Western imperialism, Marxism, or capitalism (Hutcheon, 1989;

Russell, 2010). Critics like Jürgen Habermas, however, questioned whether all metanarratives are dogmatic and if all metanarratives should be discarded on the basis of some that are oppressive. Feminism, for example, could be perceived as another metanarrative that emerged as a counterweight to the metanarrative of patriarchy (Hutcheon, 1989).

Narratologists, on the other hand, seem to be undecided whether metanarratives could be understood (1) in Lyotard's sense—but taking a softer note on the postmodernist criticism and endorsing metanarratives with personal experiences—or whether metanarratives are (2) a way to delineate the position of a narrator in a story (Bamberg, 2004). When narratologists perceive metanarratives as inspired by (1) Lyotard then they refer to the dominance of stories that, through a process of manufactured consent, claim to be universal and interrelating to the personal experience by the recipient (Herman, 2009; Russell, 2010). In this perspective, metanarratives are mainly coined as master narratives and contrasted to counternarratives, which are "the stories which people tell and live which offer resistance, either implicitly or explicitly, to dominant cultural narratives," that is, the master narratives which "offer people a way of identifying what is assumed to be a normative experience" (Andrews, 2004, p. 1). For example, motherhood is a topic that is interwoven with people's personal experiences, i.e., being mothered and/or mothering, and that may be impacted by the idealized and homogenized metanarrative of the 'good mother' (Andrews, 2004). Similarly, there are cultural expectations of what constitutes a typical pregnancy, or of elderly being asexual; these cultural frames are then considered master narratives (Bamberg, 2004). Hence, in this line of research, metanarratives "are 'frames' according to which courses of events can easily be plotted, simply because one's audience is taken to 'know' and accept these courses" (Bamberg, 2004, p. 360). In this view, metanarratives give guidance and direction to everyday expectations and actions. In general, metanarratives can be identified by storylines that appear simplified, idealized, or simply universal, and that line up with one's own experience.

Other narratologists, however, take a more confined approach to metanarratives and define them as (2) the act and/or process of narration, or as a way to indicate the directing function of the narrator (Neumann & Nünning, n.d.). The former refers to any self-reflexive manner in the narrative or the concrete reference to a narrator, while the latter refers to stories within stories as expounded by Gérard Genette in 1988. Both approaches have in common that they make the recipient aware of the fact that they are dealing with a narrative. In this line of research, different types of metanarratives are elicited in a qualitative and/or descriptive analyses, and based on formal, structural, content-related, and reception-oriented types of metanarrative (Neumann & Nünning, n.d.). For example, a metanarrative is assessed by analysing diegetic, extradiegetic or paratextual types, depending on the level at which the narrator is situated. While some post-classical scholars distinguish metanarratives from master narratives and from metafiction (e.g., Fludernik, Nünning, or Prince), others use master narratives and metanarratives as interchangeable terms. Indeed, many scholars in each camp seem to be unaware that the terms are used to mean different things by scholars in the other camp, which can make it a frustrating process to grapple with metanarratives from a semiotic perspective.

In summary, both postmodernism and narratology are working with metanarratives, but come with different implications: For postmodern thinkers, metanarratives once offered a comprehensive account of experience and knowledge in order to achieve universal truth and applicability, but were repurposed to preserve the status quo of suppression and ignorance. In this line of thinking, a metanarrative could be considered the social theory or philosophical work of colonialism, patriarchy, or capitalism. Some narratologists claim that they hark back to that idea of metanarrative, but they actually make two adjustments: They back away from the critical perspective and add the assumption of personal experience to it. In this line of research, metanarratives as master narratives are generic and universal stories that are pervasive and recall personal experiences. Other narratologists, however, consider metanarratives merely as a technique to discover anti-illusions in texts, for example when a narrator addresses the reader directly. All three approaches have in common that metanarratives reveal the relationship between the content and the societal discourse.

4.3.2 Precision of Metanarratives

In order to assess the level of clarity for the assumptions and propositions for the concept of metanarratives, the level of precision is gauged. As the brief overview of the understanding of metanarratives in other disciplines revealed, the explanations of what exactly a metanarrative is differ between scholars from cultivation theory, postmodernism, and narratology. For cultivation scholars, metanarratives are pervasive messages that permeate various types of genres and programs, and that either come in the form of a moral conclusion or in a description about the world and its agents. For example, a metanarrative would be considered the moral that 'good wins out over evil,' or the description of doctors being courageous. In comparison to the understanding of metanarratives in postmodernism and narratology, however, the social discourse aspect is missing in cultivation theory: Postmodernist thinkers take an almost antipathetic position towards metanarratives because they assume that metanarratives express support for an oppressive and ignorant status quo of activities and institutions. Consequentially, for postmodern thinkers a metanarrative could be considered the patriarchy, Western imperialism, or capitalism. Hence, the understanding of metanarratives happens on a global level of concept and with a normative focus. For narratologists, however, a metanarrative either indicates the position of a narrator in a story and how the recipient is forced into a reflexive and monitoring state; or a metanarrative refers to dominant stories that relate to the personal experiences by the recipient. A metanarrative from these two perspectives could be either when a narrator talks directly to the audience on the TV screen as in the Netflix's series *A Series of Unfortunate Events* (2017–2019), or when recurrent stories are portrayed that are perceived as common-sense and stereotypical such as 'good motherhood.' Hence, metanarratives as cultivation scholars understand them do not relate to metanarratives as understood by postmodernists or narratologists. Naturally, this indicates a lack in precision since cultivation scholars cannot draw the underlying assumptions and presuppositions from a discipline that has an established line of study on metanarratives. This calls for a careful consideration of what the presuppositions of metanarratives are. To provide a starting point, next we walk briefly through two assumptions, namely multi-generic status and nested structure, that—when carefully implemented—may be promising in increasing the precision of metanarratives as cultivating messages.

4.3.2.1 Multi-Generic Status

As outlined, metanarratives are not restricted by genres, but cross genre borders liberally. This means that it is not authorative for scholars anymore to assess to what genre a movie or TV show belongs to, but instead to determine the abstract moral or semantic pattern that underlies it. This is the reason why movies or TV shows from different genres can share the same metanarrative. As Bilandzic and Rössler (2004) exemplify,

> "It is, for instance, conceivable that crime drama and situation comedy share the same meta-narrative, e.g., 'no matter what problems occur, everything will turn out just fine'. In this case, traditional genre cat-

egories would be the wrong indicators for television use; instead, we should start looking for programs sharing similar meta-narratives, and cluster them in meta-units."
— Bilandzic and Rössler (2004, p. 309)

Two presuppositions for metanarratives can be drawn from this: First, movies and TV shows from different genres can share the same metanarrative(s), as the example above shows. Second, a single movie or TV show can be described by more than a single metanarrative. For example, the metanarrative above may apply to a show from crime drama and situational comedy, but the more dominant metanarrative for crime drama may be that 'good wins out over evil.' The second presupposition is known to semioticians as the multi-generic status of a text and has been established nearly 90 years ago with the Bakhtinian approach (Stam et al., 2005). Thus, a movie or a TV show would be attributed with several metanarratives that describe, for example, its moral.

In order to assess the main categories for metanarratives that are based on morality, Potter (1990) proposed to use the categories that Selnow (1986) detected from a content analysis. From analyzing 222 sub-plots in prime-time fictional television, Selnow (1986, p. 70) concluded that there are only seven rules by which 96 percent of the stories were resolved, namely,

- Truth wins out in the end/honesty is the best policy (24.2 percent of all resolutions),
- Hard work yields rewards (6.3 percent),
- Ingenuity finds a solution (17.8 percent),
- Good wins out over evil (36.2),
- Evil wins out over good (3.4 percent),
- Might makes right (3.4 percent),
- Luck is important (4.6 percent).

Accordingly, the argument that is being made by Potter (1990, 1993) and Bilandzic and Rössler (2004) is that these seven morals of a story are the metanarratives that cultivate heavy viewers. A single TV show or movie may contain several of these rules, and it is the scholar's task to determine which of these metanarratives apply, and how dominant they are. The latter is of importance because even though several (if not most) of the seven metanarratives may apply to a single object, they will probably vary in their importance and dominance. For example, even though crime drama and situation comedy share the same meta-narrative ('good wins out over evil'), for situation comedy the metanarratives that are even more pressing may be that 'luck is important' or 'honesty is the best policy.' It is an important task for future scholars to develop a measurement that captures this multi-generic status and weight of metanarratives accordingly to increase precision.

4.3.2.2 Nested Structure

Another presupposition of metanarratives that may increase precision is the observation that metanarratives can be nested. This suggestion is based on the notion by Bilandzic and Rössler (2004) that scholars "should start looking for programs sharing similar metanarratives, and *cluster* them in meta-units" (p. 309; emphasis added). Similarly, Selnow (1986) suggested that the seven rules of a story (outlined above) could be summarized further. By nested structure, we mean that some metanarratives are not independent of each other and are likely to be more related to each other than they are to other metanarratives. This means that two metanarratives are nested if the levels of the first metanarrative are observed in conjunction with one level of the second metanarrative. For example, Selnow (1986) argues that the four metanarratives 'truth wins out in the end,' 'hard work yields rewards,' 'ingenuity finds a solution,' and 'good wins out over evil' are likely to exhibit a clustering effect, e.g., Judeo-Christian themes. The other three metanarratives ('evil wins out over good,' 'might makes right,' and 'luck is important') are unrelated. However, we suggest that the nested structure does not stop at this first level but goes further: For example, the two metanarratives 'hard work yields rewards' and 'ingenuity finds a solution' can be clustered on another level, e.g., American dream, which is a sub-cluster of the Judeo-Christian cluster. In addition, metanarratives are also nested within more than one cluster where the clusters are not structurally related. For example, aside from Judeo-Christian themes, the metanarratives 'good wins out over evil' and 'bad wins out over good' allow another clustering, e.g., in terms of black-and-white thinking. Figure 4.1 illustrates the example of this nested and clustering structure, including two orphaned metanarratives ('luck is important' and 'might makes right').

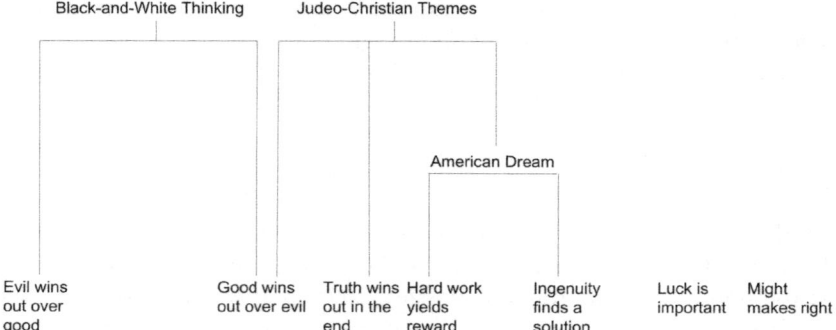

Figure 4.1 Example for nested structure of metanarratives

Hence, to the former two presuppositions from the multi-generic status, there are two more additions: First, metanarratives can have a nested structure, i.e., they can be clustered on a higher level of abstraction. And second, metanarratives can be cross-clustered, which means that metanarratives can be included in more than one cluster.

In summary, to increase the precision for metanarratives as another concept to describe cultivating messages, it is important to acknowledge that the concept as envisioned by cultivation scholars does not hark back to the understanding of metanarratives by postmodern thinkers or narratologists. It is fundamental that scholars investigate the underlying assumptions of metanarratives further before studying metanarratives empirically. Two suggestions for presuppositions for metanarratives were outlined here, namely that several metanarratives coexist in one object, and that these metanarratives are (cross-) nested. Only if scholars keep these underlying assumptions in mind or develop them further, they can start to address them by research.

4.4 Novel Concept: Subgenre Messages

4.4.1 Consequences from Former Message Concepts

Currently, there are three ways to categorize cultivating messages: Either as uniform messages, as genre-specific messages, or as metanarratives. The three types differ in terms of their underlying assumptions, the super-theory they may draw upon, and their level of precision.

The presuppositions for uniform messages assume that there is a fixed set of messages that are ubiquitous on television, such as 'the world is a mean and dangerous place.' Hence, there is no fragmentation within or between genres, but the messages are equally distributed on television. Moreover, Gerbner and his associates believed that viewers are not selective in their viewing. But actually, following the same logic, it does not matter whether viewers are selective in their viewing (with regard to, for instance, particular genres), because they are exposed to the same, uniform messages either way. Some critique has been raised with regard to these two assumptions. For example, empirical findings show that the assumption of a continuous stream of uniform message is faulty when tested on a content level (e.g., Greenberg, 1980; Potter & Ware, 1987; Tamborini & Choi, 1990). Hence, if viewers were to be selective in their viewing, it would have an impact on the messages they receive. Moreover, on a theoretical level some scholars such as Potter (1993) state that an unselective use of television was defensible decades ago when television content was dominated by three commercial networks. But with the development in technology and accompanying changes in the economy, i.e., increased number and variety of television networks and channels, the assumption of unselective viewing is strained. That is, even decades ago it was possible for a person to watch television and see very little violence, even though the rate of depictions of violence in television was in general high (Hawkins & Pingree, 1981a). We note that the arguments against uniform messages are made from different perspectives than that from which its tenets stem. Nonetheless, these critiques led to several further developments such as genre-specific messages and metanarratives.

The concept of genre-specific messages emerged as a reaction to the doubts of the presuppositions of uniform messages, namely that all content on television follows a rigid and pervasive formula, and that viewers are unselective. Instead, genre-specific messages assumes that there are messages on television that only apply to certain genres, and that viewers watch television selectively with regard to genres. In direct comparison to the concept of uniform messages, the concept of genre-specific messages also actually assumes the uniformity of messages, but only within a genre. Hence, genre-specific messages assumes that there are uniform messages that differ from genre to genre. This enables the approach to account for selective viewing, i.e., viewers have preferences for certain genres and stick to movies and/or TV shows from these genres. This phenomenon may be even more prevalent in today's era of online television. However, in the interim, alternative message categorization frameworks such as metanarratives emerged that account for viewers watching selectively but not with regard to genres.

For the concept of metanarratives the viewer is not required to view genres selectively, but rather to spend time with highly fragmented messages across all television that cluster in metanarratives (or meta-units at a higher level of abstraction). For example, the metanarrative 'no matter what problems occur, everything will work out fine' does not only occur in crime drama, but also romantic comedy and family adventure. Moreover, it is even possible that metanarratives are overlapping in different genres: In an empirical study by Potter (1990), it was found that primetime soaps, daytime soaps and sports viewing were related to the belief that 'truth wins out in the end,' while the metanarrative 'good wins over evil' was only traceable to two types of program, namely daytime soaps and sports.

As metanarratives do not necessarily require viewers to select their program by genre, the question arises how the concept of metanarratives changes if viewers in fact do choose their program by genre. Likewise, the question arises of how the concept of genre-specific messages would change if the degree of fragmentation of messages within genres were growing. For instance, due to the economic forces there is a trend towards addressing a greater number of messages in a single TV show or a single movie in order to increase the audience reach. Likewise, VOD and SVOD services, which use genres to 'help' the viewers select the content, are gaining increasing popularity (Nielsen, 2016, 2017, 2018).

Naturally, the concepts of messages in cultivation theory can only be understood with regard to the institutions that produce and distribute them as well as with regard to the audience that receives them (and is expected to be cultivated by them). Therefore, the new era of online television that we live in is also imperative to the concept of cultivating messages. For example, half of all households in the U.S. already have access to SVOD services such as Netflix, Hulu, Amazon Video, or Disney+ (Nielsen, 2016, 2017); similarly "Subscription video-on-demand (SVOD) services are in a growth phase in Europe. A variety of different platforms are increasing their market penetration while boosting their in-house production to retain subscribers and conform to new European audiovisual regulations" (Castro & Cascajosa, 2020, p. 154).

VOD and SVOD services enable the production and presentation of content in a hypertargeted way (Jenner, 2016): After creating a profile at the services, the information of each TV show and movie that the viewer watches is not only stored but also used (Lobato, 2018). This refers to VOD and SVOD services employing algorithms that determine the preferences of a viewer and that predict future preferences for certain TV shows or movies which are then suggested to the viewer. For example, with regard to the SVOD service Netflix, Lobato (2018, p. 251) explains, "Netflix users do not experience the catalog as a static list or schedule, but rather as a series of interactive, personalized recommendations that are algorithmically sorted according to user viewing history, demographic and location data." Hence, the more often the viewer uses the SVOD service, the more they are paying into a spiral of algorithmically derived recommendations, which in turn lock the viewer further in in their genre selection. Thus, genres are an important economic concept for VOD and SVOD services. Meanwhile, formerly distinct genres are being increasingly casually intermixed to serve the hyper-targeting strategy of VOD and SVOD services: For example, the TV show *Life's Too Short* (2011–2013)—which depicts fictional content with and about actor Warwick Davis in a style that is known for documentaries—tries to reach an audience that has an aptitude for satire and documentaries, in short for the novel genre 'mockumentary' (a hybridization of mock and documentary). Similarly, viewers with preferences for romance and horror do not have to search in two separate genre corpora when they search for content to watch, but can instead search in the genre 'romantic horror.' This fragmentation of genres in online television has led, for instance at Netflix, to the creation of over 75,000 non-classical genres (Madrigal, January 2, 2014). These types of novel genre creations or hybridizations are actually 'subgenres.' Subgenres are genres that are part of a larger genre. This means that 'romantic horror' is a subgenre that stems from the two genres 'romance' and 'horror.' These trends of genre fragmentation and (sub-)genre selective viewing call for yet another alternative concept of cultivating messages. In order to consider today's highly selective viewing of subgenres, we coin this novel concept in cultivating messages: 'subgenre messages.' After a short introduction on the emergence of subgenres in online television, we explain the presuppositions of subgenre messages further.

4.4.2 Subgenres and Online Television

While broadcast television was defined by a linear schedule of a few mass channels, today's era of online television is defined by "services that facilitate the viewing of editorially selected audiovisual content through internet-connected devices and infrastructure" (Johnson, 2019, p. 167). Components such as advanced technology including digital infrastructure and 4G, the fragmentation of services with mass and niche channels but also SVOD, or the algorithms that constitute a 'TV guide' shape online television further (see Section 2.2.2 for further information). Online television, and especially the VOD and SVOD services, also facilitate the segmentation of content due to their efficient access to and effective use of larger data sets. This has resulted in the emergence of more subgenres and an abundance of microgenres. For example, with reference to Netflix, Napoli (2016) explains,

> "Indeed, one of the less-discussed aspects of Netflix's evolution is that the company's analytics and decision-making now also rely upon granular content analysis of all video content in the Netflix library (Madrigal, 2014). Each piece of content is coded across dozens of variables, allowing the company to segment its content offerings into over 75,000 'microgenres' on the basis of content characteristics alone."
> — Napoli (2016, p. 1)

Madrigal (January 2, 2014) wrote a script to run through the complete set of microgenres by Netflix and found a total of 76,897 unique labels to categorize TV shows and movies. These microgenres, as he further specifies, follow a rigid formula with a specific hierarchy for each category of descriptor:

> *Microgenre = Region + Adjectives + Noun Genre + Based On... + Set In... + From The... + About... + For Age X to Y*

Hence, a microgenre is formed by creating a subset of these components. This results in microgenres ranging from 'Emotional Fight-the-System Documentaries' to 'Violent Suspenseful Action & Adventure from the 1980s' and 'Time-Travel Movies Starring William Hartnell.' Hypothetically, if all components were to apply, the longest option for such a microgenre label would be: 'American Oscar-winning Romantic Dramas based on classic literature set in Adwardian Era from the 1950s about marriage for ages 8 to 10.' Similarly, Miller (2012) points out that in today's online television era we have microgenres on YouTube such as 'shrieking-kid-with-toy,' 'cats-being-mean' or 'speed-painting.' These microgenres, however, "appeal to just a few and probably for just a short time" (Miller, 2012, p. 128).

Subgenres, on the other hand, are located between genre and microgenre: They subsume several microgenres, but are more fragmented than genres. For example, the aforementioned abundance of (roughly 75,000) microgenres on Netflix are subsumed by 400 subgenres, which are further encompassed by 19 umbrella categories, i.e., the genres, as an analysis by Smith- Rowsey (2016) revealed:

> "Many of Netflix's 400 subcategories [i.e., subgenres] suggest common-alities that might have been heretofore heterodox: under the Horror umbrella, one can click Vampires, Werewolves, Zombies, and even Teen Screams; under Children and Family, one sees subs like Book Characters and Dinosaurs; under Music, a person can click Gospel Music, Show Tunes, World Fusion, Reggae, and separately Reggaeton; under Special Interest, users are offered Sculpture, Tap and Jazz Dance, Hunting, Magic and Illusion, Wine and Beverage Appreciation, Perfor-mance Art and Spoken Word, Shakespeare, as well as Healing and Reiki."
>
> — Smith-Rowsey (2016, p. 71)

In comparison to microgenres, notably none of these 400 subgenres are restricted to any specific period which supports Altman's notion that the definition of a genre is fluid over time. Instead, Netflix, and presumably other VOD and SVOD services, confirm Altman's suggestion that any genre can be merged with any other genre at any time to create a new subgenre. Put simply: "In the genre world, however, every day is Jurassic Park day" (Altman, 2000, p. 70). While subgenres have long played a central role in musical theory, with the emergence of online television, subgenres have also gained increasing attention by scholars and industry alike. Some SVOD services such as Netflix monetarize the genre and sub-genre listing such that studios can, to some extent, pay to have movies or TV shows appear in listings from which they would otherwise be excluded. This capitalist-driven postmodernist process, however, is invisible to the users since there are no additional labels that indicate any sponsorship or advertisement (Smith-Rowsey, 2016).

In summary, both subgenres and microgenres are emerging trends in online television and "a direct result from increased access to popular culture, hypermedia devices, social media, and new marketing techniques" (Popescu, 2013, p. 568). However, microgenres appear to be highly frag-mented and one could question to what degree microgenres still belong to the concept of genres *per se*. For example, since microgenres can in princi-ple refer to a certain period of time, they are violating the assumption that genres are fluid over time (linguistic perspective); likewise, given that the economic perspective tries to attach multiple labels to a single TV show or a single movie, it is questionable how many movies and TV shows actually can receive multiple of the highly specified microgenre labels. Subgenres, in comparison, have a higher fragmentation degree than genres but avoid this hyper-specialization that is part of microgenres. While both subgenre and microgenre appear to be concepts that are relevant in today's new media environment, only the concept of subgenre seems to fill a void in a conceptualization of cultivating messages that accounts for a greater fragmentation within a genre as well as the assumption that viewers are inevitably selective in their viewing habits—either by choice or by the algorithmic settings employed by the online television service.

4.4.3 Assumptions of Subgenre Messages in Cultivation

The original concept of 'subgenre messages' that is introduced here stems from the notion that genres are becoming increasingly fragmented by the production system (e.g., studios and services of online television) and that viewers are increasingly watching content based on the algorithmic recommendations which are, along with location and demography, based on existing subgenre preferences. For example, viewers do not watch 'horror' anymore, but have a preference for vampires, zombies, or werewolf movies (Lobato & Ryan, 2011). This means that viewers do not watch simply movies and TV shows from a specific genre, but subgenres with a specific focus. For example, on a genre level, viewers may prefer 'horror' but on a subgenre level, there are viewers who have a stronger preference for TV shows and movies from the subgenre 'zombie' (e.g., *Zombieland*, 2009; or *World War Z*, 2013), while others prefer 'slashers & serial killers' (e.g., *The Strangers: Prey at Night*, 2018; or *Friday the 13th*, 2009). While the subgenres entail similar visual or audience effects, they may differ in the messages they cultivate: For example, the subgenre 'zombie' may cultivate the message that one needs to set aside differences to fight a common enemy; whereas the subgenre 'slashers & serial killers' may convey the message that one should be suspicious about one's surroundings such as strangers or abandoned buildings.

Hence, the concept of subgenre messages in cultivation theory derives as a hybridization of genre-specific messages and metanarratives. To this end, the novel concept includes some of the basic tenets from genre-specific messages and metanarratives: From genre-specific messages, the concept of subgenre messages takes over the accounting for genre-specific lock-in effects from online television. Based on the algorithmically generated recommendation system in online television, and especially VOD and SVOD services, that is based on subgenres, genres and subgenres play an increasingly important role compared to previous television eras. From metanarratives, the concept of subgenre messages borrows the assumption that there are several messages lying at the base of a genre, i.e., multi-generic status. These messages, however, can be clustered by the subgenres. This also implies that a genre now consists of multiple messages, namely its subgenre messages. Naturally, this may lead to an overlap between genres, however, the argument is that the dominant message in each genre differs. For example, while 'crime drama' and 'family adventure' share the messages 'no matter what problems occur, everything will work out fine' and 'ingenuity finds a solution,' the order of emphasis of these messages varies such that 'ingenuity finds a solution' is more dominant in 'crime drama,' whereas 'family adventure' consists mainly of the message 'no matter what problems occur, everything will work out fine.'

Hence, thinking about cultivating messages using subgenre concepts provides a different way of addressing some of the typical concerns of genre-specific messages and uniform messages. Moreover, the original concept hews closely to recent technological and economic trends towards online television. The concept of subgenre messages in cultivation also complements the former three ways to categorize cultivating messages, as discussed in the next Chapter.

Chapter Five Synthesis: Postulates, Lemmas, & Research Question

My model was complex when I started, too, but I just kept working on it till
it got simple!
Varian, 1997, p. 4

Previously, an elite cohort of scholars have started to call for "a clear rationale for how they [genre-specific messages or metanarratives] are similar to or different from the more global concept of cultivation" (Morgan & Shanahan, 2010, p. 341), yet this call remained heretofore unanswered. Having outlined what each concept of cultivating messages entails and developed an additional concept of subgenre messages in Chapter 4, we now turn towards a way to relate them to one another. The goal is not to give a definite *yes* or *no* answer to the question of whether these concepts fall within the scope of cultivation theory, but rather to show on a continuum how close the concepts are to one another. The result is a visual two-dimensional space to illustrate commonalities and differences among all four message concepts, to enable common substantial progress in cultivation theory. This process involves a decomposition of the message concepts into their most relevant parts that permit a definition of their properties to relate between them. Hence, the in-depth exploration and assessment of the propositions of each message concept in Chapter 4 enables us to simplify in this Chapter, allowing for the creation of an original framework to situate the message concepts.

5.1 Postulates and Lemmas of Message Conceptualizations

Each message concept comes with its own set of presuppositions that defines its degree of precision for cultivation theory. The four message concepts, namely uniform messages, genre-specific messages, metanarratives, and subgenre messages, can also be related to one another in terms of how they differ or are similar. Hawkins and Pingree (1981a) claimed that Gerbner's original idea of a "ubiquitous, unified, and undifferentiated 'stream' of messages" (Morgan et al., 2015, p. 677) can be broken into the assumptions of uniformity of messages and unselective viewing.

We suggest that these assumptions can serve as the basic principles for all concepts of cultivating messages if they are rephrased and abstracted further: (1) the degree of fragmentation of messages on online television, and (2) the necessity of selective viewing. These two principles serve as the basis of the cultivating effects of online television exposure. The two assumptions are based on the notions from previous Chapters that there is an on-going increase of fragmentation of genres towards subgenres with a greater range of messages that they convey. Similarly, there is a trend towards selective viewing, either actively sought out by the audience, or unbeknownst to them as they are not aware of the algorithmically derived recommendations in online television based on previous subgenre viewing behavior along with demography and location.

The relationship between online television exposure, fragmentation of messages, and selective viewing, hence, can be put in the general form:

Postulate 1: Cultivating message exposure is based on the relationship between the degree of fragmentation of messages in a genre and the level of necessarily selective viewing of genres.

For example, uniform messages are characterized by a consistent set of messages that is embedded across varying genres with the assumption that "the same viewers watch them all" (Gerbner, 1977, p. 147). In this idea of cultivating messages, a heavy viewer is determined by the amount of time they spend watching TV. Thus, there are no differences between genres in terms of the system of messages they convey. This implies that even if viewers were to be selective in their viewing, they would be exposed to the same system of messages as are the viewers who are unselective in their viewing behavior. For instance, the message that the world is a dangerous and mean place appears as a global concept in all of online television and all viewers are exposed to it. From this derives the first Lemma of Postulate 1:

Lemma 1: In the concept of uniform messages, both the degree of fragmentation of messages in a genre and the necessity of genre-selective viewing are minimized.

The concepts of genre-specific messages and metanarratives differ from this formula of uniform messages in terms of both the degree of fragmentation of messages in a genre and the necessity of genre-selective viewing: Genre-specific messages require a greater degree of selective viewing as the viewers are expected to prefer certain genres over others. Thus, a heavy viewer is a person who watches one or more genres more frequently than others. The degree of fragmentation of messages within a genre, however, is rather low, since the focus is on differences between genres. This leads to the second Lemma of Postulate 1:

> **Lemma 2:** In the concept of genre-specific messages, the degree of fragmentation of messages in a genre is minimized while the necessity of genre-selective viewing is maximized.

The concept of metanarratives, however, assumes that genres possess a great level of fragmentation of messages, which are the metanarratives. Here a heavy viewer is considered a person who watches and prefers a certain set of metanarratives that appears across genres. Since in this line of study it is not required that viewers watch genre-specifically, this leads to the third Lemma of Postulate 1:

> **Lemma 3:** In the concept of metanarratives, the degree of fragmentation of messages in a genre is maximized while the necessity of genre-selective viewing is minimized.

In comparison, Lemma 2 and Lemma 3 are inverse, hence, genre-specific messages and metanarratives are inverted concepts. This assumption is supported by the fact that genre-specific messages focus on the heterogeneity of television content, whereas metanarratives consider subtle commonalities across television (Bilandzic & Rössler, 2004).

The original concept of subgenre messages as introduced in Chapter 4 derives as a hybridization of metanarratives and genre-specific messages: It is based on the observations that there is at once an increase of fragmentation of genres towards subgenres (and even microgenres), and that online television fosters selective viewing on the part of viewers. Therefore, the concept of subgenre messages maximizes the extrema of fragmented messages in genres, and the level of selective viewing. A heavy viewer in this concept is a person who watches one or more subgenres more often than others. Accordingly, Lemma 4 of Postulate 1 is:

> **Lemma 4:** In the concept of subgenre messages, both the degree of fragmentation of messages in a genre and the necessity of genre-selective viewing are maximized.

Since the concept of subgenre messages is a hybridization of genre-specific messages and metanarratives, with regard to Postulate 1, the concept of subgenre messages derives naturally as the inverse of uniform messages. In this way, subgenre messages require the strongest assumptions, but account for recent developments in online television. We suggest that all

Lemmas can be visualized in a two-dimensional space guided by Postulate 1. Accordingly, Figure 5.1 summarizes Postulate 1 and its Lemmas.

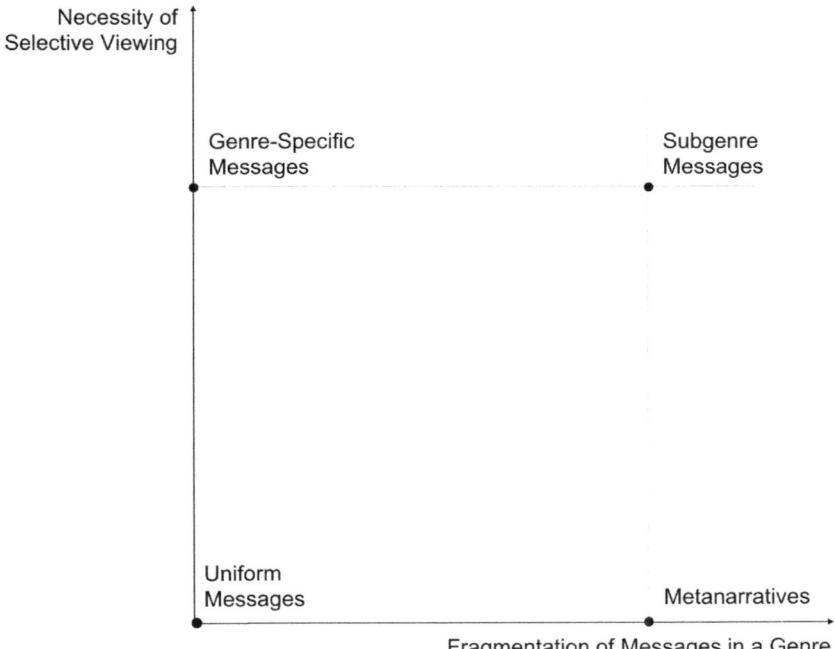

Figure 5.1 Dimensions of Cultivating Messages

Notably, genres are the element that shape Postulate 1, its Lemmas, and the two-dimensional space in Figure 5.1 further: It is about the fragmentation of messages *in a genre*, and the necessity of *genre-selective* viewing. Of course, one could shift the focus from within genres towards across genres as the concept of metanarratives assumes: Then the framework would be the fragmentation of messages across genres, and the necessity of selective viewing of specific messages across genres. However, this would not change the distance of the four concepts to one another: The level of fragmentation and the necessity of selective viewing would still be minimized for uniform messages; although genre-specific messages and metanarratives would switch places, they still remain inverse; and the concept of subgenre messages would still maximize the assumptions of message fragmentation and selective viewing. Thus, even though Postulate 1, Lemma 1 to 4, and the two-dimensional space as in Figure 5.1 rely on the framework of genres, their distance to one another remains true even if one were to apply a different framework.

Since genres constitute the framework, we also add a second Postulate that defines genres further: Advancing on the definitions by Altman (1984, 2000), Cobley (2001), and Mittell (2001), our second Postulate emphasizes the influence of perspectives on the definition of genres:

> **Postulate 2:** Genres reveal the negotiation of the relationship between a specific production system and a given audience, and are moderated by factors that differ with regard to the discipline.

To examine Postulate 2, it is necessary to look closely at genre conceptualizations by applying a linguistic, economic, sociological, or psychological filter through which the relationship between a production system and an audience can be viewed. Based on the deliberations in Section 3.2 the dominant factor which moderates the relationship between the production system and an audience is either history (linguistic perspective), financial forces (economic perspective), or individual knowledge structures and attitudes (psychological perspective). The reality observation level from the sociological perspective, on the other hand, clusters genres further into programs.

5.2 Summary and Research Question

As the previous Chapters have revealed, messages and genres are a central element to cultivation theory: The synthesis on defining genres, narratives, and messages from Chapter 3 enabled an evaluation of the precision for each of the message concepts in cultivation theory as presented in Chapter 4. Accordingly, the recapitulation of the theoretical concepts started with the original conceptualization of uniform messages, before moving on to genre-specific messages and metanarratives. In each of the Sections, the respective message construct and its set of propositions was explored by assessing the philosophical strand or super-theory that underlies them. Finally, a novel conceptualization was introduced, namely subgenre messages, that arises naturally from the implications of online television on viewing habits and message concepts such as the trend towards subgenres and microgenres in SVOD services. As outlined in Section 5.1, viewed from afar, the four message concepts differ in terms of their level of fragmentation of messages in a genre and their degree of necessity of genre-selective viewing. Given these differences, the four concepts moreover can be placed in a 2x2 space in which pairs of the concepts are inverted. The two-dimensional space that is defined by Postulate 1 and Lemmas 1 through 4 allows an estimation of how similar the concepts are to one another. The synthesis of message concepts and the original abstraction in form of the Postulate, the Lemmas and the two-dimensional space provide an answer to the question of the book in terms of defining the constructs and the set of propositions that compose media messages in cultivation theory. Hence, here we provided an answer to the call by Morgan and Shanahan (2010) who stated that it hitherto remained a black box how the alternative message concepts such as genre-specific messages and metanarratives are similar or different to the initial concept of uniform messages in cultivation theory. Moreover, we developed a novel concept that completes the set of cultivating messages that can be employed by scholars—either in theory or in research.

Here, we want to expand the call by Morgan and Shanahan (2010) and also ask further: After assessing how similar the message concepts are, how can we know that this impacts the research in cultivation? As outlined before, some scholars have pointed out that cultivation studies measured on the level of uniform message have returned weaker confirmation than studies conducted with genre-specific messages. For example, as early as 1981, Hawkins and Pingree showed that discarding the initial assumptions about uniform messages and instead applying program-specific messages strengthened rather than weakened the cultivation hypothesis. This could indicate that the analysis perspective of genre-specific messages was closer to the reality of viewers who watch television genre-specifically. But what kind of bias would appear if viewers were to choose their program actually by metanarratives yet scholars apply a genre-specific message approach? Or how would the cultivation results be affected if scholars investigate the total amount of television viewing but the viewers actually watch subgenre-specifically? Hence, the research question that guides the final part of the book is,

> **Research Question:** How does a bias between true and estimated message concepts affect the results from cultivation analysis?

With true and estimated message concepts, we refer to the occurrence of the four message concepts in the reality of the viewers and the ways that scholars investigate the cultivation effects through a certain message perspective. For example, proponents of the uniform message perspective assume that viewers watch television unselectively and are exposed to a unified stream of messages. Therefore, a uniform message approach is the accurate way to measure the effects of uniform messages in the viewers' reality. Proponents of the concept of genre-specific messages, however, challenge this view and assume that scholars apply a uniform message approach on data that is actually genre-specific. This is because proponents of genre-specific messages assume that viewers watch genres (and not just TV in general). Thus, they presume a bias between the true and applied message concepts. This bias may then explain why cultivation studies with genre-specific messages show a greater magnitude of effect than studies with uniform messages' perspective.

In order to investigate the Research Question, next we conduct a computational simulation that explores how the bias between true and estimated message concepts impacts the estimates of cultivation effects for heavy and light viewers. Hence, the simulation allows us to go from the verbal model that we defined through the Postulates and Lemmas above that explain the pattern of the four cultivating messages to a formal model that illustrates how the mechanisms work with much clearer precision. The simulation also tests the original concept of subgenre messages to reveal its mechanisms when scholars undertake the important efforts in implementing it in their future research.

Chapter Six Simulation of the Impact of Message Categorizations

Be as simple as you can be, as complicated as you need to be.
Smaldino, 2020, p. 213

6.1 Simulation Model

In the preceding Chapter, a verbal model of message conceptualizations was proposed that consists of the Postulate 1 and Lemma 1 through 4. This verbal model defines the parameters and model specifications for the simulation to investigate how a bias between true and estimated message concepts affects the results from cultivation analysis. Verbal models are a way to decompose a system by postulating its properties and the relationship between them (Smaldino, 2017, 2020). Verbal models are an ideal starting point to simplify complex processes in order to reveal their most central parts. However, "the danger with most verbal models is that there are many ways to specify the parts and relationships of a system that are consistent with such a model" (Smaldino, 2017, p. 315). Hence, the drawback of relying solely on verbal models is that they are oftentimes vague, or their interpretation can vary from scholar to scholar. As Smaldino (2017, p. 317) points out, "by being vague, verbal models simultaneously afford many interpretations from among which any reader can implicitly, perhaps even unconsciously, choose his or her favorite." Computational models such as simulations, on the other hand, enable scholars to model elements of their verbal model as computational objects with a *precise* array of properties that can be translated into numerical values (Smaldino, 2017, 2020).

How does simulation fit in with the general approaches of deduction and induction in science? With deduction, scholars derive theorems from assumptions, and with induction they search for according patterns in empirical data. Simulation, however, can be seen as an additional alternative approach. As Axelrod and Tesfatsion (2006) point out,

"Simulation, like deduction, starts with a set of explicit assumptions. But unlike deduction, simulation does not prove theorems with generality. Instead, simulation generates data suitable for analysis by induction. Nevertheless, unlike typical induction, the simulated data come from a rigorously specified set of assumptions regarding an actual or proposed system of interest rather than direct measurements of the real world. Consequently, simulation differs from standard deduction and induction in both its implementation and its goals. Simulation permits increased understanding of systems through controlled computational experiments."

— Axelrod and Tesfatsion (2006, p. 4)

Hence, simulation permits the rigorous testing of our research question, namely, how a bias between true and estimated message concepts affects the results from cultivation analysis, under the assumptions of the outlined Postulate 1 and its Lemmas, that would be too difficult in a traditional empirical makeup. Simulation is defined as "'running' the model forward through (simulated) time and watching what happens" (Gilbert & Troitzsch, 2005, p. 16). It is the aim of a simulation to create a model of the real world phenomenon (coined 'target') that the scholar has specified. The target is a dynamic entity since it reacts to environmental changes and changes over time. The model, which is represented here by the Postulate and Lemmas, is a dynamic specification of the target using logical or mathematical reasoning. Similar to empirical models, in simulations the scholar develops a model by abstracting from observations, collects data, and analyses it. However, in contrast to an empirical study, in a simulation the scholar creates artificial data by computing pseudo-random numbers by use of a computer program that runs the model and measures behavior. The simulated data is then analyzed to predict or explain the target. In some cases in which the scholar already possesses empirical data they can then compare the simulated with the collected data (Gilbert & Troitzsch, 2005). Since this is not the case here, we rather use the simulated data to investigate how a bias between true and estimated message concepts affects cultivation analysis results.

While simulation allows the rigorous testing of a research question, this approach also means that the scholar is using an idealized and simplified model that serves as a tool for a thought experiment and as an aid for reasoning (O'Connor, 2019; Smaldino, 2017). Hence, while the simulation permits us to study the processes for cultivating messages thoroughly, it may be that the results will not be replicable in reality. However, from this idealized case that builds on the two-dimensional space for cultivating messages, inferences can be drawn that explain why cultivation effects may differ. The simulation results will therefore focus on general, qualitative patterns in the data instead of reproducing exact measurements (Smaldino, 2020).

6.1.1 Data Generating Framework: True Message Concepts

The data generating framework (DGF) is the part of the simulation where we specify the true state of the (simulated) world, which includes how *viewers* behave (do they watch specifically; how much do they watch) as well as how *messages* are distributed. In a second step, we analyze each data set generated through the lens of one of the four message concepts by one of the four message concept approaches. For example, the data that was generated under the assumptions of uniform messages, is analyzed under the assumption of uniform messages, of genre-specific messages, of metanarratives, and of subgenre messages.

The first step in the simulation model is to generate data from pseudo-random numbers in R (v. 3.6.0; R Core Team, n.d.) in order to provide the values for the true message exposure (DGF). The model simulates a number of (v) viewers, N. Each iteration in the simulation involves several stages with both viewer-specific and content-specific parameters. During the stage with viewer-specific parameters, with some probability each viewer watches some amount of television (w_v), selects certain genres (g_v), and selects certain programs $(p_v^T$; these could be, for example, TV shows or movies) that contain a certain message (m). The overall viewing amount is sampled randomly from a probability distribution that is identical across all DGFs and DAFs (specified below). The viewing weight for every genre/program combination takes some value between $[0,1]$, depending on the DGF (see below), reflecting the proportion of time a particular viewer spends with each specific program in each genre. During the stage with content-specific parameters, each genre and program is attributed with a certain message (m_{gp}), in a way that again aligns with the DGF. In particular: For uniform messages, the m_{gp} matrix is 1; for genre-specific messages, the m_{gp} matrix is 1 for genre and message; for metanarratives, the m_{gp} matrix is 1 for message and program; and for subgenre messages, the m_{gp} matrix is 1 for genre and message but swaps one pair in n programs for a randomly sampled number without replacement. This means that for subgenre messages, we start with a genre-specific matrix of for example 5 genres with each 5 programs, each containing the same message. However, we replace 2 out of 5 messages by random numbers. This is done without replacement to ensure that each genre consists of a dominant subgenre message, but is fragmented as a single genre now contains between 1 to 3 subgenres. Put simply: For uniform messages, the messages are uniformly distributed across all genres and programs; for genre-specific messages the ith message only appears in i^{th} genre programs; for metanarratives, the ith message appears in i^{th} program across genres; and for subgenre messages, the ith message appears in more than half of the ith genre programs while less than half of ith message are associated with other i^{th} genre programs. Figure 6.1 illustrates an example of the m_{gp} matrix for uniform messages, genre-specific messages, metanarratives, and subgenre messages.

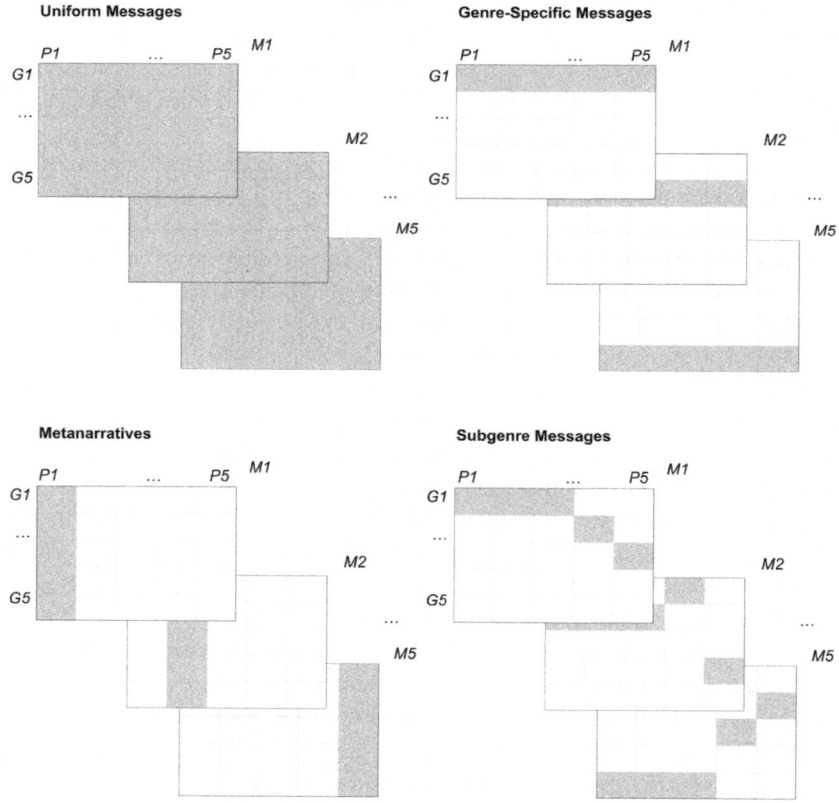

Figure 6.1 Graphical illustration for m_{gp} matrix for uniform messages, genre-specific messages, metanarratives, and subgenre messages

Simulations using these model parameters proceed as follows. First, N = 5 genres with N = 5 programs per genre and N = 5 messages (distributed as described above) is initialized. The viewing amount for N = 100 viewers (v) is sampled as a gamma distribution $\Gamma(k)$:

$$f(x; k, \theta) = \frac{x^{k-1}e^{-x \div \theta}}{\theta^{k}\Gamma(k)} \text{ for } x > 0 \text{ and } k, \theta > 0$$

To simulate viewing of messages a matrix (gp_v) is created by multiplying the viewer-specific vectors g_v and p_v^T. This multiplication produces a matrix that specifies, for each program in each genre, how likely the viewer is to view it given their selectivity of genres and programs in general. Finally, in order to compute how much time each viewer spent with each message, we take the element-wise product of each viewer's gp_v with the m_{gp} matrix, and sum across all genres and programs: $v_g \times g_{pm} \times v_p^T \times v_w$. In other words, the amount of time a given viewer is exposed to message i is simply a function of 1) in which genres and programs message i appears, and 2) with which genres and programs the viewer spends her time.

6.1.2 Data Analytical Framework: Estimated Message Concepts & Strength of Belief

The data analytical framework (DAF) represents the analysis that a scholar would run in order to distinguish heavy from light viewers, and to determine cultivation effects. Of course, from the data generation framework above we know the true values as they are defined by the parameters in the simulation; however, in a real-world empirical study these true values are unknown and it is the purpose of the data analytical framework to estimate them. Typically, cultivation scholars start by assessing the amount of viewing in accordance to their applied message concept, and then distinguish between heavy and light viewers in terms of some measure of message acceptance (e.g., as discussed earlier, a forced choice between two values relating to crime rates). Here, based on the parameters used for the (gamma-distributed) overall viewing time, four hours was applied across all DAFs as the cut-off point. Hence, a light viewer is a viewer who watches four or less hours of the sort of online television specified by the current DAF—for example, all television if the current DAF is uniform, or genre X if the current DAF is genre-specific. Meanwhile a heavy viewer is defined by watching more than four hours of a specific

155

subset of programs/ genres (potentially including all programs/ genres in the case of uniform messages). For example, message 1 could be that the world is a mean and dangerous place, message 2 is the assumption that love overcomes all difficulties, and so forth. For simplicity, and without loss of generality because the simulation is symmetric and balanced, we will focus our analyses on message 1; the results would be qualitatively identical with a focus on any of the other messages.

This general approach is further specified by the four message concepts: In the concept of uniform messages, the cut-off point for heavy and light viewer applies to all of television; for genre-specific messages, the cut-off point refers to watching genre 1 (which is presumed to contain message 1; for instance, given the mean-world message of message 1, this might be the genre 'horror'); for metanarratives, it refers to watching program 1 (which likewise is presumed to contain message 1 across genres); and for subgenre messages a heavy viewer watches more than four hours of sub-genre 1 (which again is presumed to contain message 1; for instance, the subgenre 'serial killer & slasher'). As described above, the actual amount of time each viewer was exposed to each message depends on their specific overall sampled viewing amount, their specific g_v and p_v^T vectors, and the m_{gp} matrix defined by the DGF.

After defining heavy and light viewers according to each message concept, the mean differences between the two viewer groups in accordance to the data generating and data analysis framework are computed. This means that each data set generated through the lens of one of the four message concepts each is analyzed by each of the four message concept approaches in turn. For example, the data that was generated under the assumptions of uniform messages, is analyzed under the assumption of uniform messages, of genre-specific messages, of metanarratives, and of subgenre messages; the raw difference in message-exposure hours between heavy and light viewers for each are recorded respectively in Table 6.2. Next, we compute the degree of cultivation effects. This is the degree to which heavy and light viewers incorporate the ith message into their conception of the world. For example, if a viewer is frequently exposed to message 1, which tells the viewer that the world is a mean and dangerous place, then how likely is it that their worldview mirrors this portrayal from television? To measure the strength of belief (s) in message 1, an exponential function of hours is computed with $\lambda = .2$ (nb, we provide the full equation for completeness; in this application, hours viewed must be ≥ 0):

$$F(x; \lambda) = \begin{cases} 1 - e^{-\lambda x} & x \geq 0, \\ 0 & x < 0 \end{cases}$$

The above function is deterministic, i.e., a particular number of hours will always translate to a particular strength of belief. In order to simulate noise in the data, the output of the above exponential functions, which is bounded on the range [0,1], is used as input to parameterize a beta probability distribution (with shape parameter set as $\alpha = 50 \times s$ and $\beta = 50 \times (1 - s)$):

$$f(x; \alpha, \beta) = constant \times x^{\alpha - 1} \left(1 - x\right)^{\beta - 1},$$

from which we draw a single sample. The drawn sample from distribution f serves as an alternative measure to indicate degree of belief. Noise can reflect any other third variables that lead to a greater degree of belief in message 1. For example, if message 1 were the mean world syndrome, then the according belief would be that the world is a mean and dangerous place which we expect to be greater in heavier than in light viewers. Noise could be the dangerous neighborhood that the viewer lives in and that contributes to the enhanced belief in either light or heavy viewers. We repeat the sampling of overall viewing, viewer-specific allocations to genres and programs, and calculations of total hours with message 1, belief, and noisy belief, separately for heavy and light viewers, for K = 1,000 iterations.

For the analysis of the results, mean differences, boxplots, and empirical density functions are computed. The analyses have been chosen as sufficient because "if you have been trained in the traditions of most of the behavioral and social sciences, you will likely be tempted to use inferential statistics such as regression. Although there are exceptions, this is almost never the right decision" (Smaldino, 2020, p. 214). The reason to avoid inferential statistics (such as regression) in simulation is that computing inferential statistics involves constructing a model of the data-generating process that comes with strong assumptions about the distributions of the parameter values, e.g., a Gaussian distribution (Smaldino, 2017). However, we already have a better model than this available to us, since the DGF *is* the actual model. Thus, there is no reason to model our model with a worse model (Smaldino, 2020). The R code for both the data generating framework and the data analytical framework can be found in Appendix C.

6.2 Results

The goal of the simulation study is to determine how the bias between true and estimated message concepts affects the results from heavy and light viewers in cultivation analysis. First, we present the results from the analysis for distinguishing heavy and light viewers with respect to DGF and DAF. Afterwards we present the results from the belief effects with and without noise.

6.2.1 Differences in Determining Heavy and Light Viewers

In general, cultivation scholars begin their analysis by dividing the viewers into viewing groups, e.g., heavy and light viewers, that (presumably) differ in their amount of exposure to the message 1 on online television. In order to determine the differences between heavy and light viewers for each message concept, four DGFs were computed which represent the true values for the respective four message concepts; the data from the four frameworks were then analyzed in accordance to each specific DAF, i.e., from the perspective of uniform messages, genre-specific messages, meta-narratives, or subgenre messages. This means that in a first step, according to each message concept the heavy and light viewers were determined by the cut-off point of four hours, e.g., a heavy viewer in uniform message has watched more than four hours of overall online television; a heavy viewer in genre-specific messages has watched more than four hours of a specific genre on online television; for metanarratives, a heavy viewer had exposure to more than four hours of a certain metanarrative; and for subgenre, the heavy viewer is determined by the exposure of more than four hours to a certain subgenre, respectively.

However, the two groups of heavy and light viewer from each message concept were then analyzed through a certain lens with regard to their actual exposure to message 1. This information is usually unavailable in an empirical setting, but accessible in the simulation. Table 6.1 then presents the mean differences between heavy and light viewers of exposure to message 1 in hours under the assumptions of each message concept with respect to DGF and DAF.

Table 6.1 Mean differences in hours of exposure to message 1 between heavy and light viewers with respect to DGF and DAF

		DAF			
		Uniform	Genre-Specific	Metanarratives	Subgenre
DGF	Uniform	10.30	15.26	15.24	26.23[*]
	Genre-Specific	2.06	4.36	3.06	6.61
	Metanarratives	2.06	3.10	4.36	5.45[**]
	Subgenre	2.07	3.18	1.94	4.44

Note. K = 1,000 simulations. Cases per cell > 996, except for [*]=720 and [**]=856. Loss is due to non-classifiable cases.

In the Table 6.1, the diagonal represents the mean difference between heavy and light viewers when the data is analyzed with the matching analytic framework: Accordingly, when DGF and DAF are matching then the mean difference between heavy and light viewers in terms of exposure to message 1 is 10.30 hours in the uniform framework, 4.36 hours in the genre-specific messages framework, 4.36 hours in the metanarratives framework, and 4.44 hours in the subgenre framework.

Next we walk through each DGF and the according results from the DAF analysis. In addition to Table 6.1 that conveyed the mean differences, Table 6.2 shows the means of exposure to the cultivating message (message 1) for an average heavy (hv) and light (lv) viewer with respect to each DGF and DAF; their differences result in Table 6.1.

Table 6.2 Means of exposure to message 1 for heavy and light viewers with respect to DGF and DAF

			DAF			
			Uniform	Genre-Specific	Metanarratives	Subgenre
	Uniform	hv	13.20	25.63	25.63	38.43
		lv	2.90	10.37	10.38	12.20
	Genre-Specific	hv	2.64	6.03	5.14	8.79
		lv	0.58	1.67	2.08	2.17
DGF	Metanarratives	hv	2.64	5.17	6.02	7.83
		lv	0.58	2.07	1.67	2.38
	Subgenre	hv	2.65	5.08	4.08	6.67
		lv	0.57	1.89	2.14	2.24

Note. Initial conditions according to Table 6.1. hv = heavy viewer; lv = light viewer.

6.2.1.1 DAF Results for Viewing Groups when Uniform Messages as DGF

The first row of Table 6.1 presents the mean differences between heavy and light viewers when message 1 is distributed uniformly across all genres and programs, and viewers allocate their time equally to all genres and programs. When the applied DAF is that of uniform messages, then the mean difference between heavy and light viewers in terms of hours spent with message 1 is 10.30 hours. Put simply: It is correctly assumed that viewers have watched unselectively and received message 1 in all genres and programs that they watched, therefore, the only variable that matters is the total amount of viewing in order to determine heavy and light viewers. The average light viewer in this case has watched 2.90 hours of message 1, while the average heavy viewer has watched 13.20 hours of that message. This is in line with the cut-off point of 4 hours to distinguish between heavy and light viewers.

However, when the uniformly distributed data is analyzed via the other (mismatching) analytical frameworks, the mean difference between heavy and light viewers increases: In both the analytical framework of genre-specific messages and metanarratives, the mean difference between heavy and light viewer in terms of exposure to message 1 is 15.3 hours; and in the subgenre messages framework, the difference between the two viewing groups is 26.23 hours. How do these greater mean differences between heavy and light viewers in all three alternative DAF occur? In all cases the initial cut-off point remains the same, e.g., in the analytical framework of genre-specific messages, a heavy viewer is a person who watches more than 4 hours of genre 1, whereas a light viewer is determined by watching 4 hours or less of genre 1. In the analytical framework of genre-specific messages, the underlying assumption is that only the specific genre 1 contains message 1, therefore, the classification of heavy and light viewer is based on the exposure to genre 1. However, the actual exposure to message 1 is higher in both viewer groups since the generated data is based on a uniform distribution of message 1 across all genres. This means that both heavy and light viewers of genre 1 are actually exposed to message 1 in all other genres as well. Given the initial conditions of the DGF of 5 genres, this means that the sampled viewing amount is divided by 5 in order to receive the viewing time for genre 1. This results in greater overall viewing amount: Although per definition of genre-specific messages, a light viewer has only been exposed to genre 1 for 4 hours or less, they have been exposed to message 1 for 10.37 hours on average; and the average heavy viewer has watched 25.63 hours of that message. The same process occurs in the DAF of metanarratives (light viewers: 10.38; heavy viewers: 25.63), with programs set to 5. In the analytical framework of subgenre messages, the viewing amount is divided by (genre n=5 ◇ program n=5 =) 25 over (subgenre n=) 3, which results in an average light viewer watching 12.20 hours of message 1, while the average heavy viewer has spent 38.43 hours with that message.

Thus, in all three data analytical frameworks that are a mismatch with regard to the uniformly distributed data, the mean differences between heavy and light viewers in their exposure to message 1 are increasing. However, this is due to a misrepresentation of heavy and light viewers: Light viewers, in particular, have been classified as such correctly by each DAF (e.g., watching four hours or less of a genre, a metanarrative, or a subgenre), but in terms of exposure to message 1 they have received more than 15 hours. Put simply: the light viewers from all three DAF are actually misclassified heavy viewers. Section 6.2.2 discusses the implication of this when measuring cultivation effects.

6.2.1.2 DAF Results for Viewing Groups when Genre-Specific Messages as DGF

In the case of genre-specific messages as DGF, the data is distributed as such that only genre 1 entails message 1 (and likewise for messages and genres 2–5). When the data is analyzed correctly with the according DAF of genre-specific messages, the mean difference between heavy and light viewers in terms of their exposure to message 1 is 4.35 hours. The average light viewer in this case has watched 1.67 hours of message 1, while the average heavy viewer has watched 6.03 hours of that message.

When the genre-specific distributed data is analyzed via the (mismatching) analytical framework of uniform messages, the mean difference between heavy and light viewers in terms of exposure to message 1 is 2.06 hours. An average light viewer in that DAF watches 0.58 hours of message 1, whereas an average heavy viewer receives 2.64 hours of the respective message. Hence, although the heavy viewers watch more than 4 hours of online television, they actually receive less of message 1 than is expected from them (2.64 hours instead of > 4 hours).

When the data is analyzed through the lens of metanarratives, the mean difference between heavy and light viewers in terms of exposure to message 1 is 3.06 hours; an average light viewer watches 2.08 hours of message 1, whereas an average heavy viewer watches 5.14 hours of message 1. Analyzing the data through the DAF of subgenre messages, the mean difference between heavy and light viewers in terms of exposure to message 1 is 6.61 hours; an average light viewer watches 2.17 hours of message 1, whereas an average heavy viewer watches 8.79 hours of message 1. Hence, in both DAF of metanarratives and subgenre messages, the mean difference varies in comparison to the correct DAF results from genre-specific messages. Yet, the cut-off point for heavy and light viewers set in each DAF matches the reception in hours of message 1 for both groups. For example, in the DAF of subgenre messages, a heavy viewer is a person who watches more than 4 hours of a specific subgenre, and the results reveal that this person also is exposed to more than 4 hours of message 1; meanwhile a light viewer watches 4 hours or less of the specific subgenre, and the results show that they also receive less than 4 hours of message 1. In other words, the degree of misclassification of heavy and light viewers when the data derives from genre-specific (or metanarrative; see below) DGFs and is analyzed by any framework other than uniform or genre-specific (respectively, metanarrative) is less than in the case of uniform DGF.

6.2.1.3 DAF Results for Viewing Groups when Metanarratives as DGF

In the case of metanarratives as DGF, the data is distributed as such that across all genres a certain program X entails message 1. When the data is analyzed correctly with the according DAF of metanarratives, the mean difference between heavy and light viewers in terms of their exposure to message 1 is 4.35 hours. The average light viewer in this case has watched 1.67 hours of message 1, while the average heavy viewer has watched 6.03 hours of that message. Analyzing the data through the DAF lens of uniform messages, the mean difference between heavy and light viewers in terms of exposure to message 1 is 2.06 hours. An average light viewer in that DAF watches 0.58 hours of message 1, whereas an average heavy viewer receives 2.64 hours of the respective message. For the DAF of genre-specific messages, the mean difference between heavy and light viewers in terms of exposure to message 1 is 3.10 hours; an average light viewer watches 2.07 hours of message 1, whereas an average heavy viewer watches 5.17 hours of message 1. Analyzing the data through the DAF of subgenre messages, the mean difference between heavy and light viewers in terms of exposure to message 1 is 5.45 hours; an average light viewer watches 2.38 hours of message 1, whereas an average heavy viewer watches 7.83 hours of message 1. Thus, the DAF results for heavy and light viewers with metanarratives as DGF are similar to the results with genre-specific messages set as DGF. The same implications that were drawn in Section 6.2.1.2 also apply here.

6.2.1.4 DAF Results for Viewing Groups when Subgenre Messages as DGF

When the DGF is subgenre messages, the message 1 is only present in a specific subgenre which in the analysis was defined as consisting of 3 out of 5 programs within genre 1, while the other two programs then represent separate subgenres. The mean difference between heavy and light viewers in terms of their exposure to message 1 is 4.44 hours, when the data is analyzed correctly with the according DAF of subgenre messages. The average light viewer in this case has watched 2.24 hours of message 1, while the average heavy viewer has watched 6.69 hours of that message.

Meanwhile, when the data is analyzed in the data analytical framework of uniform messages, the mean difference between heavy and light viewers of message 1 decreases to 2.07 hours. An average light viewer in that DAF watches 0.57 hours of message 1, whereas an average heavy viewer receives

2.65 hours of the respective message. Hence, although a heavy viewer is defined as watching more than 4 hours of online television, they actually receive less of message 1 than is expected from them (2.65 hours instead of > 4 hours).

Although the mean difference between heavy and light viewer of message 1 is also decreasing when the DAF of genre-specific messages ($mean_{dif}$ = 3.18 hours) and metanarratives ($mean_{dif}$ = 1.94 hours) is applied, the distribution of people in heavy and light viewers matches the average exposure to message 1. In the case of analyzing the data in the framework of genre-specific messages, an average light viewer receives 1.89 hours of message 1, whereas an average heavy viewer watches 5.08 hours of the respective message. And when analyzing the data in the framework of metanarratives, an average light viewer watches 2.14 hours of message 1, whereas an average heavy viewer watches 4.08 hours of the respective message. The greater similarity between the results of the DAF of genre-specific messages and subgenre messages (in comparison to metanarratives) is due to the distribution of subgenre messages within genres.

6.2.2 Differences in Belief Effects between Heavy and Light Viewers

In general, the next step in a typical cultivation analysis (i.e., after defining heavy/light viewers as described above) consists of analyzing the degree of belief in the message from online television in the real world, with the hypothesis that for heavy viewers the conception of the world mirrors more closely the message that is distributed on online television. For example, it is investigated whether heavy viewers of the mean world syndrome are also more likely to believe that the real world is a mean and dangerous place. Here, we present the results of the degree of belief in message 1, which is the cultivating message, for heavy and light viewers with respect to each DGF and DAF. Given the information about the exposure to message 1 for heavy and light viewers from the previous Section, the underlying question is: How are differential means of the exposure to message 1 and the degree of belief in message 1 informative variables of one another? Put simply: Does a heavy viewer as defined in each message concept reveal a stronger cultivation effect than a light viewer regardless of the way they receive the message in reality? Or does the cultivation effect differ with regard to the congruence between the data analytical framework and the data generating framework?

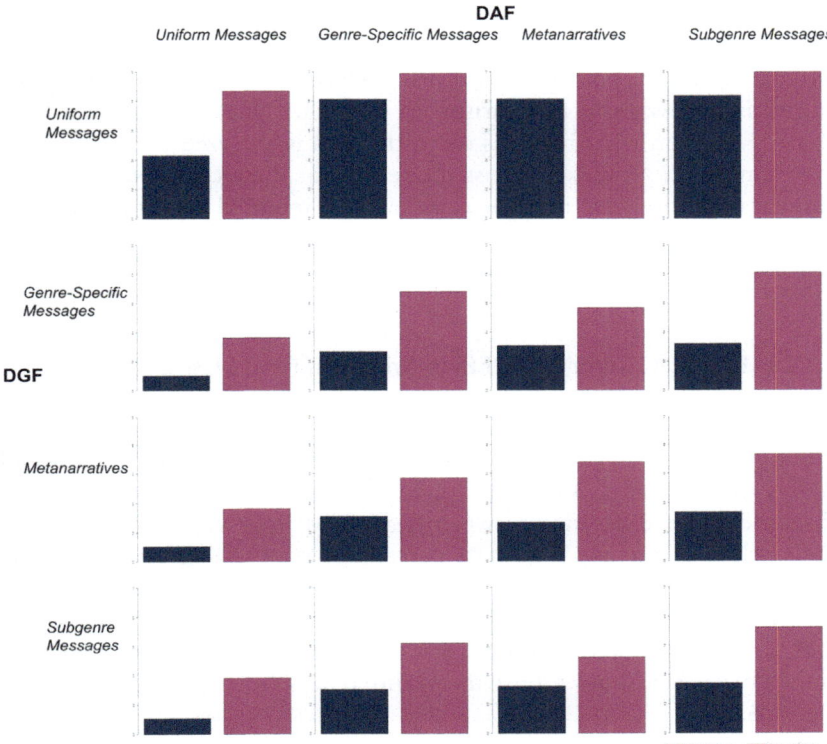

Figure 6.2 Degree of belief in cultivating message for heavy and light viewers
with respect to DGF and DAF

Accordingly, Figure 6.2 shows the degree of belief in message 1 for both viewer groups with respect to DGF and DAF. In other words, the degree of belief in message 1 was generated for heavy and light viewers from each DGF and then analyzed through the perspective of uniform messages, genre-specific messages, metanarratives, or subgenre messages. In Figure 6.2, the diagonal shows the degree of belief for both heavy and light viewers when the data is analyzed with the matching analytic framework: Accordingly, when DGF and DAF are matching then the mean difference between heavy and light viewers in terms of their degree of belief in message 1 is 44.02 percentage points in the uniform framework, 41.22 percentage points in the genre-specific messages framework, 41.01 percentage points in the metanarratives framework, and 38.59 percentage points in the subgenre framework. Thus, when message 1 is present in all genres and

165

programs in online television, and when the viewer watches unselectively, heavy and light viewers show the greatest difference in their cultivation effects. Moreover, both groups reveal a stronger degree of belief in the cultivating message in comparison to the other three frameworks from above. However, what happens when the data is analyzed by a mismatching framework? Next, we discuss the results for these cases. Note that the empirical density functions for each case are reported in Figure A.5; the mean differences in the degree of belief in the cultivating message between heavy and light viewers are reported in Table A.4.

6.2.2.1 DAF Results for Belief Effects when Uniform Messages as DGF

The first row of Figure 6.2 presents the degree of belief in message 1 for heavy and light viewers when message 1 is distributed uniformly across all genres and programs. When the applied DAF is that of uniform messages, then the mean difference between heavy and light viewers in terms of their belief in message 1 is 44.02 percentage points. Thus, it is correctly assumed that viewers have watched unselectively and received message 1 in all genres and programs that they watched, and the amount of message 1 that they received predicts the magnitude of their cultivation effect. Heavy and light viewer show robust mean differences (see also the boxplot in Figure 6.3).

However, when the uniform data is analyzed via the other (mismatching) analytical frameworks, the mean difference of the cultivation effect between heavy and light viewers decreases: In the analytical framework of genre-specific messages, the heavy and light viewers differ by 17.61 percentage points in their cultivation effects; in the framework of metanarratives, they differ by 17.51 percentage points; and in the framework of subgenre messages, they differ by 16.08 percentage points. How does this decreasing trend in cultivation effects across these three alternative DAF occur, when the difference between heavy and light viewer has been increasing instead (see Table 6.1)? As revealed in the former Section, the mean differences of exposure to message 1 between heavy and light viewers are the greatest when the uniform data is analyzed through the lens of genre-specific messages, metanarratives, and subgenres. While the mean difference through the proper lens of uniform messages was 10 hours, for the alternative (mismatching) analytical frameworks the difference between heavy and light viewers has been ranging from 15 to 26 hours. However, the mean values for the viewer groups were disproportionately high in these three frameworks as well: For example, in the DAF of genre-specific messages as well as in metanarratives, a light viewer was exposed to message 1 for 10 hours, a heavy viewer for 26 hours; and in subgenre messages, a light viewer was someone who has spent 12 hours with message 1, and a heavy viewer watched 38 hours of message 1. Given that the function we used to derive a strength of belief from hours is asymptotic, these great differences between heavy and light viewers then exhibit a lower cultivation effect than the lower values for heavy and light viewers from uniform messages. Hence, the analytical framework of uniform messages shows the greatest mean differences in the degree of belief in cultivating message for heavy and light viewers; this robust mean difference diminishes when the uniform data is analyzed through the other concepts of genre-specific messages, metanarratives, and subgenre messages.

6.2.2.2 DAF Results for Belief Effects when Genre-Specific Messages as DGF

When the DGF is genre-specific messages, message 1 is only distributed in the specific genre 1. When the applied analytical framework is that of the corresponding genre-specific messages, then the degree of belief in message 1 differs by 41.22 percentage points between heavy and light viewers. Moreover, as Figure 6.3 reveals the two viewer groups are distinct. However, when the genre-specific distributed data is analyzed via the other (mismatching) analytical frameworks, the mean difference of the cultivation effect between heavy and light viewers is decreasing for uniform messages and metanarratives, but increasing for subgenre messages. More precisely, in the analytical framework of uniform messages, the heavy and light viewers differ by 26.03 percentage points in their cultivation effects; in the framework of metanarratives, they differ by 26.01 percentage points; yet in the framework of subgenre messages, they differ by 49.19 percentage points. With regard to the DAF of uniform messages, as Table 6.1 has revealed, the heavy viewers from that analytical framework are actually light viewers since they are only watching 2.64 hours of the cultivating message. Thus, the mean difference between heavy and light viewers with regard to the degree of belief in message 1 decreases since both groups are light viewers. This trend is also visible in the corresponding boxplot in Figure 6.3.

With regard to the DAF of metanarratives, the former analysis revealed that an average heavy viewer received 5.14 hours of message 1, while a light viewer watched 2.08 hours of message 1. This is similar to the results from the DAF from genre-specific messages (heavy viewers: 6.03 hours; light viewers: 1.66 hours). While the median for both DAF is almost identical as well, for the DAF of metanarratives, however, the data for heavy viewers is more disperse than for light viewers (see corresponding boxplot; Figure 6.3). This is due to the assumption of metanarratives that message 1 appears across all genres, while it is actually genre-specific.

Taking subgenre messages as DAF, however, the magnitude of the cultivation effect even increases for heavy viewers, as well as the mean difference between heavy and light viewers. However, as the density function in Figure A.5 shows is there a great skewness in the data and the number of cases on which the analysis is based has decreased by nearly 95 percent. Moreover, as the cases classified as light viewers has increased, the degree of cultivation effects has become more disperse as well. Put simply: There are only few cases in which a person is classified as a heavy viewer of subgenre 1 when the data is distributed genre-specifically, while the number of cases in the light viewer group increases; the great mean for the degree of belief in cultivating message for heavy viewers may be the result from an overly homogeneous group, whereas the relatively low degree of cultivation effects for the group of light viewers may be a result from the greater variance within the group.

6.2.2.3 DAF Results for Belief Effects when Metanarratives as DGF

When the DGF is metanarratives, message 1 is distributed in specific programs across genres. When the applied analytical framework is that of the corresponding metanarratives, then the magnitude of cultivation effect differs by 41.06 percentage points between heavy and light viewers. Moreover, as the corresponding boxplot in Figure 6.3 reveals, the two viewer groups are distinct.

Yet, when the data is analyzed via the other (mismatching) analytical frameworks, the mean difference of the cultivation effect between heavy and light viewers is decreasing. In the analytical framework of uniform messages, the heavy and light viewers differ by 25.84 percentage points in their cultivation effects; in the framework of genre-specific messages, they differ by 26.05 percentage points; and in the framework of subgenre messages, they differ by 39.58 percentage points. Given that genre-specific messages and metanarratives are inverted concepts, the DAF results from uniform messages and genre-specific messages for the degree of belief in message 1 for heavy and light viewers with metanarratives as DGF are similar to the results with genre-specific messages set as DGF. Thus, the same implications that were drawn in section 6.2.2.2 also apply here.

However, when the data is analyzed through the lens of subgenre messages, the magnitude of cultivation effect is closer again to the reported effect from metanarratives as DAF, since they differ by 1.48 percentage points. Moreover, the heavy viewers of subgenre messages reveal a stronger degree of belief in message 1 than the heavy viewers of metanarratives, even though in reality message 1 was appearing in programs across genres (instead of appearing in a particular subgenre) and the viewers had a preference for these. As the boxplot (see Figure 6.3) and density function (see Figure A.5) suggest, the median for heavy viewers is greater in the DAF of subgenre messages compared to the DAF of metanarratives. Notwithstanding the magnitude of the cultivation effect for the DAF of subgenre messages is smaller because the group of heavy viewers exhibits a more disperse structure and a larger number of outliers. In summary, given the case that the data is distributed in terms of metanarratives, then through the lens of uniform messages, the assigned heavy viewers are actually light viewers which is also expressed in their low degree of belief in the cultivating message. When the scholars analyze the data as genre-specific, then the cultivation effect also decreases because the data for heavy viewers is more disperse than for light viewers. And in the (mismatching) DAF of subgenre messages the mean difference of cultivation effect between heavy and light viewer is similar to the (accurate) DAF of metanarratives, however, the data is more disperse and shows a great number of outliers.

6.2.2.4 DAF Results for Belief Effects when Subgenre Messages as DGF

When the data is distributed as in the concept of subgenre messages, message 1 appears in a certain subgenre. Applying the corresponding analytical framework, i.e., of subgenre messages, then the degree of belief in message 1 differs by 38.58 percentage points between heavy and light viewers. Moreover, as the boxplot in Figure 6.3 reveals, the two viewer groups are distinct.

However, the mean difference of the cultivation effect between heavy and light viewers is decreasing, when the data is analyzed via the other (mismatching) analytical frameworks: In the analytical framework of uniform messages, the heavy and light viewers differ by 27.39 percentage points in their cultivation effects; in the framework of genre-specific messages, they differ by 31.52 percentage points; and in the framework of metanarratives, they differ by 19.81 percentage points.

More precisely, when the data distributed according to the framework of subgenre messages is analyzed via the analytical framework of uniform messages, again a person has been assigned a heavy viewer even though they only watched on average 2.65 hours of the cultivating message. This leads to a greater overlap in the cultivation effects between heavy and light viewers, and the relatively low mean differences between the two groups (see the empirical density function in Figure A.5).

With regard to the DAF of genre-specific messages, the mean differences for the degree of belief in message 1 between heavy and light viewers are relatively similar to the (accurate) DAF of subgenre messages, as they differ by 7.06 percentage points. Moreover, the density function reveals a similar structure compared to the one from subgenre messages. However, both groups of heavy and light viewers in the DAF of genre-specific messages are more disperse (see boxplot; Figure 6.3). This is because the cultivating message only appears in a certain subgenre of genre-specific messages, i.e., while the DAF of genre-specific messages assumes that message 1 can be found in all 5 programs, in the DAF of subgenre messages only 3 out of the 5 programs (which are clustered as single subgenre) entail the cultivating message. Put simply: In the DAF of genre-specific messages, a heavy viewer can be a heavy viewer of the subgenre with the message 1; however, a heavy viewer can also be a viewer who has watched all subgenres in the according genre, except for the subgenre of interest that entails message 1. Therefore, the group of heavy viewers has a greater variance which results in a lower cultivation effect.

With regard to the DAF of metanarratives, the former analysis revealed that the exposure to message 1 only differs by 1.94 hours between heavy and light viewers (in comparison to 4.44 hours in the DAF of subgenre message). This relatively small mean difference is also mirrored in the small mean difference of cultivation effects between heavy and light viewers. As the empirical density function reveals, both viewer groups overlap in their strength of belief in message 1, which is due to the dispersion in the group of heavy and light viewers, with a great number of outliers for the light viewers. This is because light viewers have been more exposed to message 1 than expected since in the DAF of metanarratives any program is taken into account that could entail message 1, while in the subgenre messages framework only a certain genre (i.e., the subgenre) is analyzed.

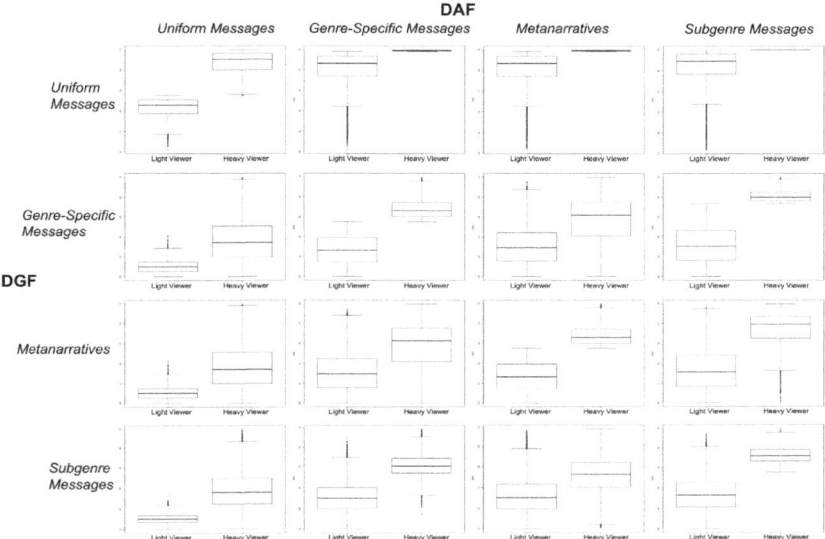

Figure 6.3 Degree of belief in cultivating message for heavy and light viewers with respect to DGF and DAF without noise

6.2.3 Impact of Third Factors on Differences between Heavy and Light Viewers & Belief Effects

Next, we present the results when noise is added to the model. Noise can be any third factors that impact the degree of belief in the cultivating message, for example, a dangerous neighborhood or the experience of being robbed can impact the perception of the world as a mean and dangerous place in both heavy and light viewers. To this end, noise was added to the belief definition function. The results of the mean differences of the degree of belief in message 1 between heavy and light viewers remains the same as reported above (see Figure 6.2 and Table A.4 accordingly), therefore they will not be reported again. However, the formerly reported empirical density function (see Figure A.5) and the boxplots (see Figure 6.3) differ since the skewness and dispersion shift with the additional noise. The shifts are recorded in Figure A.6 and Figure 6.4, accordingly, and compared visually.

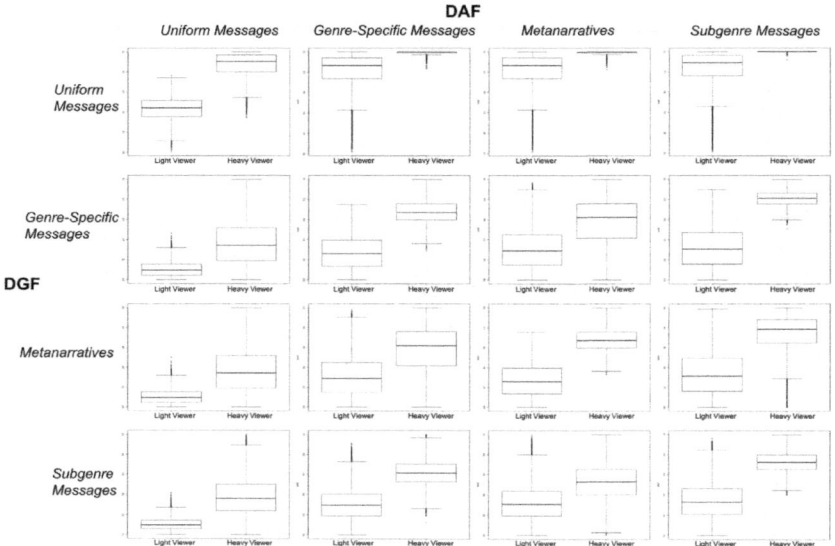

Figure 6.4 Degree of belief in cultivating message for heavy and light viewers with respect to DGF and DAF with noise

First, in terms of skewness, the empirical density functions with and without noise are compared. Notably, noise flattens the distributions of the probability and the strength of belief for heavy and light viewers across all DGF and DAF. Moreover, all distributions of the DGF with uniform messages (i.e., first row of Figure 6.4) exhibit a trend towards right-skewness for the groups of light viewers. With regard to the other three DGF—namely genre-specific messages, metanarratives, and subgenre messages—all distributions show a trend towards right-skewness for light viewers, and left-skewness for heavy viewers. This trend is especially visible in the cases when DGF and DAF are corresponding, i.e., in the diagonal of Figure 6.4. Thus, the additional noise leads to a greater overlap between heavy and light viewers in terms of their strength of belief in the cultivating message.

Second, for dispersion the boxplots with and without noise are compared. The greatest changes in the interquartile range are notably in the diagonal, i.e., in the cases when DGF and DAF are corresponding. The maximum for the light viewers is raised, while the minimum for the heavy viewers is lowered. In addition, across all DGF and DAF, the noise added more outliers for both light and heavy viewers. Particularly noteworthy is the increased dispersion for the DGF of genre-specific messages and DAF of subgenre messages, and vice versa. Given that subgenre messages are related to genres, the dependency leads to a greater increase of dispersion in these cases. In the case of DGF of uniform messages, the dispersion increases mainly for the cases of heavy viewers across all DAF, given the increase of outliers. Thus, the additional noise added more dispersion to the data and blurred the belief effect for heavy and light viewers further.

Chapter Seven Implications & Discussion

Models necessarily simplify [...] but this is a feature rather than a bug
Smaldino, 2020, p. 207

7.1 Implications of the Simulation Results for Assessing the Impact of Message Concepts

The simulation was carried out to investigate how a bias between true and estimated message concepts affects the putative cultivation effect. The parameters and model specifications stem from Chapter 5 in which a Postulate and a number of Lemmas define in a two-dimensional space how the four message concepts relate to one another. Taken together, the simulation has provided converging evidence for three main aspects, each of which is discussed in further detail below: (1) the 'winner' if the analysis matches the reality; (2) the 'winner' if the analysis differs from the reality; and (3) the robustness of the patterns for (1) and (2).

First, although the simulation is a highly simplified model of reality and comes with certain limitations that we discuss in Section 7.2, there is converging evidence that one concept of cultivating messages is superior to the other concepts if the analysis that the scholar performs matches the reality: uniform messages. When DGF and DAF are a match, then the concept of uniform messages outperforms the other three concepts both in terms of finding great viewing differences between heavy and light viewers, and in the magnitude of the cultivation effect. More precisely, the mean difference between heavy and light viewers was twice the number of hours than for the other three message concepts. While the differences in terms of the cultivation effect are not as substantial, they are still higher by 3 to 6 percentage points in comparison to the other concepts. Hence, in a reality in which messages are uniformly distributed across online television and the viewers watch everything unselectively, and the scholar chooses the number of hours spent with overall television as the decisive variable, then the results show the greatest differences. However, the simulation does not tell the modeler how likely it is that our reality is shaped by the concept of uniform messages. Indeed, in an era of online television that among other factors contributes to a greater fragmentation of the production, distribution, and selection of content, the assumption of uniform messages seems in question. Thus, the more pressing result from this simulation may be which message concept outperforms the alternatives when the analysis does not match the reality.

Second, from the simulation there is also converging evidence for a 'winner' when the analysis run by the scholar does not match the reality: subgenre messages. In 66 percent of all cases, subgenre messages seems to be the go-to analysis if scholars apply a mismatching analysis to the data (which by simple probability measure is more likely than the case of a match). More precisely, in both the DGF of genre-specific messages and metanarratives, subgenre messages revealed the greatest mean differences between heavy and light viewers in terms of exposure to the cultivating message in comparison to the other mismatching analytical frames in each DGF. Moreover, the actual average viewing hours of the cultivating messages for the heavy and light viewer groups were within the cut-off of four hours. Hence, a defined heavy viewer by the analysis was also an actual heavy viewer by the actual distribution of viewing time in the simulated reality, and vice versa with regard to light viewers. In addition, subgenre messages also showed the greatest differences in the magnitude of cultivation effect between heavy and light viewers when compared to other mismatching DAF. The only exception to this pattern is the case of uniformly distributed messages: While uniform messages was the 'winner' when the analysis matches the reality, applying other analysis to this data results in the least favorable outcome: In all alternative analysis, light viewers are actually misidentified heavy viewers which results in biased results in terms of distinguishing heavy from light viewers and cultivation effects, respectively. This seems at first counter-intuitive since the alternative analysis on uniformly distributed data produced greater differences between heavy and light viewers. However, this difference is rapidly diminishing in the cultivation effect since it is based on a bias. Thus, greater differences between heavy and light viewers do not necessarily predict a stronger magnitude in cultivation effects, especially if the analysis performed is not congruent with reality. While the analytical framework of subgenre messages is the winner in all other mismatching scenarios, of course, the question occurs which alternative analysis is preferred if subgenre messages is the framework in reality. Given the interdependency between subgenres and genres, the preferred (mismatching) analysis in a reality shaped by subgenre messages is the analytical framework of genre-specific messages. In comparison to the other two alternatives, the results from the analytical framework of genre-specific messages reveal the greatest similarity to the results subgenre messages both in terms of differences in viewing hours of the cultivating messages as well as the putative cultivation effect.

Third, the simulation provides converging evidence for the robustness of the patterns of (1) the 'winner' if the analysis matches the reality, and for (2) the 'winner' if the analysis differs from the reality. The first indicator for the robustness of the results is that, unsurprisingly, the best analytical framework is the one that matches the reality. The second indicator for the robustness of the results stems from the additional analysis with noise that was performed: Noise added variance and skewness to each case, but overall, the patterns remain.

In summary, the simulation suggests that the analysis in the form of uniform messages is only convincing if in reality the messages are uniformly distributed and the viewing behavior is unselective. In all other cases, the analytical framework of uniform messages was outperformed by the alternatives and produced biased results especially with regard to distinguishing heavy and light viewers and their true exposure to the cultivating message. Moreover, the simulation provides converging evidence that analyzing heavy and light viewers and their cultivation effects through the lens of subgenre messages, offers robust results even in cases when the data is actually distributed as in the framework of genre-specific messages or metanarratives. However, the drawback of this analytical framework was an increased variance within groups and skewness. Thus, to ensure the exact cut-off point for heavy and light viewers, it is suggested to include a receiver operating characteristic curve which allows an estimation how dependent the results are on the choice of the cut-off. This aspect is discussed further below as an implication for the limitations.

7.2 Limitations of Simulation Choices

7.2.1 Common Limitations of Simulation

The goal of this simulation was to serve as a proof of concept to demonstrate the impact of the message concepts in reality (DGF) and as an analytical framework (DAF), as well as the impact of a mismatch between these two in some sort-of toy model of the real world. There are some common limitations of simulations that also apply to some degree here: the objection that simulations are unrealistic, and the objection that simulations rely on choices made by the modeler.

First, a common objection is that simulations are unrealistic. This is correct, since simulations imply a simplification of the real world that ignores large parts of reality such as details of human behavior or complexity of system. However, this is done to ensure that the models are "tractable, [and] easy to understand, and to get a clear picture of the causal processes occurring in the simulations" (O'Connor, 2019, p. 28). Thus, simulations enable scholars to precisely note what their most central parameters and specifications of their theories are because they simplify. As Smaldino (2017) explains,

> "However, the stupidity of a model is often its strength. By focusing on some key aspects of a real-world system (i.e., those aspects instantiated in the model), we can investigate how such a system would work if, in principle, we really *could* ignore everything we are ignoring. This only sounds absurd until one recognizes that, in our theorizing about the nature of reality—both as scientists and as quotidian humans hopelessly entangled in myriad webs of connection and conflict—*we ignore things all the time.*"
> — Smaldino (2017, p. 317)

Simulation is not data driven, meaning that it is not trying to fit the data, but rather to find out how systems behave in a simplified way. Hence, the goal cannot be to produce precise estimates that apply one-to-one to the real world. For the simulation here this means that instead of capturing the absolute estimates in the cells in our DGF x DAF matrix, the simulation rather captured patterns in relative terms across the cells in our matrix. As Weisberg (2012) points out, no model can capture every desideratum a scholar might have, i.e., one cannot expect a model to be maximally simple while being maximally realistic. Thus, the aim was not to try to build a truly realistic model but to capture certain aspects of reality and idealize them to make them tractable in the model. Therefore, we expect that none of the estimations from the DGF are correct in their absolute terms, but we expect that each DGF computed is closer to the corresponding conceptualization of reality than the others. Hence, the process of simplification in simulations "is a feature rather than a bug" (Smaldino, 2020, p. 207).

The second general limitation of simulations that also applies here is that the parameters and model specifications are choices made by the modeler. Hence, if the scholar were to make a change in any of the simulation parameters and model specifications, then the results would change. However, the goal is to make reasonable and logical choices in such a way that a moderate change of the parameters and model specifications would not change the *pattern* of the results. Of course, if one were to change the Postulate and Lemmas that underlie the simulation model then the results could fundamentally change—but this also involves the introduction of new Postulates and Lemmas that require logical reasoning. Thus, the aim here was to specify a model and choose parameters that fit the Postulate and Lemmas from Chapter 5, while both being as realistic as possible and making the results as robust as possible against modest changes. For example, given our parameters and model specifications a change of the cut-off point for distinguishing heavy and light viewers from 4 hours to 6 hours is not expected to change much of the reported pattern. There is also converging evidence for the robustness of our results given that the addition of noise to our model did not change the patterns much.

Nonetheless, there are two parameters that need to be discussed in more detail: The choices for modeling viewing choice behavior, and the distinction between heavy and light viewers.

7.2.2 Modelling Viewing Choice Behavior

The simulation modeled viewing choice behavior in such a way that heavy viewers definitionally have a high preference for one certain genre, program, or subgenre, but that all other types are equally preferred, on average. This means that in the DGF of genre-specific messages, heavy viewers preferred the genre 1, but their preferences for genres 2 through 5 were equal; for metanarratives, the viewers had a preference for program 1, but the preference values for the other programs were the same; and for subgenres, they preferred subgenre 1, but had no preference of subgenre 2 over 3 or vice versa. Of course, this does not apply to the DGF of uniform messages in which the viewers did not have any preferences at all since they are supposed to watch unselectively. However, in the DGF of genre-specific messages, metanarratives, and subgenre messages the chances for the alternatives to be watched were equally distributed. Presumably, this hardly matches reality, in which a viewer with a strong preference for, for example, the genre 'horror' likely also prefers TV shows and movies from the genre 'action' rather than from 'romance.' Statistically, this is represented in a covariance matrix in which all covariances are equal except for the diagonal that repeats a different value. This is consistent with the classic repeated measures design in which each realization would be white noise with the mean of the white noise varying from realization to realization. Note that in the case of uniform messages, we produced a degenerate process since the elements of the covariance matrix are identical including the diagonal.

While this model of viewing choice behavior marks a certain departure from reality, the choice to model viewing choice behavior this way was made on the assumption that this matches the cleanest statement of the Postulates and Lemmas from Chapter 5. It goes beyond the scope of this book to empirically test how a change of these parameters would impact the results of the simulation as this requires novel theorizing. For example, future research could begin to theorize how the genre-selection covariance matrix shifts if the viewing behavior is modeled more realistically. Nonetheless, intuition suggests that changing this parameter would impact variance rather than means—with the result that the pattern of the simulation results holds up.

7.2.3 Distinction between Heavy and Light Viewers

Another choice in the parameters and model specifications of the simulation that was made by the modeler, which we now discuss critically, is the demarcation between heavy and light viewers. As a brief reminder: The cut-off point for heavy and light viewer in any DGF was set to 4 hours. For example, in the DGF of uniform messages, a heavy viewer was defined by watching more than four hours of online television in general (e.g., per week); while in the DGF of genre-specific messages, a heavy viewer was a person who watched more than four hours of genre 1 per week. Several questions can be raised: First, how would the results change if the cut-off point were to be raised or lowered? Second, how would a median split, rather than a fixed cut-off, affect the results? And third, how would the creation of more than two groups impact the results? Next, we walk through all three questions.

First, is the scenario that the cut-off point is raised or lowered, e.g., instead of 4 hours, it is raised to 30 hours, or lowered to 2 minutes. In this scenario, the means for heavy and light viewers are expected to change, however, the pattern of the results are unlikely to be impacted. The reason lies in the parameters for viewing amount and message reception amount in the simulation that are defined in an order-preserving function: Given that the simulation satisfies the monotonicity of the order-preserving function, a change only impacts the absolute values but not the pattern. However, this argument is only valid if the changes to the cut-off points apply to all DGF and DAF. A change to this assumption, however, would imply a change to the Postulate and Lemmas since these assumed translational invariance, i.e., not the exact position in the two-dimensional space is important but the distance between the concepts. This stresses the importance for scholars to choose cut-off points in a principled way, because a non-monotonic change naturally impacts the results. For example, in order to break monotonicity, a scholar would have to assert that exposure to a message resulted in lower rates of belief—which in general seems farfetched given the assumptions of cultivation theory.

Second, is the scenario that a median split is employed which dichotomizes heavy and light viewers by taking the median of amount of viewing. This means that for example in the DGF of uniform messages, the median for the total amount of viewing determines which viewers are sorted in the group of heavy or light viewers; meanwhile in the DGF case of genre-specific messages, the median for the viewing amount of genre 1 sorts the viewers into the respective groups. There is a certain appeal for a median split since it ensures that the groups consist of an equal number of cases. However, the drawback is that a median split does not hold constant the values but the operation. This implies that each case in the DGF and DAF would then be based on different principles. For example, let's assume that in reality the messages are uniformly distributed and the viewers are unselective in their viewing behavior (DGF: uniform messages); the scholar, however, assumes that viewers watch genre-specifically and that each genre consists of a unique message (DAF: genre-specific messages). If the scholar then were to apply a median split by creating two groups based on the amount of watching genre 1, while in reality the cultivating message is distributed across all genres, then the light viewers actually would have received a greater amount of the cultivating message than is expected from them. Vice versa applies, if the DGF is the case of genre-specific messages while the DAF is set to uniform messages. Thus, in the case of a median split the scholar ends up with fewer true light viewers. Moreover, in our simulation each case in the DGF and DAF would then be based on different principles, i.e., in some cases a heavy viewer is defined by watching 4 hours, while in another case the distinction may be drawn at 10 hours, while in another case it is 30 hours. Given that the values are not held constant anymore, a median split, hence, would represent a violation of each case in the DGF and DAF, and is therefore not a technique that can be considered.

Third, is the scenario to create more than two groups, either by adding more categories of viewers (e.g., heavy, medium, and light viewer), or by employing a linear function (e.g., the more a person watches online television, the more they are cultivated). For the former, more categories of viewers are likely to result in more noise in the simulation. However, there is converging evidence that the patterns that the simulation computed are robust to noise given the results from additional third variables. With regard to the latter, it can be assumed that a non-linearity will exert a bigger effect in this non-group scenario with n groups given that the relationship between belief and viewing was modeled as non-linear. Nonetheless, given the aforementioned monotonicity, it is expected the same overall patterns would hold.

In summary, the absolute cut-off points are expected to impact the means of each group, however, they are less likely to affect the variance which is mainly important. Moreover, a misspecification of the cut-off points by the scholar is more likely to result in Type 2 errors rather than Type 1 errors. For example, a median split is more likely to result in smaller mean differences in the cultivation effect between the groups rather than to overestimate the effect. However, in order to avoid misspecifications, here we suggest that cultivation scholars begin to employ the receiver operating characteristic (ROC) curve.

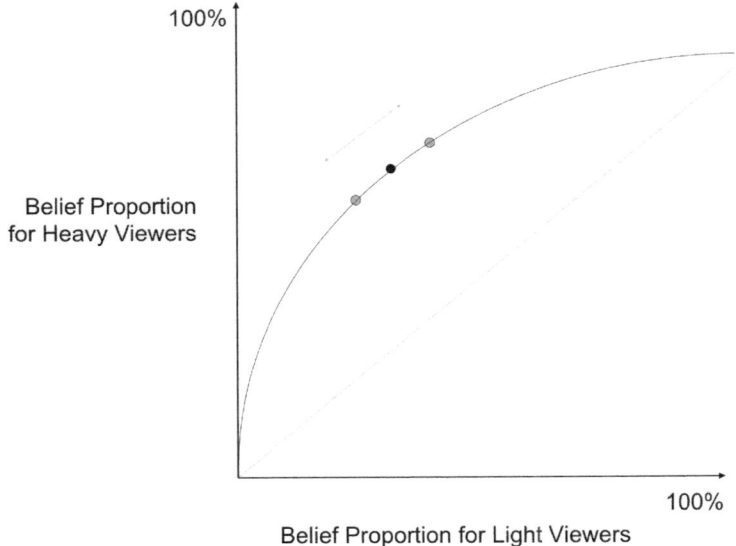

Figure 7.1 Example of ROC curve to estimate the dependency of cultivation effects on cut-off point choices; each point would derive from a single choice of cut-off

Initially, ROC curves were invented to study discriminator systems for the detection of radio signals in the presence of noise in the 1940s. They are a graphical way to reveal the trade-off between sensitivity and specificity for every possible cut-off for a (or a combination of) test. More precisely, the ROC curve is used to plot the true positives against the false positives at various threshold settings. This results in an estimation of how dependent the results are on the choice of the cut-off. For example, a cultivation scholar could set cut-offs in deciles (i.e., light/heavy cut-off at the 10*th*, 20*th*, etc. percentiles) to calculate the ROC curve and plotting the belief proportion of heavy viewers against the belief proportion of light viewers. Figure 7.1 shows an example how the various cut-off points are set to estimate how the results for heavy and light viewers change based on the cut-off chosen.

7.3 General Implications for the Future of Cultivation Theory

The Postulates and Lemmas and their visualization in the two-dimensional space have proven to be powerful in guiding the simulation to assess how a bias between true and estimated message concepts affects the results from cultivation analysis. While they do not reveal whether each message concept in fact deserves to be labeled as 'cultivation,' the proposed framework explains how similar or different the alternative message concepts are from the original concept of uniform messages. This answers the call from Morgan and Shanahan (2010) for a clear rationale to relate the concepts on an abstract level. Thus, future cultivation scholars may refer to this framework when they begin to assess what message concept may underlie their theoretical model. The second step then would be to refer to the tenets and level of precision for each concept as we outlined before, and to determine whether the underlying super-theory and philosophical strand aligns with their approach as well. It seems indispensable for future cultivation scholars to be aware of the implications of the tenets and presuppositions that come with each concept. Moreover, as the simulation has demonstrated, the degree of congruence between real and estimated message concepts is responsible for whether there is a small or large bias in the measurement of cultivation effects. The concept of subgenre messages has surprisingly emerged as the winner to reduce the bias in the results when there is a mismatch between reality and measurement. This is surprising insofar as the novel concept arrives with the strongest implications on the degree of fragmentation of messages within a genre and on the level of genre-selective viewing behavior. However, this result from the simulation may be another argument for why the consideration of subgenre messages is a fruitful path for future cultivation scholars. Especially given the changes in the media landscape since the introduction of cultivation theory, subgenre messages may mirror more closely than the alternative concepts the institutional forces towards online television and the selective behavior of viewers.

The next steps to develop the concept of subgenre messages further, therefore, involve the methodology as well as induction. To measure the cultivation effect from subgenre messages, a sufficient content analysis is required that measures the dominant messages in each subgenre. Here, Gerbner's idea of assessing the existence, importance, sentiment, and relationship of the research object (Gerbner, 1969a) appears as a way to facilitate the subgenre message system analysis. Afterwards the novel concept can be tested in reality. Since the difference between heavy and light viewers is also central to all message concepts to measure the putative cultivation effect, we further propose that scholars begin to use the ROC curve. While in the past, scholars suggested a greater number of viewer groups or a continuous variable to indicate the amount of exposure to the cultivating messages, the ROC curve actually enables the cultivation scholar to estimate how the cultivation effects vary when the cut-off points for distinguishing the groups are changed. Thus, this approach allows greater transparency why scholars chose a certain cut-off point over another, and avoids the drawbacks that comes with other techniques such as a median split.

At this point, we hasten to point out that cultivation scholars, of course, are encouraged to continue to use the alternative concepts of genre-specific messages and metanarratives as these concepts showed reasonable results in the simulation as well. However, from the previous notions, scholars have to be aware that metanarratives as they are considered in cultivation theory are neither narratives nor are they related to postmodernism or narrativity. Here, we proposed two elements of metanarratives in cultivation theory, namely nested structure and multi-generic status, that serve as a stepping stone for future scholars to continue their research on metanarratives but with greater precision. Genre-specific messages can also emerge as a powerful concept if they are anchored to a specific field such as economy, semiotics, or psychology. When future cultivation scholars begin to define which perspective shapes their definition of genre, not only do they increase the precision of the concept but allow other scholars to assess whether the study can be compared to their own. This is especially relevant for meta-analyses which currently distinguish between different topics of the studies but do not take into consideration that these studies may actually differ in the way that they assign genre labels to movies and TV shows. The four perspectives on genres as synthesized here may serve as a starting point to distinguish between the various ways to define genres and assign them to TV shows and movies in future research.

Finally, both future cultivation theory and research is encouraged to once more consider Gerbner's initial idea of a tripartite concept of cultivation theory: The three prongs of media institutions, media messages, and cultivating effect are highly entangled, thus, a change in one of the prongs may cause a shift in the others. Here we argued that the change towards online television on an institutional level may have caused changes with regard to the media messages—such as subgenre messages—and the cultivating effect. When cultivation scholars begin to consider all three prongs together and determine if, and which, shifts have occurred in comparison to previous cultivation studies, then they can make common progress and ensure that cultivation remains a theory that is of relevance for contemporary communication sciences.

Chapter Eight Conclusion

Cultivation theory has emerged as one of the most widely known theories in communication and has led to over 650 studies ever since its introduction to the field five decades ago (Morgan et al., 2015). The theory assumes that the exposure to messages on television affects people's conception of social reality. Initially, it was assumed that these cultivating messages are uniformly distributed and that the viewers are unselective in their viewing habits. Over the last five decades, a large volume of empirical studies has investigated this cultivation effect further and produced significant development and refinement of the theoretical premises. One of the most substantial developments is the introduction of genre-specific messages and metanarratives as alternative concepts of how the messages are conveyed on television and how the viewer receives them. Genre-specific messages assumes that viewers have preferences for certain genres and that each genre consists of a unique message; metanarratives, on the other hand, assumes that there are messages that are conveyed across different genres which are sought out actively by the viewers. Much of the criticism around these alternative concepts of cultivating messages centers around the question of how these concepts differ from the original concept of uniform messages. Moreover, some critiques doubt that there is a need for alternative concepts despite the changes in the media landscape towards online television. In addition, some scholars have begun to question the relevance of cultivation theory for the field altogether given its focus on television (e.g., Singer, 2018). This book addressed all three concerns: We elaborated how cultivation theory continues its journey in the era of online television and how the use and development of alternative concepts of cultivating messages are increasingly important for this continuation. Guided by the overarching question of which constructs and set of propositions compose media messages in cultivation theory, we started by comparing the tenets on television of the Cultural Indicators Project to contemporary conceptualizations of television by institutional scholars. While proponents of the original cultivation theory argue that it is merely the number of screens that has multiplied since the broadcast era, this is only one aspect among many that has changed for television scholars. Accordingly, scholars such as Johnson (2019) and Lotz (2017a, 2017b) argue that today's era of online television marks a departure from former television eras in terms of its technological, cultural, industrial, organisational and experiential components. For example, broadcast television and online television are not only distinct with regard to the sheer number of screens on which viewers can watch TV shows and movies, but also with regard to implications on mobility, availability, content fragmentation, individuality, engagement levels, and algorithmic recommendation systems.

And with SVOD services such as Netflix, Hulu, Amazon Video, or Disney+ on the rise, there is also a greater pull in online television towards fragmentation and selectivity: Subgenres and microgenres are a symptom of this trend. The emergence of subgenres and microgenres reveals a greater segmentation of content on the production side and preferences for certain genres' topics on the audience side. Given that SVOD services operate with algorithmically derived recommendations, it may even be that viewers who perceive themselves as unselective are actually selective due to the algorithm.

Our argument was that these changes in the media landscape naturally call for a reconsideration of the current message conceptualizations in cultivation theory. This argument is based on Gerbner's notion that cultivation is not a cause-and-effect theory but consists of three interrelated prongs, namely media institutions, media messages, and the cultivating effect. Although the book mainly focused on the second, that is media messages, we were later only able to advance the understanding of media messages by taking current developments in the media landscape into account, such as online television and the emergence of subgenres. These notions then allowed us to disentangle the constructs and set of propositions that compose the concept of uniform messages, genre-specific messages, and metanarratives. For all three existing concepts, an underlying super-theory was asserted which then allowed an evaluation of the degree of precision of each respective concept.

More precisely, it was found that Gerbner's original concept of uniform messages is related to Herbert Schiller, who in turn was inspired by Critical Theorists from the Frankfurt School such as Theodor Adorno and Max Horkheimer. It was found that Gerbner's assumptions about a uniform stream of messages on television and the unselective viewing behavior of the audience were similar to the assumptions of the Critical Theorists, which implies a high degree of precision. Furthermore, uncovering an underlying super-theory of the concept of uniform messages also revealed why proponents of this original idea seem to be rather immune to the objections by other scholars: The critiques about the uniformity of messages and the unselective viewing behavior are made from perspectives *other* than Critical Theory. Thus, while critiques reiterate their calls for revision of the underlying propositions of uniform messages, their arguments are actually based on different premises such as economy or psychology, and therefore unheard by the Cultural Indicators Project team that does not see the applicability given their roots in Critical Theory. Thus, to foster the dialogue it is recommended that critiques re-shift their focus in their objections by arguing against the backdrop of Critical Theory—and vice versa that proponents of the original idea of cultivating messages question whether their perspective of Critical Theory still applies to the contemporary production and distribution of media messages.

Similarly, it was found for the concept of genre-specific messages that the critiques are based on different perspectives. For example, the concern that there is a dissonance between viewers and scholars with regard to their definition of genres, hews closely to the psychological perspective; the criticism that studying genre-specific messages may be tautological refers to the linguistic perspective; and the argument that genres are not distinct because messages cut across genres alludes to the economic perspective. However, our argument was not that one of these perspectives is superior to the others in terms of addressing the critiques but rather that scholars should increase their awareness regarding what perspective they are applying when they work with or criticise the concept of genre-specific messages. As we outlined in Chapter 3, there are several ways to refine the definition of a genre. A genre is a corpus, category or class that reveals the relationship between a production system and a given audience. As we argued, this relationship is further shaped by different factors associated with each perspective: According to the linguistic perspective, history shapes the relationship between the production system and the audience; from an economic perspective, it is the financial forces; and from a psychological perspective, the relationship is shaped by the viewer's knowledge structures. System theory offers a framework to cluster genres further into programs such as news and entertainment, or respectively sub-programs such as fictional entertainment or reality TV, each with reference to the level of reality observation. Thus, the precision of the concept of genre-specific messages is increased when a particular perspective is applied—especially since each perspective has its own merits and drawbacks. We encourage future scholars, and cultivation scholars in particular, to clearly articulate what perspective they are applying to their definition of genres. This call for the importance of genre distinction has also been identified in the past by scholars from other areas than cultivation, for example Steininger and Woelke (2008) argued that the "effective enforcement of the separation principle [of TV ads from TV program ...] also depends on consistent definitions of forms and genres to serve as a basis for the interpretation of such rules" (p. 460). Hence, our notion that the definition of genres (and the decision which TV show and movie is associated with a certain genre label) varies according to the applied perspective, may be of relevance for scholars outside of cultivation theory as well.

In the same way, our notion on narratives provides a gateway to understand narratives as a fragmented concept that is shaped distinctly by each strand of classical and post-classical narratology. The recent works by post-classical narratologists appear to be highly promising for communication scholars who focus on narratives in their study. Moreover, from the notions of narratives it was found that the concept of metanarratives in cultivation neither is associated to narratives nor to metanarratives in the perspective by narratologists or postmodern thinkers. This is an important and surprising result of the synthesis since this implies that there is currently no super-theory or grand perspective supporting cultivation scholars' idea of metanarratives. By referring to linguistics, we therefore proposed two presuppositions for the concept of metanarratives to increase its level of precision in cultivation: The assumption that several metanarratives coexist in one object (multi-generic status), and that these metanarratives are (cross-) nested. However, these presuppositions serve as a starting point and require more work from future cultivation scholars especially in terms of practicality, i.e., how can these two presuppositions be measured in a content analysis.

After considering the constructs and set of propositions that underlie the concepts of uniform messages, genre-specific messages, and metanarratives, we then took into consideration the relevance of online television for cultivating messages. We argued that the change in the media landscape towards a greater fragmentation of genres towards subgenres and the greater selectivity by viewers (either by choice or by algorithmic recommendation) calls for an additional alternative concept, which we coined subgenre messages. This original concept implies that viewers do not simply select movies and TV shows from a specific genre, but rather from specific subgenres with a specific focus. Each subgenre then entails a certain cultivating message, for example the subgenre 'zombie' may cultivate the message that one needs to set aside differences to fight a common enemy; whereas, the subgenre 'slashers & serial killers' may convey the message that one should be suspicious about one's surroundings. To show how the novel concept fits in with the original concept of cultivating messages and its established alternatives, we then synthesized the key components in order to assess how similar or different they are to one another. As a result, we found that the underlying Postulate of cultivating messages formalizes the relationship between the degree of fragmentation of messages and the level of necessity of selective viewing, both with respect to genre boundaries (Postulate 1). In the concept of uniform messages, both the degree of message fragmentation in a genre and necessity level of genre-selective viewing are minimized (Lemma 1). In comparison, the concepts of genre-specific messages and metanarratives entail stronger assumptions: Genre-specific messages require a higher level of genre-selective viewing while there is no fragmentation of messages in a genre (Lemma 2); on the other hand, metanarratives assume a greater degree of fragmentation in genres but do not require viewers to watch specific genres, i.e., allow a low level of genre-selective viewing (Lemma 3). As a consequence, these alternative concepts are inverse. The concept of subgenre messages then derives as a hybridization of genre-specific messages and metanarratives: Both the degree of fragmentation of messages in a genre as well as the necessity to watch selectively are maximized (Lemma 4). Thus, the concept of subgenre messages filled the last quadrant when we visualized Postulate 1 and its Lemmas topologically. An additional Postulate 2 completed this set by emphasizing the importance of perspective-taking when defining a genre. The Postulates, Lemmas and their visualization as a two-dimensional space answer the call and guiding question for this book, namely, to clearly outline the constructs and set of propositions that compose media messages in cultivation theory.

The validity and implications of the Postulates, Lemmas, and two-dimensional space were then tested in a simulation model that we developed. The simulation investigated how a bias between true and estimated message concepts affects the results from cultivation analysis. With true and estimated message concepts, we referred to the occurrence of the four message concepts in the reality of the viewers and the ways that scholars investigate the cultivation effects through a certain message perspective. The simulation consisted of a data generating framework in which the true state of the simulated world was defined, such as the way viewers behave and how messages are distributed. The four generated frameworks, each guided by an according message concept, were then analyzed in a second step by a data analyzing framework. This ensured that data from each message concept was analyzed through the lens of each message concept. The results showed that the cultivation effects differ substantially, though to varying degrees, depending on the message concept that is applied. Generally speaking, the concept of uniform messages was only convincing when the analysis matched the reality. In the cases when there was mismatch between reality and analytical framework, however, the concept of subgenre messages emerged as the winner. Hence, the simulation provides converging evidence that subgenre messages derives as a powerful new concept to measure cultivation effects. Moreover, subgenre messages mirrors more closely the changes in the media landscape towards online television and the selective viewing behavior of the audience. That being said, more work is necessary to validate the concept in the real world.

Over the last five decades, cultivation theory has been established as one of the core theories in the field of communication. With the era of online television, it is at a crossroads. Scholars can continue to employ the original concept of uniform messages, or they can adjust to the new set of propositions that come with the new era of online television and begin to use subgenre messages in cultivation. As cultivation scholars, our goal is not to study enculturation in a vacuum, but to assess the impact of real messages in a real environment on real viewers. And if the reality of the environment and of the viewers changes, we should seek to adjust our idea of cultivating messages as well. The framework here permits us to determine how we model the reality of the media institutions and of the audience—and to decide which path of the crossroad we are going to take in the future.

REFERENCES

Abbott, H. P. (2008). *The Cambridge introduction to narrative*. Cambridge: Cambridge University Press. doi:10.1017/CBO9780511816932

Adorno, T. W. (1991[1972—1981]). *The culture industry: Selected essays on mass culture*. London: Routledge.

Alber, J. (n.d.). Unnatural narrative. In P. Hühn & et al. (Eds.), *The living handbook of narratology*. Retrieved from http://www.lhn.uni-hamburg.de/article /unnatural – narrative

Alber, J. & Fludernik, M. (Eds.). (2010). *Postclassical narratology. Approaches and analyses*. Columbus, OH: The Ohio State University Press.

Altman, R. (1984). A semantic/syntactic approach to film genre. *Cinema Journal, 23* (3), 6–18. doi:10.2307/1225093

Altman, R. (2000). *Film/genre*. Bloomington: Indiana University Press.

Andrews, M. (2004). Counter-narratives and the power to oppose. In M. Bamberg & M. Andrews (Eds.), *Considering counter-narratives: Narrating, resisting, making sense* (pp. 1–6). Amsterdam: John Benjamins.

Axelrod, R. & Tesfatsion, L. (2006). A guide for newcomers to agent-based modeling in the social sciences. In L. Tesfatsion & K. Judd (Eds.), *Handbook of computational economics* (pp. 1647–1659). Amsterdam: Elsevier.

Bakhtin, M. (1981). *The dialogical imagination*. Austin: University of Texas.

Bakhtin, M. & Medvedev, P. (1985). *The formal method of literary scholarship*. Cambridge, MA: Harvard University Press.

Bamberg, M. (2004). Considering counter narratives. In M. Bamberg & M. Andrews (Eds.), *Considering counter-narratives: narrating, resisting, making sense* (pp. 351–371). Amsterdam: John Benjamins Publishing Company.

Bandura, A. (1965). Influence of models' reinforcement contingencies on acquisition of imitative responses. *Journal of Personality and Social Psychology, 1* (6), 589–595. doi:10. 1037/h0022070

Bartlett, F. C. (1932). *Remembering: A study in experimental and social psychology*. Cambridge: Cambridge University Press.

Bezdek, M. A. & Gerrig, R. J. (2017). When narrative transportation narrows attention: Changes in attentional focus during suspenseful film viewing. *Media Psychology, 20* (1), 60–89. doi:10.1080/15213269.2015.1121830

Bilandzic, H. & Busselle, R. W. (2008). Transportation and transportability in the cultivation of genre-consistent attitudes and estimates. *Journal of Communication, 58* (3), 508- 529. doi:10.1111/j.1460 – 2466.2008.00397.x

Bilandzic, H. & Busselle, R. W. (2012a). A narrative perspective on genre-specific cultivation. In M. Morgan, J. Shanahan, & N. Signorielli (Eds.), *Living with television now: Advances in cultivation theory and research* (pp. 261–285). New York: Peter Lang.

Bilandzic, H. & Busselle, R. W. (2012b). Narrative persuasion. In J. P. Dillard & L. Shen (Eds.), *The Sage handbook of persuasion. Developments in theory and practice* (pp. 200-219). Los Angeles, CA: Sage.

Bilandzic, H. & Busselle, R. W. (2017). Beyond metaphors and traditions: Exploring the boundaries of narrative engagement. In F. Hakemulder, M. M. Kuijpers, E. S. Tan, K. Bálint, & M. Diocaru (Eds.), *Handbook of narrative absorption* (pp. 11–28). Amsterdam: John Benjamins Publishing Company.

Bilandzic, H. & Rössler, P. (2004). Life according to television. Implications of genre-specific cultivation effects: The Gratification/Cultivation model. *Communications, 29*, 295-326. doi:10.1515/comm.2004.020

Bodenhausen, G. V., Macrae, C. N., & Hugenberg, K. (2003). Social cognition. In I. B. Weiner, T. Millon, & M. J. Lerner (Eds.), *Handbook of psychology: Personality and social psychology* (Vol. 5, pp. 257–282). Hoboken, NJ: Wiley.

Bordwell, D. (1989). A case for cognitivism. *Iris, 5* (2), 11–40.

Braddock, K. & Dillard, J. P. (2016). Meta-analytic evidence for the persuasive effect of narratives on beliefs, attitudes, intentions, and behaviors. *Communication Monographs, 83* (4), 446–467. doi:10.1080/03637751.2015.1128555

Brown, C. & Augusta-Scott, T. (2006). *Narrative therapy: Making meaning, making lives.* Thousand Oaks, CA: Sage.

Bryant, J. & Miron, D. (2004). Theory and research in mass communication. *Journal of Communication, 54* (4), 662–704. doi:10.1111/j.1460 – 2466.2004.tb02650.x

Bunia, R. (2010). Diegesis and representation: Beyond the fictional world, on the margins of story and narrative. *Poetics Today, 31* (4), 679–720. doi:10.1215/03335372–2010–010

Busselle, R. W. (2003). Television exposure, parents' precautionary warnings, and young adults' perceptions of crime. *Communication Research, 30* (5), 530–556. doi:10.1177/ 0093650203256360

Busselle, R. W. & Bilandzic, H. (2008). Fictionality and perceived realism in experiencing stories: A model of narrative comprehension and engagement. *Communication Theory, 18* (2), 255–280. doi:10.1111/j.1468 – 2885.2008.00322.x

Busselle, R. W. & Bilandzic, H. (2009). Measuring narrative engagement. *Media Psychology, 12*, 321–347. doi:10.1080/15213260903287259

Busselle, R. W., Ryabovolova, A., & Wilson, B. (2004). Ruining a good story: Cultivation, perceived realism and narrative. *Communications, 29* (3), 365–378. doi:10.1515/comm. 2004.023

Castro, D. & Cascajosa, C. (2020). From Netflix to Movistar+: How subscription video-on- demand services have transformed Spanish TV production. *JCMS: Journal of Cinema and Media Studies, 59* (3), 154–160. doi:10.1353/cj.2020.0019

Chapman, O. (2008). Narratives in mathematics teacher education. In D. Tirosh & T. Wood (Eds.), *Tools and Processes in Mathematics Teacher Education* (pp. 15–38). Rotterdam: Sense Publishers.

Chong, Y. M. G., Teng, K. Z. S., Siew, S. C. A., & Skoric, M. M. (2012). Cultivation effects of video games: A longer-term experimental test of first- and second-order effects. *Journal of Social and Clinical Psychology, 31* (9), 952–971. doi:10.1521/jscp.2012.31.9.952

Cobley, P. (2001). Analysing narrative genres. *Sign system studies, 29* (2), 479–502.

Cohen, B. C. (1963). *The press and foreign policy*. Princeton, NJ: Princeton University Press.

Cohen, J. & Weimann, G. (2000). Cultivation revisited: Some genres have some effects on some viewers. *Communication Reports, 13* (2), 99–114. doi:10.1080/08934210009367728

Connelly, F. & Clandinin, D. (1990). Stories of experience and narrative enquiry. *Educational Researcher, 19* (5), 2–14. doi:10.3102/0013189X019005002

Craig, R. (1999). Communication theory as a field. *Communication Theory, 9* (2), 119–161. doi:10.1111/j.1468 – 2885.1999.tb00355.x

Cumberbatch, G., Jones, I., & Lee, M. (1988). Measuring violence on television. *Current Psychology: Research & Reviews, 7* (1), 10–25. doi:10.1007/BF02686661

Danesi, M. (2004). *Messages, signs, and meanings: A basic textbook in semiotics and communication theory*. Toronto: Canadian Scholars' Press Inc.

Davis, N. (2012). Rethinking Narrativity: A Return to Aristotle and Some Consequences. *Storyworlds: A Journal of Narrative Studies, 4*, 1–24. doi:10.5250/storyworlds.4.2012. 0001

Diefenbach, D. L. & West, M. D. (2012). Cultivation and the third-person effect. In M. Morgan, J. Shanahan, & N. Signorielli (Eds.), *Living with television now: Advances in cultivation theory and research* (pp. 329–346). New York: Peter Lang.

Dogra, S. (2017). The thirty-one functions in Vladimir Propp's morphology of the folktale: An outline and recent trends in the applicability of the Proppian taxonomic model. *Rupkatha Journal on Interdisciplinary Studies in Humanities, 9* (2), 410–419. doi:10. 21659/rupkatha.v9n2.41

Doob, A. & Macdonald, G. (1979). Television viewing and fear of victimization: Is the relationship causal? *Journal of Personality and Social Psychology, 37* (2), 170–179. doi:10.1037/0022–3514.37.2.170

Duchan, J. F., Bruder, G. A., & Hewitt, L. E. (1995). *Deixis in narrative: a cognitive science perspective*. Hillsdale, NJ: Lawrence Erlbaum.

Eden, A., Tamborini, R., Grizzard, M., Lewis, R., Weber, R., & Prabhu, S. (2014). Repeated exposure to narrative entertainment and the salience of moral intuitions. *Journal of Communication, 64* (3), 501–520. doi:10.1111/jcom.12098

Eleey, M. F., Gerbner, G., & Tedesco, N. (1972). Apples, oranges, and the kitchen sink: An analysis and guide to the comparison of violence ratings. *Journal of Broadcasting, 17* (1), 21–31.

Endrass, B., Klimmt, C., Mehlmann, G., Andre, E., & Roth, C. (2014). Designing user- character dialog in interactive narratives: An exploratory experiment. *IEEE Transactions on Computational Intelligence and AI in Games, 6* (2), 166–173. doi:10.1109 / tciaig.2013.2290509

Eschholz, S., Chiricos, T., & Gertz, M. (2003). Television and fear of crime: Program types, audience traits, and the mediating effect of perceived neighborhood racial composition. *Social Problems, 50* (3), 395–415. doi:10.1525/ sp.2003.50.3.395

Fuchs, C. (2014). *Digital labour and Karl Marx.* New York: Routledge.

Galbraith, M. (1995). Deictic shift theory and the poetics of involvement in narrative. In J. F. Duchan, G. A. Bruder, & L. E. Hewitt (Eds.), *Deixis in narrative: A cognitive science perspective* (pp. 19–60). Hillsdale, NJ: Lawrence Erlbaum.

Gehrau, V. (2003). (Film-) Genres und die Reduktion von Unsicherheit [(Movie) genres and the decrease in uncertainty]. *Medien & Kommunikationswissenschaft, 51* (2), 213–231.

Gerbner, G. (1956). Toward a general model of communication. *Audio Visual Communication Review, 4* (3), 171–199.

Gerbner, G. (1958). On content analysis and critical research in mass communication. *Audio Visual Communication Review, 6* (2), 85–108.

Gerbner, G. (1964). Ideological perspectives and political tendencies in news reporting. *Journalism Quarterly, 41,* 495–509.

Gerbner, G. (1966). Images across cultures: Teachers in mass media fiction and drama. *The School Review, 74* (2), 212–230.

Gerbner, G. (1969a). Toward 'cultural indicators': The analysis of mass mediated public message systems. *AV Communication Review, 17* (2), 137–148.

Gerbner, G. (1969b). Toward 'cultural indicators': The analysis of mass mediated public message systems. In G. Gerbner, O. Holsti, K. Krippendorff, W. J. Paisley, & P. J. Stone (Eds.), *The analysis of communication content: developments in scientific theories and computer techniques* (pp. 123–132). New York: John Wiley & Sons.

Gerbner, G. (1970). Cultural indicators: The case of violence in television drama. *The ANNALS of the American Academy of Political and Social Science, 388* (1), 69–81. doi:10.1177/000271627038800108

Gerbner, G. (1972a). Communication and social environment. *Scientific American, 227* (3), 153–160.

Gerbner, G. (1972b). Teacher image and the hidden curriculum. *The American Scholar, 42* (1), 66–92.

Gerbner, G. (1973). Cultural indicators: The third voice. In G. Gerbner, L. P. Gross, & W. H. Melody (Eds.), *Communication technology and social policy* (pp. 555–573). New York: John Wiley & Sons.

Gerbner, G. (1977). Television: The new state religion? *Et Cetera: A Review of General Semantics, 34* (2), 145–150.

Gerbner, G. (1980a). Death in prime time: Notes on the symbolic functions of dying in the mass media. *The ANNALS of the American Academy of Political and Social Science, 447* (1), 64–70. doi:10.1177/000271628044700109

Gerbner, G. (1980b). Trial by television: Are we at the point of no return. *Judicature*, *63* (9), 416–426.

Gerbner, G. (1983). The importance of being critical—in one's own fashion. *Journal of Communication*, *33* (3), 355–362. doi:10.1111/j.1460 – 2466.1983.tb02435.x

Gerbner, G. (1984). Defining the field of communication. *Association for Communication Administration Bulletin*, *48*, 10–11.

Gerbner, G. (1985). Mass media discourse: Message system analysis as a component of cultural indicators. In T. A. van Dijk (Ed.), *Discourse and communication. New approaches to the analysis of mass media discourse and communication* (pp. 13–25). Berlin: Walter de Gruyter.

Gerbner, G. (1987). Science on television: How it affects public conceptions. *Issues in Science and Technology*, *3* (3), 109–115.

Gerbner, G. (1990). Epilogue: Advancing on the path of righteousness (maybe). In N. Signorielli & M. Morgan (Eds.), *Cultivation analysis: New directions in media effects research* (pp. 249–262). Newbury Park, CA: Sage.

Gerbner, G. (1995). Marketing global mayhem. *Javnost – The Public*, *2* (2), 71–76. doi:10.1080/13183222.1995.11008595

Gerbner, G. (1998). Cultivation analysis: An overview. *Mass Communication and Society*, *1* (3–4), 175–194. doi:10.1080/15205436.1998.9677855

Gerbner, G. (1999). What do we know? In J. Shanahan & M. Morgan (Eds.), *Television and its viewers: Cultivation theory and research* (pp. ix–xiii). New York: Cambridge University Press.

Gerbner, G. (2001). The cultural arms of the corporate establishment: Reflections on the work of Herb Schiller. *Journal of Broadcasting & Electronic Media*, *45* (1), 186–190. doi:10.1207/s15506878jobem4501_14

Gerbner, G. (2012[1998]). The stories we tell and the stories we sell. *Journal of International Communication*, *18* (2), 237–244. doi:10.1080/13216597.2012.709928

Gerbner, G. & Gross, L. (1976a). Living with television: The violence profile. *Journal of Communication*, *26* (2), 172–194. doi:10.1111/j.1460 – 2466.1976.tb01397.x

Gerbner, G. & Gross, L. (1976b). The scary world of TV's heavy viewer. *Psychology Today Magazine*, *16* (3), 1–8.

Gerbner, G. & Gross, L. (1979). A reply to Newcomb's 'humanistic critique'. *Communication Research*, *6* (2), 223–230. doi:10.1177/009365027900600206

Gerbner, G., Gross, L., Eleey, M. F., Jackson-Beeck, M., Jeffries-Fox, S., & Signorielli, N. (1977). TV Violence Profile No. 8: The highlights. *Journal of Communication*, *27* (2), 171–180. doi:10.1111/j.1460 – 2466.1977.tb01845.x

Gerbner, G., Gross, L., Jackson-Beeck, M., Jeffries-Fox, S., & Signorielli, N. (1977). One more time: An analysis of the CBS "final comments on the violence profile." *Journal of Broadcasting*, *21* (3), 297–303. doi:10.1080/08838157709363839

Gerbner, G., Gross, L., Jackson-Beeck, M., Jeffries-Fox, S., & Signorielli, N. (1978). Cultural indicators: Violence Profile No. 9. *Journal of Communication*, *28* (3), 176–207. doi:10. 1111/j.1460 – 2466.1978.tb01646.x

Gerbner, G., Gross, L., Morgan, M., & Signorielli, N. (1979). On Wober's "televised violence and paranoid perception: The view from Great Britain". *Public Opinion Quarterly*, 43 (1), 123–124. doi:10.1086/268499

Gerbner, G., Gross, L., Morgan, M., & Signorielli, N. (1980a). Some additional comments on cultivation analysis. *Public Opinion Quarterly*, 44 (3), 408–410.

Gerbner, G., Gross, L., Morgan, M., & Signorielli, N. (1980b). The "mainstreaming" of America: Violence Profile No. 11. *Journal of Communication*, 30 (3), 10–29. doi:10.1111/j.1460 – 2466.1980.tb01987.x

Gerbner, G., Gross, L., Morgan, M., & Signorielli, N. (1981a). A curious journey into the scary world of Paul Hirsch. *Communication Research*, 8 (1), 39–72. doi:10.1177/ 009365028100800102

Gerbner, G., Gross, L., Morgan, M., & Signorielli, N. (1981b). Final reply to Hirsch. *Communication Research*, 8 (3), 259–280. doi:10.1177/009365028100800301

Gerbner, G., Gross, L., Morgan, M., & Signorielli, N. (1981c). Health and medicine on television. *The New England Journal of Medicine*, 305 (15), 901–904. doi:10. 1056 / NEJM198110083051530

Gerbner, G., Gross, L., Morgan, M., & Signorielli, N. (1981d). On the limits of "the limits of advocacy research": Response to Hirsch. *Public Opinion Quarterly*, 45 (1), 116–118. doi:10.1086/268639

Gerbner, G., Gross, L., Morgan, M., & Signorielli, N. (1981e). Scientists on the TV screen. *Society*, 18 (4), 41–44. doi:10.1007/bf02701349

Gerbner, G., Gross, L., Morgan, M., & Signorielli, N. (1982a). Charting the mainstream: Television's contributions to political orientations. *Journal of Communication*, 32 (2), 100–127. doi:10.1111/j.1460 – 2466.1982.tb00500.x

Gerbner, G., Gross, L., Morgan, M., & Signorielli, N. (1982b). What television teaches about physicians and health. *Möbius: A Journal for Continuing Education Professionals in Health Sciences*, 2 (2), 44–51. doi:10.1002/chp.4760020209

Gerbner, G., Gross, L., Morgan, M., & Signorielli, N. (1984). Political correlates of television viewing. *Public Opinion Quarterly*, 48 (1), 283–300. doi:10.1086/268826

Gerbner, G., Gross, L., Morgan, M., & Signorielli, N. (1986). Living with television: The dynamics of the cultivation process. In J. Bryant & D. Zillmann (Eds.), *Perspectives on media efects* (pp. 17–40). Hillsdale, NJ: Lawrence Erlbaum Association.

Gerbner, G., Gross, L., Morgan, M., Signorielli, N., & Shanahan, J. (2002). Growing up with television: Cultivation processes. In J. Bryant & D. Zillmann (Eds.), *Media effects: Advances in theory and research* (Vol. 2, pp. 43–67). Mahwah, NJ: Lawrence Erlbaum Associates.

Gerbner, G., Gross, L., Signorielli, N., & Morgan, M. (1980a). Aging with television: Images on television drama and conceptions of social reality. *Journal of Communication*, 30 (1), 37–47. doi:10.1111/j.1460 – 2466.1980.tb01766.x

Gerbner, G., Gross, L., Signorielli, N., & Morgan, M. (1980b). Television violence, victimization, and power. *American Behavioral Scientist, 23* (5), 705–716. doi:10.1177/ 000276428002300506

Gerbner, G., Gross, L., Signorielli, N., Morgan, M., & Jackson-Beeck, M. (1979). The demonstration of power: Violence Profile No. 10. *Journal of Communication, 29* (3), 177–196. doi:10.1111/j.1460 – 2466.1979.tb01731.x

Gerbner, G. & Signorielli, N. (1979). *Women and minorities in television drama, 1969–1978 [A research report by George Gerbner and Nancy Signorielli. For release on October 29, 1979 in collaboration with The Screen Actors Guild].* The Annenberg School of Communications, University of Pennsylvania, Philadelphia, PA. Retrieved from https://files.eric.ed.gov/fulltext/ED185178.pdf

Gilbert, N. & Troitzsch, K. (2005). *Simulation for the social scientist.* London: McGraw-Hill Education.

Grabe, M. E. & Drew, D. G. (2007). Crime cultivation: Comparisons across media genres and channels. *Journal of Broadcasting & Electronic Media, 51* (1), 147–171. doi:10.1080/ 08838150701308143

Green, M. C. & Brock, T. C. (2000). The role of transportation in the persuasiveness of public narratives. *Journal of Personality and Social Psychology, 79* (5), 701–21. doi:10. 1037/0022–3514.79.5.701

Green, M. C. & Brock, T. C. (2013). In the mind's eye: Transportation-imagery model of narrative persuasion. In M. C. Green, J. J. Strange, & T. C. Brock (Eds.), *Narrative impact: Social and cognitive foundations* (pp. 516–539). New York: Psychology Press.

Greenberg, B. S. (1980). *Life on television.* Norwood, NJ: Ablex.

Gross, K. & Aday, S. (2003). The scary world in your living room and neighborhood: Using local broadcast news, neighborhood crime rates, and personal experience to test agenda setting and cultivation. *Journal of Communication, 53* (3), 411–426. doi:10.1111/j.1460- 2466.2003.tb02599.x

Gunter, B. (1981). Measuring television violence: A review and questions for a new analytical perspective. *Current Psychological Reviews, 1,* 91–112. doi:10.1007/ BF02979256

Hakemulder, F., Kuijpers, M. M., Tan, E. S., Bàlint, K., & Doicaru, M. M. (Eds.). (2017). *Narrative Absorption.* Amsterdam: John Benjamins Publishing Company.

Hannula, M. S. (2006). Motivation in mathematics: Goals reflected in emotions. *Educational Studies in Mathematics, 63* (2), 165–178. doi:10.1007/s10649–005–9019–8

Hawkins, R. P. & Pingree, S. (1980). Some processes in the cultivation effect. *Communication Research, 7* (2), 193–226. doi:10.1177/009365028000700203

Hawkins, R. P. & Pingree, S. (1981a). Uniform messages and habitual viewing: Unnecessary assumptions in social reality effects. *Human Communication Research, 7* (4), 291–301. doi:10.1111/j.1468 – 2958.1981.tb00576.x

Hawkins, R. P. & Pingree, S. (1981b). Using television to construct social reality. *Journal of Broadcasting, 25* (4), 347–364. doi:10.1080/08838158109386459

Hawkins, R. P. & Pingree, S. (1982). Television's influence on social reality. In D. Pearl, L. Bouthilet, & J. Lazar (Eds.), *Television and behavior: Ten years of scientific progress and implications for the 80's* (pp. 224–227). Rockville, MD: NIMH.

Hawkins, R. P., Pingree, S., & Adler, I. (1987). Searching for cognitive processes in the cultivation effect: Adult and adolescent samples in the United States and Australia. *Human Communication Research, 13* (4), 553–577. doi:10. 1111 /j. 1468 – 2958. 1987. tb00118.x

Herman, D. (1997). Scripts, sequences, and stories: elements of a postclassical narratology. *PMLA, 112* (5), 1046–1059.

Herman, D. (2002). *Story logic. Problems and possibilities of narrative.* Lincoln: University of Nebraska Press.

Herman, D. (Ed.). (2007). *The Cambridge companion to narrative.* Cambridge: Cambridge University Press.

Herman, D. (2009). *Basic elements of narrative.* Malden, MA: Wiley-Blackwell. doi:10.1002/ 9781444305920

Herzig, B. & Assmann, S. (2014). How to define media in a mediatized society? A media pedagogical proposal inspired by theoretical ideas of Castells, Luhmann and Peirce. *MedienPädagogik, 24,* 18–29. doi:10.21240/mpaed/24/2014.07.18.X

Hetsroni, A. & Lowenstein, H. (2012). Cultivation and agenda setting: Conceptual and empirical intersections. In M. Morgan, J. Shanahan, & N. Signorielli (Eds.), *Living with television now: Advances in cultivation theory and research* (pp. 307–328). New York: Peter Lang.

Himmelweit, H., Oppenheim, A., & Vince, P. (1958). *Television and the child: An empirical study of the efect of television on the young.* New York: Oxford University Press.

Hirsch, P. M. (1980). The 'scary world' of the nonviewer and other anomalies: A reanalysis of Gerbner et al.'s findings on cultivation analysis part I. *Communication Research, 7* (4), 403–456. doi:10.1177/009365028000700401

Hirsch, P. M. (1981). On not learning from one's own mistakes: A reanalysis of Gerbner et al.'s findings on cultivation analysis part II. *Communication Research, 8* (1), 3–37. doi:10.1177/009365028100800101

Holbert, R., Shah, D., & Kwak, N. (2004). Fear, authority, and justice: Crime-related TV viewing and endorsements of capital punishment and gun ownership. *Journalism & Mass Communication Quarterly, 81* (2), 343–363. doi:10.1177/107769900408100208

Horkheimer, M. & Adorno, T. W. (1973). *Dialectic of enlightenment.* London: Allan Lane.

Horkheimer, M. & Adorno, T. W. (1993[1944]). The culture industry: Enlightenment as mass deception. In M. Horkheimer & T. W. Adorno (Eds.), *Dialectic of enlightenment* (pp. 94–136). New York: Continuum.

Hughes, M. (1980). The fruits of cultivation analysis: A re-examination of the effects of television watching on fear of victimization, alienation, and the approval of violence. *Public Opinion Quarterly, 44* (4), 287–302.

Hühn, P. & et al. (n.d.). *The living handbook of narratology*. Retrieved from http://www. lhn.uni-hamburg.de/

Hutcheon, L. (1989). Incredulity toward metanarrative: Negotiating postmodemism and feminisms. *Tessera*, 7, 39–44. doi:10.25071/1923–9408.23598

Hyvärinen, M. (2010). Revisiting the narrative turns. *Life Writing*, 7 (1), 69–82. doi:10.1080/ 14484520903342957

Jeffres, L. W., Neuendorf, K., Bracken, C. C., & Atkin, D. (2008). Integrating theoretical traditions in media effects: Using third-person effects to link agenda-setting and cultivation. *Mass Communication and Society*, 11 (4), 470–491. doi:10.1080/15205430802375303

Jenner, M. (2016). Is this TVIV? On Netflix, TVIV and binge-watching. *New Media & Society*, 18 (2), 257–273. doi:10.1177/1461444814541523

Jin, D. Y. (2020). *Globalization and media in the digital platform age*. New York: Routledge.

Johnson, C. (2019). *Online TV*. New York: Routledge.

Katz, E., Gurevich, M., & Haas, H. (1973). On the use of the mass media for important things. *American Sociological Review*, 38 (2), 164–181. doi:10.2307/2094393

Katz, E. & Lazarsfeld, P. (1955). *Personal influence: The part played by people in the flow of mass communications*. New York: Free Press.

Kim, B. S. & Alamilla, S. G. (2007). Acculturation and enculturation: A review of theory and research. In F. Leong, A. Ebreo, L. Kinoshita, A. Inman, L. Yang, & M. Fu (Eds.), *Handbook of Asian American psychology*. Thousand Oaks, CA: Sage Publications.

Kreuter, M. W., Green, M. C., Cappella, J. N., Slater, M. D., Wise, M. E., Storey, D., Woolley, S. (2007). Narrative communication in cancer prevention and control: A framework to guide research and application. *Annals of Behavioral Medicine*, 33 (3), 221–235. doi:10.1007/BF02879904

Leech-Wilkinson, D. (2017). Musical shape and feeling. In D. Leech-Wilkinson & H. M. Prior (Eds.), *Music and shape* (pp. 359–382). New York: Oxford University Press.

Lobato, R. (2018). Rethinking international tv flows research in the age of netflix. *Television & New Media*, 19 (3), 241–256. doi:10.1177/1527476417708245

Lobato, R. & Ryan, M. D. (2011). Rethinking genre studies through distribution analysis: Issues in international horror movie circuits. *New Review of Film and Television Studies*, 9 (2), 188–203. doi:10.1080/17400309.2011.556944

Lotz, A. (2017a). Linking industrial and creative change in 21st-century US television. *Media International Australia*, 164 (1), 10–20. doi:10.1177/1329878X17707066

Lotz, A. (2017b). *Portals: A treatise on internet-distributed television*. Ann Arbor: Maize Publishing.

Luhmann, N. (2000). *The reality of the mass media*. Stanford, CA: Stanford University Press.

Madrigal, A. (January 2, 2014). *How netflix reverse engineered hollywood*. Retrieved from https://www.theatlantic.com/technology/archive/2014/01/how-netflix-rever se-engineered-hollywood/282679/

Marsen, S. (2014). "Lock the Doors": Toward a narrative–semiotic approach to organizational crisis. *Journal of Business and Technical Communication, 28* (3), 301–326. doi:10.1177/ 1050651914524781

McQuail, D. (2010). *Mass communication theory*. London: Sage.

McQuail, D. & Windahl, S. (1981). *Communication models: For the study of mass communications*. New York: Longman.

Metag, J. (2016). Content analysis in climate change communication. In M. Nisbet (Ed.), *The Oxford encyclopedia of climate change communication*. Oxford: Oxford University Press. doi:10.1093/acrefore/9780190228620.013.486

Miller, C. R. (2012). New genres, now and then. In S. Hulan, M. McArthur, & R. A. Harris (Eds.), *Literature, rhetoric and values: selected proceedings of a conference held at the University of Waterloo, 3–5 june 2011* (pp. 127–148). Newcastle: Cambridge Scholars Publishing.

Mittell, J. (2001). A cultural approach to television genre theory. *Cinema Journal, 40* (3), 3–24.

Morgan, M. & Shanahan, J. (1997). Two decades of cultivation research: An appraisal and meta-analysis. In B. R. Burleson & A. W. Kunkel (Eds.), *Communication yearbook 20* (pp. 1–45). Thousand Oaks, CA: Sage.

Morgan, M. & Shanahan, J. (2010). The state of cultivation. *Journal of Broadcasting & Electronic Media, 54* (2), 337–355. doi:10.1080/08838151003735018

Morgan, M. & Shanahan, J. (2017). Television and the cultivation of authoritarianism: A return visit from an unexpected friend. *Journal of Communication, 67* (3), 424–444. doi:10.1111/jcom.12297

Morgan, M., Shanahan, J., & Signorielli, N. (2012). The stories we tell: Cultivation theory and research. In M. Morgan, J. Shanahan, & N. Signorielli (Eds.), *Living with television now: Advances in cultivation theory and research* (pp. 1–14). New York: Peter Lang.

Morgan, M., Shanahan, J., & Signorielli, N. (2014). Cultivation theory in the twenty-first century. In R. Fortner & P. Fackler (Eds.), *The handbook of media and mass communication theory* (pp. 480–497). Walden, MA: John Wiley & Sons.

Morgan, M., Shanahan, J., & Signorielli, N. (2015). Yesterday's new cultivation, tomorrow. *Mass Communication and Society, 18* (5), 674–699. doi:10.1080/15205436.2015.1072725

Morgan, M., Shanahan, J., & Signorielli, N. (2017). Cultivation theory: Idea, topical fields, and methodology. In P. Rössler, C. A. Hoffner, & L. van Zoonen (Eds.), *The international encyclopedia of media effects* (pp. 1–14). New York: John Wiley & Sons.

Morgan, M. & Signorielli, N. (1990). Cultivation analysis: Conceptualization and methodology. In N. Signorielli & M. Morgan (Eds.), *Cultivation analysis: New directions in media effects research* (pp. 13–34). Newbury Park, CA: Sage.

Mosharafa, E. (2015). All you need to know about: The cultivation theory. *Global Journal of Human Social Science, 15* (8), 23–37.

Murdock, G. (2006). Notes from the number one country. *International Journal of Cultural Policy, 12* (2), 209–227. doi:10.1080/10286630600813727

Nabi, R. L. (2009). Cosmetic surgery makeover programs and intentions to undergo cosmetic enhancements: A consideration of three models of media effects. *Human Communication Research, 35* (1), 1–27. doi:10.1111/j.1468 – 2958.2008.01336.x

Napoli, P. M. (2016). Special issue introduction: big data and media management. *International Journal on Media Management, 18* (1), 1–7. doi:10.1080/14241277.2016.1185888

Neale, S. (2015). Studying genre. In G. Creeber (Ed.), *The television genre book* (pp. 3–4). London: British Film Institute.

Neumann, B. & Nünning, A. (n.d.). Metanarration and metafiction. In P. Hühn & et al. (Eds.), *The living handbook of narratology*. Retrieved from http://www.lhn.u ni–hamburg.de/article/metanarration-and-metafiction

Newcomb, H. (1978). Assessing the Violence Profile Studies of Gerbner and Gross. *Communication Research, 5* (3), 264–282. doi:10.1177/009365027800500303

Newhagen, J. & Lewenstein, M. (1992). Cultivation and exposure to television following the 1989 Loma Prieta earthquake. *Mass Comm Review, 18*, 49–56.

Nielsen. (2016, June). Milestone Marker: SVOD and DVR penetration are now on par with one another. *Nielsen Insights*. Retrieved from http://www.nielsen.com/u s/en/insights/news/2016/milestone-marker-svod-and-dvr-penetration-on-par-with -one-another.html

Nielsen. (2017). *The Nielsen Total Audience Report, Q1–2017*. Retrieved from http:// www.nielsen.com/us/en/insights/reports/2017/the- nielsen- total- audience- repor t- q1- 2017.html

Nielsen. (2018). *The Nielsen Total Audience Report, Q3–2018*. Retrieved from https:// www.nielsen.com/wp-content/uploads/sites/3/2019/04/q3–2018-total-audience-re port.pdf

Nünning, A. (2003). Narratology or narratologies: New perspectives on narrative analysis. In T. Kindt & H.-H. Müller (Eds.), *What is narratology?: Questions and answers regarding the status of a theory* (pp. 239–276). Berlin: De Gruyter.

O'Connor, C. (2019). The natural selection of conservative science. *Studies in History and Philosophy of Science, 76*, 24–29. doi:10.1016/j.shpsa.2018.09.007

Oliver, M. B., Dillard, J. P., Bae, K., & Tamul, D. J. (2012). The effect of narrative news format on empathy for stigmatized groups. *Journalism & Mass Communication Quarterly, 89* (2), 205–224. doi:10.1177/1077699012439020

Olsen, G. (Ed.). (2011). *Current trends in narratology*. Berlin: De Gruyter.

Oschatz, C. & Klimmt, C. (2016). The effectiveness of narrative communication in road safety education: A moderated mediation model. *Communications, 41* (2), 145–165. doi:10.1515/commun-2016-0003

Peirce, C. S. (1993[1884–1886]). *Writings of Charles S. Peirce. A chronological edition* (C. J. W. Kloesel, N. Houser, U. Niklas, M. Simon, A. Houser, A. de Tienne,... M. H. Fisch, Eds.). Bloomington: Indiana University Press.

Pelzer, E. & Raemy, P. (2020). What shapes the cultivation effects from infotaining content? Toward a theoretical foundation for journalism studies. *Journalism*. doi:10.1177/ 1464884920922704

Phelan, J. & Rabinowitz, P. (Eds.). (2005). *A companion to narrative theory*. Oxford: Blackwell.

Picard, R. G. (2003). Media economics, content, and diversity: Primary results from a Finnish study. In P. Hovi-Wasastjerna (Ed.), *Media culture research programme* (pp. 107–120). Helsinki: Academy of Finland.

Popescu, S. O. (2013). Hyper-real narratives: The emergence of contemporary film subgenres hyper-real narratives. *Journal of Literature and Art Studies, 3* (9), 568–575.

Posner, R. (2004). Basic tasks of cultural semiotics. In G. Withalm & J. Wallmansberger (Eds.), *Signs of power — power of signs. Essays in honor of Jef Bernard* (pp. 56–89). Vienna: INST.

Potter, W. J. (1981). The linearity assumption in cultivation research. *Human Communication Research, 17*, 562–583. doi:10.1111/j.1468 – 2958.1991.tb00244.x

Potter, W. J. (1990). Adolescents' perceptions of the primary values of television programming. *Journalism Quarterly, 67* (4), 843–851. doi:10.1177/107769909006700439

Potter, W. J. (1993). Cultivation theory and research. A conceptual critique. *Human Communication Research, 19* (4), 564–601. doi:10.1111/j.1468 – 2958.1993.tb00313.x

Potter, W. J. (1994). Cultivation theory and research. A methodological critique. *Journalism Monograph, 147*, 1–34.

Potter, W. J. (2012). *Media effects* (6th ed.). Thousand Oaks, CA: Sage.

Potter, W. J. (2014). A critical analysis of cultivation theory. *Journal of Communication, 64* (6), 1015–1036. doi:10.1111/jcom.12128

Potter, W. J. & Chang, I. C. (1990). Television exposure measures and the cultivation hypothesis. *Journal of Broadcasting & Electronic Media, 34* (3), 313–333. doi:10.1080/ 08838159009386745

Potter, W. J., Pashupati, K., Pekurny, R. G., Hoffman, E., & Davis, K. (2002). Perceptions of television: A schema explanation. *Media Psychology, 4* (1), 27–50. doi:10.1207/ S1532785XMEP0401_02

Potter, W. J. & Riddle, K. (2007). A content analysis of the media effects literature. *Journalism & Mass Communication Quarterly, 84* (1), 90–104. doi:10.1177/107769900708400107

Potter, W. J. & Ware, W. (1987). An analysis of the contexts of antisocial acts on prime-time television. *Communication Research, 14* (6), 664–686. doi:10.1177/009365087014006003

Prince, G. (1999). Revisiting narrativity. In W. Grünzweig & A. Solbach (Eds.), *Grenzüberschreitungen: Narratologie im Kontext [Blurring boundaries: Contextualizing narratology]* (pp. 43–51). Tübingen: Narr.

Prince, G. (2008). Classical and/or postclassical narratology. *L'Esprit Créateur, 48* (2), 115- 123. doi:10.1353/esp.0.0005

Prince, L. (2018). *Conceptualizing television viewing in the digital age: Patterns of exposure and the cultivation process* (Dissertation). Retrieved from https://scholarw orks.umass. edu/cgi/viewcontent.cgi?article=2214&context=dissertations_2

Quick, B. L. (2009). The effects of viewing Grey's Anatomy on perceptions of doctors and patient satisfaction. *Journal of Broadcasting & Electronic Media, 53* (1), 38–55. doi:10. 1080/08838150802643563

Quintero-Johnson, J. M. & Sangalang, A. (2017). Testing the explanatory power of two measures of narrative involvement: an investigation of the influence of transportation and narrative engagement on the process of narrative persuasion. *Media Psychology, 20* (1), 144–173. doi:10.1080/15213269.2016.1160788

R Core Team. (n.d.). R: a language and environment for statistical computing. In *R foundation for statistical computing*. Vienna: Austria.

Richardson, B. (2012). Unnatural narratology. Basic concepts and recent work. [Review of: Jan Alber / Rüdiger Heinze: unnatural narratives – unnatural narratology. Berlin 2011. Per Krogh Hansen / Stefan Iversen / Henrik Skov Nielsen / Rolf Reitan (eds.): strange voices in narrative fiction. Berlin 2011. David Herman / James Phelan / Peter Rabinowitz / Brian Richardson / Robyn Warhol: narrative theory: core concepts and critical debates. Columbus 2012]. *Diegesis. Interdisciplinary E-Journal for Narrative Research, 1* (1), 95–103.

Russell, D. (2010). Master narrative. In M. Ryan (Ed.), *The encyclopedia of literary and cultural theory* (Vol. 2, pp. 1–4). Wiley Blackwell. doi:10.1002/9781444337839.wbelctv2m003

Ryan, M.-L. (n.d.). Narration in various media. In P. Hühn & et al. (Eds.), *The living handbook of narratology*. Retrieved from http://www.lhn.uni- hamburg.de/article/ narration-various-media

Ryan, M.-L. (Ed.). (2004). *Narrative across media: The languages of storytelling*. Lincoln: University of Nebraska Press.

Ryan, M.-L. (2007). Toward a definition of narrative. In D. Herman (Ed.), *The Cambridge companion to narrative* (pp. 22–35). New York: Cambridge University Press.

Schiller, H. I. (2000). *Living in the number one country: Reflections from a critic of American empire*. New York: Seven Stories Press.

Schneider, F. M. (2012). *Measuring subjective movie evaluation criteria. Conceptual foundation, construction, and validation of the SMEC scales* (Dissertation). Retrieved from http://nbn-resolving.de/urn:nbn:de:hbz:lan1-7813

Schramm, W., Lyle, J., & Parker, E. (1961). *Television in the lives of our children*. Stanford, CA: Stanford University Press.

Segal, E. M. (1995). Narrative comprehension and the role of deictic shift theory. In J. F. Duchan, G. A. Bruder, & L. E. Hewitt (Eds.), *Deixis in narrative: A cognitive science perspective* (pp. 3–18). Hillsdale, NJ: Lawrence Erlbaum.

Segrin, C. & Nabi, R. L. (2002). Does television viewing cultivate unrealistic expectations about marriage? *Journal of Communication, 52* (2), 247–263. doi:10. 1111 / j. 1460 – 2466.2002.tb02543.x

Selnow, G. W. (1986). Solving problems on prime-time television. *Journal of Communication, 36* (2), 63–72. doi:10.1111/j.1460 – 2466.1986.tb01424.x

Shanahan, J. & Morgan, M. (1999). *Television and its viewers: Cultivation theory and research.* New York: Cambridge University Press.

Shanahan, J. & Scheufele, D. (2012). Cultivation and the spiral of silence: Theoretical and empirical investigations. In M. Morgan, J. Shanahan, & N. Signorielli (Eds.), *Living with television now: Advances in cultivation theory and research* (pp. 347–365). New York: Peter Lang.

Shen, F., Sheer, V. C., & Li, R. (2015). Impact of narratives on persuasion in health communication: A meta-analysis. *Journal of Advertising, 44* (2), 105–113. doi:10. 1080 / 00913367.2015.1018467

Shrum, L. J. (2002). Media consumption and perceptions of social reality: Effects and underlying processes. In J. Bryant & D. Zillmann (Eds.), *Media effects: Advances in theory and research* (Vol. 2, pp. 50–73).

Signorielli, N., Gerbner, G., & Morgan, M. (1995). Standpoint: Violence on television: The cultural indicators project. *Journal of Broadcasting & Electronic Media, 39* (2), 278- 283. doi:10.1080/08838159509364304

Signorielli, N., Gross, L., & Morgan, M. (1982). Violence in television programs: Ten years later. In D. Pearl, L. Bouthilet, & J. Lazar (Eds.), *Television and behavior: Ten years of scientific progress and implications for the 80's* (Vol. 2, pp. 158–173). Rockville, MD: NIMH.

Signorielli, N., Morgan, M., & Shanahan, J. (2019). The Violence Profile: Five decades of Cultural Indicators Research. *Mass Communication and Society, 22* (1), 1–28. doi:10. 1080/15205436.2018.1475011

Singer, J. B. (2018). Transmission creep. Media effects theories and journalism studies in a digital era. *Journalism Studies, 19* (2), 209–226. doi:10.1080/1461670X.2016.1186498

Slater, M. D. & Rouner, D. (2002). Entertainment-education and elaboration likelihood: Understanding the processing of narrative persuasion. *Communication Theory, 12* (2), 173–191. doi:10.1111/j.1468 – 2885.2002.tb00265.x

Smaldino, P. E. (2017). Models are stupid, and we need more of them. In R. R. Vallacher, S. J. Read, & A. Nowak (Eds.), *Computational social psychology* (pp. 311–331). New York: Routledge. doi:10.4324/9781315173726–14

Smaldino, P. E. (2020). How to translate a verbal theory into a formal model. *Social Psychology, 51*(4), 207–218. doi:10.1027/1864–9335/a000425

Smith, E. R. & Queller, S. (2001). Mental representations. In A. Tesser & N. Schwarz (Eds.), *Blackwell handbook of social psychology: Intraindividual processes* (pp. 111–133). Oxford: Blackwell.

Smith-Rowsey, D. (2016). Imaginative indices and deceptive domains: How Netflix's categories and genres redefine the long tail. In D. Smith-Rowsey (Ed.), *The Netflix effect: Technology and entertainment in the 21st century* (pp. 63–80). New York: Bloomsbury Academic. doi:10.5040/9781501309410.ch-005

Stam, R., Burgoyne, R., & Flitterman-Lewis, S. (2005). *New vocabularies in film semiotics. Structuralism, post-structuralism and beyond*. London: Routledge.

Stein, J.-P., Krause, E., & Ohler, P. (2019). Every (insta)gram counts? Applying cultivation theory to explore the effects of instagram on young users' body image. *Psychology of Popular Media Culture, Advance online publication*. doi:10.1037/ppm0000268

Steininger, C. & Woelke, J. (2008). Separating TV ads from TV programming. What we can learn about program-integrated advertising from economic theory and research on media use. *Communications, 33* (4), 455–471. doi:10.1515/COMM.2008.028

Tamborini, R. & Choi, J. (1990). The role of cultural diversity in cultivation research. In N. Signorielli & M. Morgan (Eds.), *Cultivation analysis: new directions in media effects research* (pp. 157–180). Newbury Park, CA: Sage.

Tamborini, R., Weber, R., Eden, A., Bowman, N. D., & Grizzard, M. (2010). Repeated exposure to daytime soap opera and shifts in moral judgment toward social convention. *Journal of Broadcasting & Electronic Media, 54* (4), 621–640. doi:10.1080/08838151. 2010.519806

Tapper, J. (1995). The ecology of cultivation: A conceptual model for cuitivation research. *Communication Theory, 5* (1), 36–57. doi:10.1111/j.1468 – 2885.1995.tb00097.x

Tarasti, E. (2004). Music as a narrative art. In M.-L. Ryan (Ed.), *Narrative across media: The languages of storytelling* (pp. 283–304). Lincoln: University of Nebraska Press.

The Cultural Indicators Research Team. (1977). "The Gerbner violence profile" —an analysis of the CBS report. *Journal of Broadcasting, 21* (3), 280–286. doi:10.1080/08838157709363837

Tsay-Vogel, M., Shanahan, J., & Signorielli, N. (2018). Social media cultivating perceptions of privacy: A 5-year analysis of privacy attitudes and self-disclosure behaviors among Facebook users. *New Media & Society, 20* (1), 141–161. doi:10.1177/1461444816660731

Uricchio, W. (2014). Film, cinema, television … media? *New Review of Film and Television Studies, 12* (3), 266–279. doi:10.1080/17400309.2014.926656

Van Cuilenburg, J. V. (2000). On measuring media competition and media diversity: Concepts, theories and methods. In R. G. Picard (Ed.), *Measuring media content, quality, and diversity* (pp. 51–80). Tuku, Finland: Suomen Akatemia.

Van den Bulck, J. (2012). International cultivation. In M. Morgan, J. Shanahan, & N. Signorielli (Eds.), *Living with television now: Advances in cultivation theory and research* (pp. 238–260). New York: Peter Lang.

Varian, H. (1997). How to build an economic model in your spare time. *The American Economist, 41* (2), 3–10.

Walsh, R. (2010). Person, level, voice. A rhetorical reconsideration. In J. Alber & M. Fludernik (Eds.), *Postclassical narratology. Approaches and analyses* (pp. 35–57). Columbus, OH: The Ohio State University Press.

Ward, L. M., Merryweather, A., & Caruthers, A. (2006). Breasts are for men: Media, masculine ideologies, and men's beliefs about women's bodies. *Sex Roles, 55*, 703–714. doi:10.1007/s11199–006–9125–9

Weisberg, M. (2012). *Simulation and similarity: Using models to understand the world.* Oxford: Oxford University Press.

Williams, D. (2006). Virtual cultivation: Online worlds, offline perceptions. *Journal of Communication, 56* (1), 69–87. doi:10.1111/j.1460 – 2466.2006.00004.x

Wober, J. (1978). Televised violence and paranoid perception: The view from Great Britain. *Public Opinion Quarterly, 42* (3), 315–321. doi:10.1086/268455

Wober, J. (1979). Televised violence and viewers' perceptions of reality: A reply to criticisms of some British research. *Public Opinion Quarterly, 43* (2), 271–273.

APPENDIX

Appendix A Tables & Figures

Table A.1 Summary of questions and terms of public message system analysis.

Questions and Terms of Public Message System Analysis.				
Dimensions	Question	Definition	Measures & terms of analysis	Brief explanations of questions
1. Existence	What Is?	Public assumptions about existence	Distribution, frequency; attention	What things (or kinds or things) does this message system call to the attention of a community?
2. Importance	What Is Important?	Context of priorities	Ordering, scaling; emphasis	In what context or order of importance are these things arranged?
3. Value	What Is Right?	Point of view, affective qualities	Semantic differential; tendency	In what light or from what point of view are these things presented?
4. Relationship	What Is Related To What?	Proximal or logical associations	Contingencies, clustering; structure	In what structure of associations with one another are these things presented?

Aggregation of notes by Gerbner (1969a, 1985), Shanahan and Morgan (1999)

Table A.2 *The components of television as a medium for delivering audiovisual content in the broadcast, cable/ satellite, digital and internet eras.*

	Infrastructure*	Viewing Device*	Add-on Device*	Service**	Frame**	Content**	Funding	Organizational structures	User experience
	The components of television as a medium for delivering audiovisual content in the broadcast, cable/ satellite, digital and internet eras.								
Broadcast era 1930s—70s	Broadcasting	TV set		Mass channels	Linear schedule	Professional programmes, ads, interstitials	State/licence fee Advertising	National/ regional/ local broadcasters Regulated	Viewing
Cable/satellite era 1970s—90s	Broadcasting Cable Satellite	TV set	Remote control VHS player Set-top box	Mass and niche channels Channel bundles	Linear schedule EPG	Professional programmes, ads, interstitials	State/licence fee Advertising Subscription Transaction	National/ regional/ local broadcasters Global conglomer ates Deregulated	Viewing Surfing Buying
Digital era 1990s—2000s	Broadcasting Cable Satellite	TV set	Remote control VHS/DVD player Set-top box/ PVR	Mass and niche channels Channel bundles PPV	Linear schedule EPG Interfaces	Professional programmes, ads, interstitials Transmedia	State/licence fee Advertising Subscription Transaction	National/ regional/ local broadcasters Global conglomer ates Deregulated	Viewing Surfing Buying Playing
Internet era 2010s+	Digital (terrestrial, satellite, cable) Digital (terrestrial, satellite, cable) Broadband/4G/ wifi Cloud computing	TV set Smart TV Desktop Laptop Tablet Smartphone	Remote control DVD player Set-top box/ PVR Digital media player Games console	Mass and niche channels Channel bundles PPV VOD P2P	Linear schedule EPG Interfaces Algorithms	Professional programmes, ads, interstitials Transmedia Semi-professional pro-amateur Amateur	State/licence fee Advertising Subscription Transaction	National/ regional/ local broadcasters Global conglomer ates Deregulated	Viewing Surfing Buying Playing Curating Sharing Uploading Downloading Liking Commenting Rating

Adapted from *Online Television* (p. 8), by Johnson, 2019. *Note:* * Technology; ** Cultural Form; EPG = electronic programme guide; P2P = peer-to-peer; PPV = pay-per-view; PVR = personal video recorder; VHS = video home system; VOD = video on demand.

Table A.3 Number of times message, narrative, story, and genre are mentioned in respective articles on cultivation by Gerbner et al.

List of coded articles by Gerbner et al.				
Reference	Messa-ge*	Narra-tiv*	Story* OR Stories	Genre*
Gerbner (1966)	3	0	26	0
Gerbner (1969a)	50	0	5	0
Gerbner (1970)	47	0	3	0
Gerbner (1972a)	33	0	2	0
Gerbner (1972b)	8	0	21	0
Eleey, Gerbner, and Tedesco (1972)	5	0	1	0
Gerbner and Gross (1976a)	19	1	9	0
Gerbner and Gross (1976b)	1	0	3	0
Gerbner (1977)	3	0	7	1
Gerbner, Gross, Eleey, et al. (1977)	1	0	0	0
The Cultural Indicators Research Team (1977)	0	0	0	0
Gerbner, Gross, Jackson-Beeck, Jeffries-Fox, and Signorielli (1977)	3	0	0	0
Gerbner et al. (1978)	15	0	8	0
Gerbner, Gross, Morgan, and Signoriel-li (1979)	2	0	0	0
Gerbner, Gross, Signorielli, Morgan, and Jackson-Beeck (1979)	2	0	10	0
Gerbner and Gross (1979)	1	0	0	0
Gerbner (1980a)	0	4	5	0
Gerbner (1980b)	1	0	2	0
Gerbner, Gross, Morgan, and Signoriel-li (1980b)	11	0	3	0
Gerbner, Gross, Signorielli, and Mor-gan (1980a)	4	0	2	0
Gerbner, Gross, Signorielli, and Mor-gan (1980b)	6	0	1	1

Continuation of Table A.3				
Reference	Messa-ge*	Narra-tiv*	story* OR stories	genre*
Gerbner et al. (1981a)	9	0	1	0
Gerbner et al. (1981b)	6	0	2	0
Gerbner et al. (1981c)	3	0	0	0
Gerbner et al. (1981d)	1	0	1	0
Gerbner et al. (1981e)	4	0	0	1
Gerbner et al. (1982a)	6	0	2	0
Gerbner et al. (1982b)	5	0	0	0
Gerbner (1983)	4	0	1	0
Gerbner (1984)	9	0	13	0
Gerbner et al. (1984)	0	0	0	0
Gerbner (1987)	2	0	1	0
Gerbner (1995)	0	0	1	1
Signorielli, Gerbner, and Morgan (1995)	3	0	3	1
Gerbner (1998)	25	0	11	2
Gerbner (2012[1998])	4	0	21	0
Gerbner (2001)	2	0	1	0
SUM	298	5	166	7
End of Table				

Table A.4 Mean differences in degree of belief in message 1 between heavy and light viewers with respect to DGF and DAF

| | | DAF | | | |
		Uniform	Genre-Specific	Metanarratives	Subgenre
	Uniform	.440	.176	.175	.161
DGF	Genre-Specific	.260	.412	.260	.492
	Metanarratives	.258	.261	.411	.396
	Subgenre	.274	.315	.198	.386

Note. K = 1,000 simulations with N > 720. See Table 6.1 for further information on initial conditions.

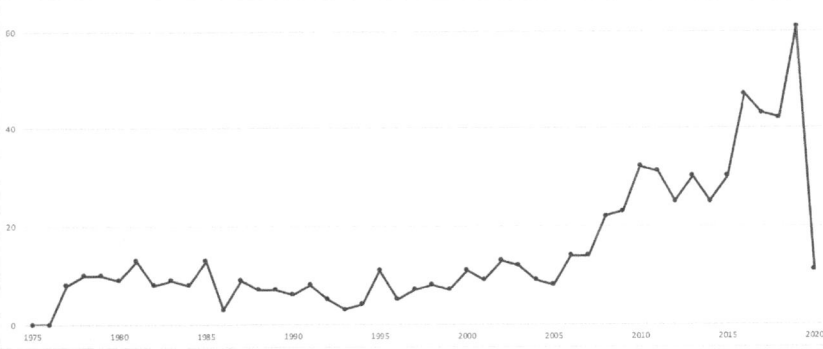

Figure A.1 Sum of times the article Living with Television - Violence Profile by Gerbner and Gross (1976a) was cited per year

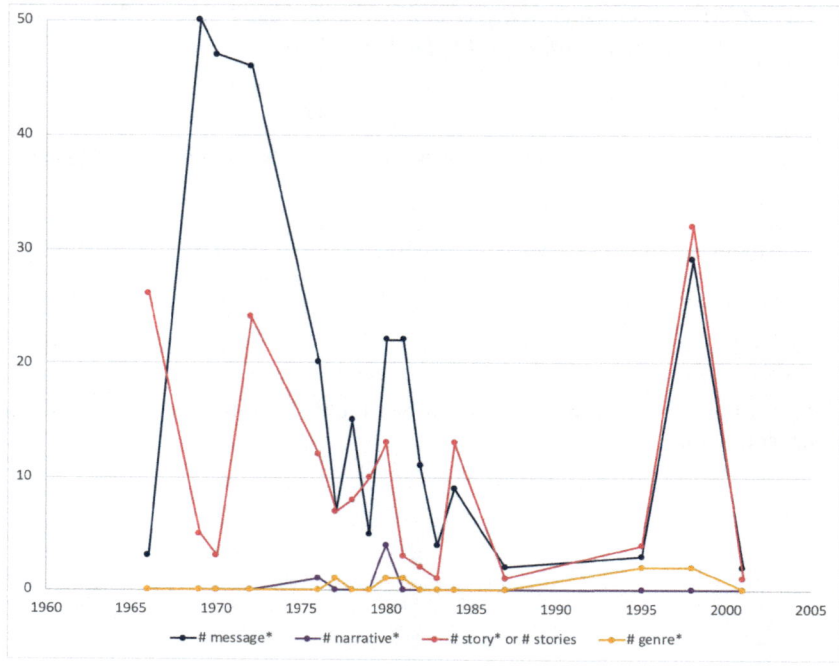

*Figure A.2 Overall number of times 'message,' 'narrative,' 'story,' and 'genre'
was mentioned in an article by Gerbner between 1966 and 2001
per year*

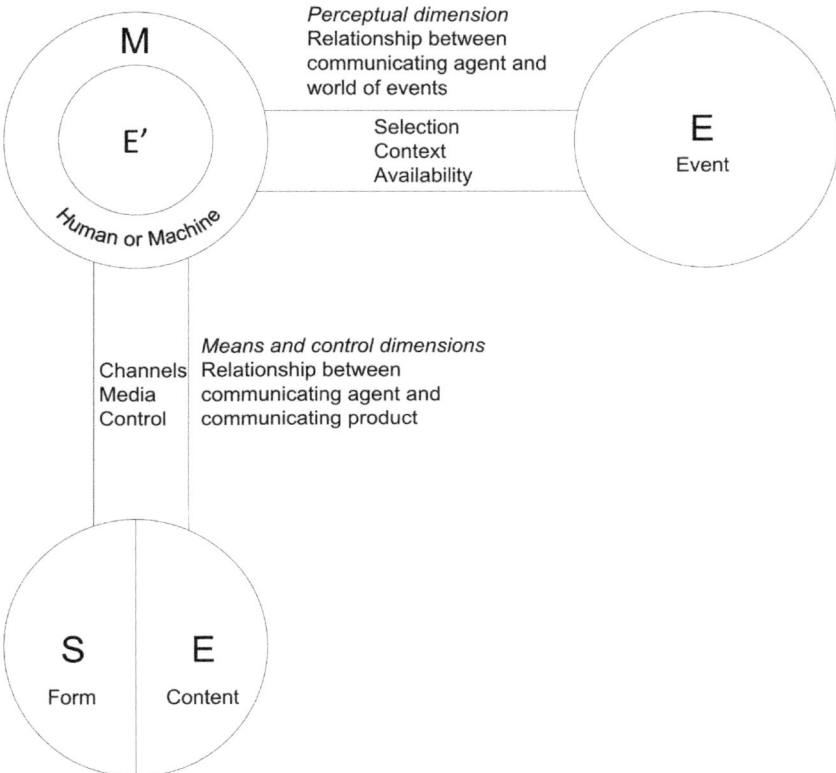

Figure A.3 Gerbner's general model of communication (after Gerbner, 1958, p. 93, McQuail and Windahl, 1981, p. 19)

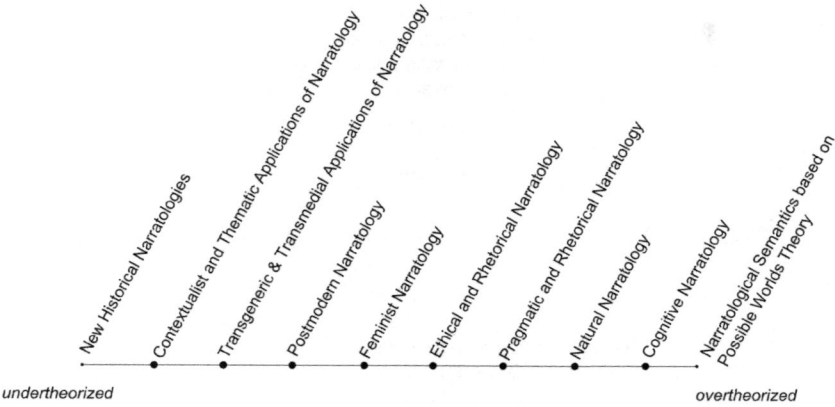

Figure A.4   Nünning's axis of degree of theoretical elaboration of legacies in post-classical narratology (after Nünning, 2003, p. 256)

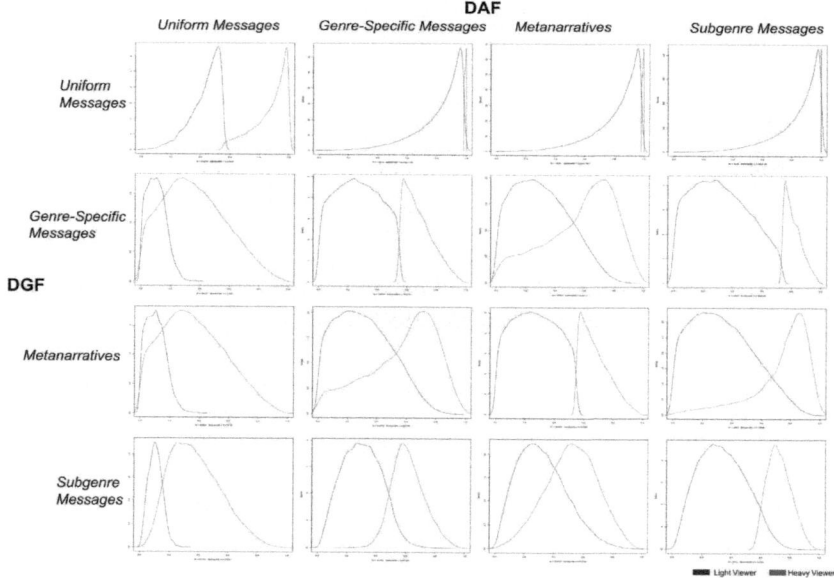

Figure A.5   Density functions for degree of belief in cultivating message for heavy and light viewers with respect to DGF and DAF without noise

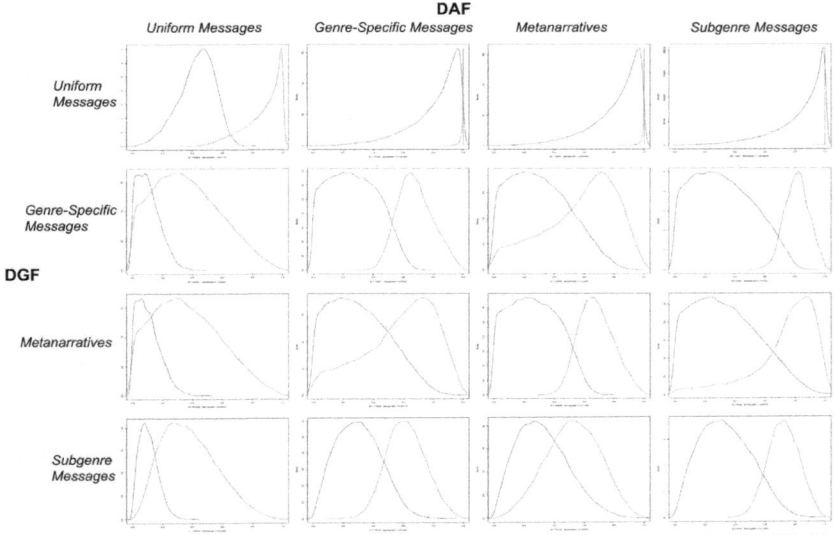

Figure A.5 Density functions for degree of belief in cultivating message for heavy and light viewers with respect to DGF and DAF with noise

Appendix B Narrative Glossary

Narrative terminology is important to learn and to understand to interpret narrative media entities. Many of the narrative terms from semiotics have analogs in psychology and communication studies, and it would be helpful if scholars would stick to one term or the other. Unfortunately, this is often not the case. Yet, scholars from different fields come across similar phenomena and ideas, but due to different terminology they miss the similarities. For example, Segal (1995) claims that "we have not seen the DST (Deictic Shift Theory) elsewhere in the cognitive psychology literature" (p. 15), although there are direct analogues yet put into other terms such as 'identification' in psychology and communication studies, respectively. At the risk of oversimplifying, we present the following brief definitions of some of the most relevant narrative terms in semiotics and their equivalents from psychology and communication studies if applicable. In isolation, these terms most likely have limited utility—nevertheless, we hope that this list will stimulate the dialogue between the different fields, and help inform the psychological approach on narratives and long-term effects to follow. For additional information about the keywords, readers are encouraged to consult other guides to the field such as by Herman (2009, 2007), Phelan and Rabinowitz (2005), M.-L. Ryan (2004), or frequently updated encyclopedia such as *The Living Handbook of Narratology* by Hühn and et al. (n.d.).

Actant. Harking back to Aristotle and Propp's approach on the spheres of action, structuralist narratologists proposed a theory of characters, the actants respectively. The typology of actants identifies general roles that are fulfilled by the characters. Initially Greimas identified six actants to which narrative actors ought to be reduced: subject, object, sender, receiver, helper, and opponent.

Agency. Within a storyworld, agency concerns the character's ability to initiate events or actions deliberately.

Anagnorisis. The Aristotelian term anagnorisis is close to 'recognition.' However, recognition only partially captures its meaning, since the transition includes an enlightening discovery of knowledge, but even further a discrediting and loss of the knowledge that has seemed entirely secure until then (Davis, 2012). Anagnorisis challenges gathered knowledge (about the narrative) and disrupts the coherent perception of the narrative.

Analepsis. This concept is analoguous to what practitioners call a flashback in a text or a movie. Analepsis indicates events that are told in an anachronic way, e.g., 2-1-3 instead of 1- 2-3. It is oftentimes employed by *backstory* which is a filling in of the events or circumstances that led to a certain momentum in the storyworld. Contrary to analepses are prolepses (i.e., flashforwards).

Conflict. As proposed by Aristotle and Todorov, an initial state of equilibrium is disrupted by a conflict during the middle of the narrative. The conflict can refer to clashes among beliefs, desires or intentions of characters in the storyworld, dissonant aspects of a single character, or—in a broader sense—to general unexpected, noncanonical events (Herman, 2009).

Counter Narratives. Counter Narratives question established accounts of how the world is portrayed. Counter narratives are most commonly considered the opposite of master narratives, although there are recent attempts to position them on a continuum (e.g., Bamberg, 2004).

Deictic Shift. The term deictic shift stems from the cognitive approach in semiotics (Segal, 1995), and is analogous to the concept of 'identification' in communication studies (Busselle & Bilandzic, 2009). Deixis is a pragmatic word that indicates temporal, spatial, and person components of a story world, for example 'here,' 'that,' 'now,' or 'you,' and was initially introduced in narratology as *Zeigfeld* by Bühler. Thus, in the act of a fictional narration one is relocated to other space-time coordinates, namely those of the events of the story (Herman, 2002, 2009; Duchan et al., 1995) —a cognitive act of imagination (*mimesis*) that was commented over 2,000 years ago by Aristotle. Directly analogues to the concept of identification in communication studies, the Deictic Shift Theory claims that how an object is interpreted depends on the cognitive stance of the recipient (Segal, 1995; Galbraith, 1995). More precisely, in order to enable a Deictic Shift the recipient has to have some degree of cognitive dissonance (Davis, 2012).

Diegesis. In general, there are three ways to define diegesis. In one sense, diegesis has been defined as the "spatiotemporal universe" of the story (by Genette in 1969), the narrated world (by Martinez and Scheffel in 2003), "the fictional world of the story" (by Bordwell in 1985), and the "world in which the situations and events narrated occur" (by Prince in 1987; all citations stem from Bunia, 2010). In this approach, diegesis serves as an analytical tool to investigate homo-, hetero-, intra- and extra-diegesis. For example, an extradiegetic narrator indicates a narrator who is outside of the storyworld. In a second sense that goes back to Greek etymology, the term diegesis is derived from the Greek word for narrative by Plato, and is meant to create some sort of distance. Understood as a *diegesis/mimesis* dichotomy, in mimesis (such as a theater play) events and figures are being presented/ staged, whereas in diegesis (such as a novel) the narrator serves as a mediating instance. In a third sense, diegesis is related to the concept of meaning by Luhmann (2000) and described as the "immediate meaning of a representational mode" (Bunia, 2010, p. 711). In this approach, diegesis is not the narrated universe but explores how recipients (or rather observers) structure representations.

Discourse. Discourse in the understanding of a *sjuzhet* by Russian Formalists refers to the manner, i.e., the semiotic cues, in which the storyworld is presented. It is contrary to story (called *fabula* by Russian Formalists) which explores what is being told in the storyworld.

Emplotment. In order to produce a plot, situations and events are linked together. This process is coined emplotment.

Episode. An episode is a narrative unit that shows internally coherent sequences of situations and events. Several episodes can be chained together to create larger narrative structures.

Focalization. Brought forward by Genette, focalization is a term for modes of perspective, and is directly analogous to the concept of 'point of view' or 'perspective' in communication studies. Genette distinguishes between zero focalization (when the viewpoint is not anchored) and internal focalization (when the viewpoint is restricted to a localized position such as a particular observer). Internal focalization can be variable, fixed, or multiple.

Hypodiegetic Narrative. This concept is analoguous to what communication scholars call a story within a story.

Master Narratives. Master or dominant narratives are culturally accepted frames. In accordance to these cultural scripts, storylines can easily be plotted, because the recipient is expected to know and accept the course of events. In order to set up actions and events in the storyline that give guidance, the range of actions in the storyline becomes limited (Bamberg, 2004). Counter narratives are most commonly considered the opposite of master narratives, although there are recent attempts to position them on a continuum. The use of the term is not coherent in narratology; see the critical discussion in section 4.3.1 for further information.

Metalepsis. Coined by Genette, metalepsis describes the transgression of boundaries between narrative levels within distinct worlds. The phenomenon is restricted to multi- layered narratives such as hypodiegetic narratives, as otherwise there is no capacity for crossing borders. Communication scholars refer to metalepsis when they describe a story with a narrators voice, which at a certain point moves from the extradiegetic level to the intradiegetic level and intervenes with the events.

Metanarrative. A metanarrative either indicates the directing function of the narrator according to Genette (in 1988), or stories about the world that strive to sum it all up in one account according to Lyotard (in 1984). The use of the term is not coherent in narratology; see the critical discussion in section 4.3.1 for further information.

Minimal Narrative. Coined minimal narrative, semioticians have in general agreed on a minimal definition on narratives which conceptualizes a narrative "as the representation of at least one event, one change in a state of affairs" (G. Prince, 1999, p. 43). This definition is further shaped by the varying assumptions and presuppositions from each strand in narratology.

Narrative Experience. By narrative experience, semiotics refers to what happens in the production and reception of a narrative. Extrapolating from Aristotelian insights, semioticians argue that the concept is constitutive of narrativity, and combines the polar opposites of *gestalt* wholeness with whole-resisting particularity (see *anagnorisis*; Davis, 2012). As for the former, the narrative is perceived coherently, because it represents an imitation (*mimesis*) of an action that is complete, whole (i.e., indicated by a beginning, middle, end) and of limited magnitude (neither too short or too long). The latter refers to the audience undergoing a cognitive transition, i.e., re-establishing of what is perceived. The concept is often put in analogue reference to 'transportation' in communication studies (see for example, Busselle & Bilandzic, 2009).

Narrative Performance. Narrative performance is anchored in conversation and discourse analyses in semiotics. To this end, in a performative role, narratives are a commentary and highlight how the content of the narrative is ordered and in which kinds of forms it is produced.

Prosody. Stemming from linguistics, the term indicates speech characteristics, including volume, tempo, voice quality, intonation, rhythm, and the qualities of pauses.

Serial Narration. Serial narration indicates a narration across multiple episodes, for example TV shows but also multiple movies, which can be autonomous (e.g., *Star Trek Enterprise*, 2001—2005) or related (e.g., *Star Wars*, 1977—2019).

Unnatural Narrative. Unnatural narratives are characterized as antirealistic as they provide improbable or impossible events that violate mimetic conventions (Richardson, 2012). For some post-classical narratology scholars such as Richardson, unnatural narratives indicate antimimetic scenes, entities, and events such as reversed causality, impossible spaces or defamiliarizing conversations, whereas unrealistic narratives relate to violations to realism as portrayed in fairy tales, ghost stories, or supernatural fiction. For other scholars such as Alber, unnatural narratives denote logically, physically, or humanly impossible events and scenarios, for instance speaking animals in fables, the use of magic in fantasy, time travel in science fiction, and so forth.

Unreliable Narration. This phenomenon applies when the narrator of a story appears untrustworthy and forces the recipient to read between the lines.

Vraisemblance. Vraisemblance equals what communication scholars call the expectation of plausibility or verisimilitude in fictional content. Vraisemblance (what ought to be) and truth (what is) are a subject of discussion in semiotics (e.g., by Genette).

Appendix C R Code for Simulation

```
 1
 2
 3    library (selectr)
 4
 5    # Define worker functions
 6    viewing_amount <- function (behavior_flag) {
 7
 8      if (behavior_flag == 'bimodal') {
 9        sampled_viewing_amount <- c( rep (4, n_users / 2), rep (20.01, n_users / 2))
10      } else if (behavior _ flag == ' gamma ') {
11        sampled_viewing_amount <- 2 * rgamma (n_users , 3.125 , .5)
12        # sampled_viewing_amount <- 4 * rgamma (n_users , 2.5 , .5)
13      }
14    }
15
16    viewer_to_category_matrix <- function (u_selectivity_flag) {
17
18      # Function will output a n_users x n_categories matrix
19
20      if (u_selectivity_flag == 0) {
21        viewer_selectivity_matrix = matrix (data = 1, n_users , n_categories )
22      } else if (u_selectivity_flag == 1) {
23        viewer_selectivity_matrix = matrix (data = runif (n_users * n_categories ), n_users , n_categories )
24      } else { print ("error") }
25
26      viewer_selectivity_matrix <- viewer_selectivity_matrix / rowSums (viewer_selectivity_matrix)
27
28      return (viewer _ selectivity _ matrix )
29
30    } # END of viewer_to_category_matrix
31
32    make_gpm_matrix <- function (c_selectivity_flag) {
33
34      # Function will output a n_genres x n_programs x n_messages matrix
35      # c_selectivity_flag : 1= uniform , 2= genre - specific , 3= metanarrative , 4= subgenre
36
37      gpm_matrix = array (data = 0, dim = c(n_genres , n_programs , n_messages ))
38
39      if (c_selectivity_flag == 1) {
40        gpm_matrix = array (data = 1, dim = c(n_genres , n_programs , n_messages ))
41      } else if (c_selectivity_flag == 2) {
42        for (genre in 1:n_genres) {
          message = genre
```

```
43        gpm_matrix[genre,,message]  = 1
44      }
45    } else if (c_selectivity_flag == 3) {
46      for (program in 1:n_programs) {
47        message=program
48        gpm_matrix[,program,message] = 1
49      }
50    } else if (c_selectivity_flag == 4) {
51      for (genre in 1:n_genres) {
52        message=genre
53        gpm_matrix[genre,,message]  = 1
54      }
55      v1 <- matrix(1:5, 5, 1)
56      v2 <- matrix(sample(v1, 5), 5, 1)
57      while (any(v1==v2)) {v2 <- matrix(sample(v1, 5), 5, 1)}
58      for (i in 1:5) {
59        gpm_matrix[v1[i],4,v1[i]]  <- 0
60        gpm_matrix[v1[i],4,v2[i]]  <- 1
61        gpm_matrix[v2[i],5,v2[i]]  <- 0
62        gpm_matrix[v2[i],5,v1[i]]  <- 1
63      }
64    } else {print ("error")}
65
66    return(gpm_matrix)
67
68    #gpm_matrix <- gpm_matrix / sum(gpm_matrix)
69
70  } # END of viewer_to_category_matrix
71
72  define_key_hours <- function(analysis_flag) {
73
74    if (analysis_flag == 1) {
75      key_hours = sum(viewer_gp_matrix)*sampled_viewing_amount[viewer]
76    } else if (analysis_flag == 2) {
77      key_hours = sum(viewer_gp_matrix[1,])*sampled_viewing_amount[viewer]
78    } else if (analysis_flag == 3) {
79      key_hours = sum(viewer_gp_matrix[,1])*sampled_viewing_amount[viewer]
80    } else if (analysis_flag == 4) {
81      key_hours = sum(viewer_gp_matrix[1,1:3])*sampled_viewing_amount[viewer]
82    } else {print ("error")}
83  }
84
85  hours_to_degree_belief <- function(noise_flag, hours) {
86
87    belief <- 1 - exp(-belief_slope*hours)
88    if (noise_flag == 1) {
89      belief <- rbeta(1, 50*belief, 50*(1-belief))
90    }
91
92    return(belief)
93
94  }
95
96  ## Define parameters
97
```

```
98  # User - specific  params
99  n_users  =  100000  #100
00  behavior_flag <-  'gamma'
01  noise_flag  =  1
02
03  # Content - specific  params
04  n_genres  =  5
05  n_programs  =  5
06
07  # Simulation control params
08  n_simulations  =  1  #1000
09  n_messages  =  n_programs
10
11  # Analysis params
12  hl_cutpoint  =  4
13  #d_primes <-  matrix(0,  n_simulations ,  1)
14  mean_difs <-  array(0,  c(4,  4,  n_simulations))
15  mean_heavy  <-  array(0,  c(4,  4,  n_simulations))
16  mean_light  <-  array(0,  c(4,  4,  n_simulations))
17
18  # Dist plotting params
19  track_hl <-  array(0,  c(4,  4,  n_users))
20  track_belief <-  array(0,  c(4,  4,  n_users))
21  plotting_flag  =  1
22  belief_slope  =  .2
23
24  for (dgf in 1:4) {
25
26     # Master control  variable   (1=uniform ,2= genre - specific ,3= metanarrative ,4= subgenre)
27     master_flag <-  dgf
28     master_vec  =  switch(master_flag,  c(0,  0,  1),  c(1,  0,  2),  c(0,  1,  3),  c(1,  1,  4))
29
30     for (daf in 1:4) {
31
32        analysis_flag <-  daf
33
34        for (sim  in  1:n_simulations)  {
35
36           sampled_viewing_amount  =  viewing_amount(behavior_flag)
37           #if  (master_flag ==1)  {sampled_viewing_amount  <-  sampled_viewing_amount *runif(n_users)*2}
38           genre_selectivity_matrix  =  viewer_to_category_matrix(master_vec[1])
39           program_selectivity_matrix  =  viewer_to_category_matrix(master_vec[2])
40
41           gpm_matrix  =  make_gpm_matrix(master_vec[3])
42
43           key_hours <-  matrix(0,  n_users,  1)
44
45           # Simulate viewing
46           viewer_to_message_matrix  =  matrix(0,  n_users,  n_messages)
47           for (viewer  in  1:n_users) {
48
49              viewer_gp_matrix  =  matrix(genre_selectivity_matrix[viewer,] ,5,1)  %*%  matrix(program_selectivity_matrix[viewer
                  ,] ,1,5)
50              viewer_gp_matrix  <-  viewer_gp_matrix / sum(viewer_gp_matrix)
51
```

```
152        m_vec <- matrix(data = 0, nrow = 1, ncol = n_messages)
153        for (message in 1:n_messages) {
154          m_vec[message] = sum(as.matrix(gpm_matrix[,,message])*viewer_gp_matrix)
155        }
156        #m_vec <- m_vec / sum(m_vec)
157
158        viewer_to_message_matrix[viewer,] = m_vec*sampled_viewing_amount[viewer]
159
160        key_hours[viewer] <- define_key_hours(analysis_flag)
161
162        if (plotting_flag == 1) {
163          track_hl[dgf,daf,viewer]   <- key_hours[viewer]>hl_cutpoint
164          track_belief[dgf,daf,viewer] <- hours_to_degree_belief(noise_flag,viewer_to_message_matrix[viewer,1])
165        }
166
167      } # End of simulate viewing
168
169      # Do analysis according to selected DAF
170      # d_primes[sim]   <-  (mean(viewer_to_message_matrix[key_hours>hl_cutpoint,1])  -
171      #   mean(viewer_to_message_matrix[key_hours<=hl_cutpoint,1]))/sqrt(.5*
172      #   (var(viewer_to_message_matrix[key_hours>hl_cutpoint,1])  +
173      #     var(viewer_to_message_matrix[key_hours<=hl_cutpoint,1])))
174
175      mean_difs[dgf,daf,sim] <-  (mean(viewer_to_message_matrix[key_hours>hl_cutpoint,1])  -
176                        mean(viewer_to_message_matrix[key_hours<=hl_cutpoint,1]))
177      mean_heavy[dgf,daf,sim]   <- mean(viewer_to_message_matrix[key_hours>hl_cutpoint,1])
178      mean_light[dgf,daf,sim] <- mean(viewer_to_message_matrix[key_hours<=hl_cutpoint,1])
179
180    } # End of simulation loop
181
182  } # End of daf loop
183
184 } # End of dgf loop
185
186 return(viewer_to_message_matrix)
```